ZANY GAMES

America at the 1900 Paris Olympics

By

Howard Burman

Master Arts Publishing

Howard Burman

Also by Howard Burman

A Story Told by Two Liars

An O. Henry Christmas

Surrounded

Paradise by Paradise

Gentlemen at the Bat

To Hate Like This is to Love Forever

Here Be Dragons

Willie, Mickey & The Duke

You Can't Win (with Barbara Zajak)

You Shoot Me Now

Duckrabbit

A Man Called Shoeless

The Secret Game

Howard Burman

THANK YOU

Nancy Miller, archivist at the University of Pennsylvania, for her gracious assistance with the Kraenzlein archives. The Olympic Multimedia Library for images. My wife, Karen, for her invaluable editorial assistance.

Howard Burman

Format and Layout by Red Raven
www.redravenbookdesign.com

Cover by Diogo Lando
www.diogolando.com

Zany Games/ Howard Burman
Master Arts Publishing
ISBN
www.howardburman.com

Howard Burman

INTRODUCTION

The Paris Olympic Games of 1900 were triumphant, they were contentious, they were bizarre. I know because I was a part of them in all their glory and all their disgrace, in all their accord and all their discord, for these were truly zany games.

I am Edward Bushnell, the son of Methodist missionaries, born in Republican City, Nebraska. I attended Hastings College in Nebraska before transferring to the University of Pennsylvania's Wharton School to prepare myself for a career in journalism. It was a wonderful school and a great place to become involved in athletics. I was a tall, thin young man at the time and I could run seemingly forever. Maybe I wasn't the fastest runner around but I was good enough to run on the Penn cross-country and track teams and even to win the intercollegiate mile a couple of times.

In my senior year they made me captain of the cross-country team, a singular honor to be sure since I wasn't the best runner on the team by a long shot.

My greatest contribution to the glorious tradition of Penn athletics, however, was not as a runner, but as a chronicler of the athletic accomplishments. While still a student I supported myself by serving as a campus correspondent for the *Philadelphia Press*. Later I worked as an editorial writer for the old *Philadelphia North American* and *The Evening Public Ledger*. I also edited *A History of Athletics at Penn*, founded *The Franklin Field Illustrated*, was for a time the editor of *Old Penn* which became *The Pennsylvania Gazette*, and wrote a book with our legendary coach, Mike Murphy, called *Athletic Training*.

I was chair of the Houston Club's Press Committee and a member of the Pennsylvania Debating Union and the Western Club.

So you can see, I had a full and rewarding experience at Penn and am forever grateful for the opportunities the university provided.

The highlight of my time there was the opportunity to participate in the wonderful, crazy, exhilarating, frustrating, unforgettable Paris Olympics and Universal Exposition of 1900. Later I attended the 1908 London Olympics where I was the official photographer for our U.S. team, but that was an altogether different experience.

The 1900 Olympics, the second modern Olympic Games, were something very special. There had never been anything like them and there never would be again. They were unique in the truest sense of the word.

Figure 1 Edward Bushnell then and now

The Paris Olympics allowed me to combine my two great loves: journalism and track and field. Once I knew I would be on the ship headed to Europe I made a commitment to myself to run to the best of my abilities and to write down my observations of the games in as journalistic a manner as I could. I also collected comments from many of those involved in the competitions or who wrote about them.

At the center of this story are three University of Pennsylvania roommates. They are track and field athletes and together they will take home 14 medals—more than any single country other than the United States. Well, actually they didn't receive medals as we have come to know them—gold for first, silver for second, bronze for third—but, as is customary, I use those colors to represent those positions.

Here then are recollections of that febrile time in Paris from the point of view of an American participant.

Howard Burman

ONE

WORD HAD GONE OUT LATE. In the summer of 1900 the second modern Olympic Games would be staged in Paris in conjunction with the Universal Exposition. The French promised the Exposition would be the grandest fair ever staged by any country. It would celebrate the coming of the new century. It would showcase the newest in technology. It would display to the world the grandeur that was France.

An open letter to the American people from the games' founder, Baron de Coubertin, promised that the Paris Games would be "the greatest athletic events ever held in the history of the world."

Then, of course, America would send a team, but which events would be held? And when? Which sports other than track and field would be represented?

Not a lot was known about the organization of the games themselves. It was all a bit sketchy, confusing.

An official invitation had come to our Secretary of State, William Chilton: "The Government of the French Republic, desirous to maintain the tradition which has established the term of 11 years as the period for renewing our international expositions, has decided that a Universal Exposition of works of art and industrial and agricultural products should take place in Paris in 1900."

In response, President McKinley appointed General Ferdinand Wythe Peck as our Commissioner-General to the Exposition. Peck had made his fortune in real estate, was politically connected, civic minded, and a supporter of the arts.

Peck's oft-stated opinion was that few foreigners appreciated the prominence of America. He would set out to change that. Could there be a better place to do that than at the Paris Exposition? He thought not.

Figure 2 Ferdinand Wythe Peck

FERDINAND WYTHE PECK   The proof of our superiority would have to be on display because all of Europe and all the Americas would attend. Paris was set to be the mecca of all the peoples of all the nations of 1900 and we needed to be a part of that. A credible exhibit would mean not only the offering of proof to the world of American greatness, an objective that should stir the patriotism of every American heart, but would also be followed by an extension of American export trade.

After setting up office and hiring a staff, he booked passage on the steamship *Tiniraine* sailing from New York to Le Havre. Once in Paris he made an early determination that the space allocated to the USA could not meet the country's needs. He turned to General Horace Porter, our ambassador to France, for assistance. Porter, who won the Medal of Honor for his role in the Battle of Chickamauga during the Civil War, demanded that French officials enlarge the USA exhibition space.

His demand was met by an official, definite and not-so-gracious Gallic refusal.

Final allotments have been made. Additional space is impossible.

You don't understand. We are the leading industrial country in the world and we need space to showcase that.

No, you don't understand. The subject is closed.

This was the situation for about a month.

Peck and Porter returned with pages of statistics emphasizing the important place our country occupied.

The French officials refused to budge.

FERDINAND WYTHE PECK   In no uncertain terms I informed the French officials that the population of the United States was 75 million. The value of the manufacturers of this country was over one-third of the total value of the manufactures of the world. Our agricultural resources represented nearly 40 percent of those of all countries combined. In railroad transportation our mileage exceeded that of the whole of Europe. Our mines produced more than those of any other nation on earth and equal to those of all Europe. The wealth of the United States amounted to nearly twice that of France, equal to that of Russia, Austria, Italy, and Spain combined and 75 percent more than that of Great Britain.

Yes, we understand you're a big country, the French responded brusquely.

Then Peck arranged for the statistics to be published throughout Europe.

Embarrassed by the publication, the French government quickly ordered the Exposition authorities to concede to our demands.

Yes, of course you can have more space. How much do you need?

An additional 40 percent.

Done.

As the French were learning, the United States was becoming—if it was not already—the most important country in the world, something our athletes would set out to demonstrate.

But Peck was an unpopular choice among many Americans who had interest in participating in the Exposition.

He's arrogant.

The slipshod manner in which he performs his duties is appalling.

He's employing many of his own relatives and the sons of friends at large salaries for which it appears they do absolutely nothing other than to turn up well-dressed and smiling at social functions.

He promises space and localities for American exhibitors and then doesn't deliver.

He showed contempt by not even showing up for the official visit of other USA dignitaries.

William Sayne, the Pennsylvania commissioner to the Exposition, expressed his frustration.

WILLIAM SAYNE   I must say that I received little courtesy from Commissioner-General Peck. As a representative of the State of Pennsylvania I was entitled to some, and instead I was treated with contumely. I showed Mr. Peck my commission and he hardly looked at it.

Peck told Sayne that since he was the designated United States representative he recognized no state authority.

Oh, yes, he was in charge and made sure everyone knew it.

But he wasn't done.

Just a few months before the Exposition was to open, he determined the neighboring Turkish building was encroaching on the building line of America's pavilion, and since it was four stories high it impeded the view of the building.

He was furious. He took photographs from the Pont des Invalides and charged back to the offices of the French Exhibition officials.

Figure 3 Pavilion of the United States

Look at these. The Turks are blocking a clear view of our building.

We have many countries' interests to protect.

You must instruct them to alter their building.

Finally, an official protest was presented to Commissioner-General Picard, who was the major domo of the entire Exposition. Picard ordered all work to stop on the Turkish building.

Naturally the Turks protested. However, concerned that their building would not be finished in time, they agreed to lower their minaret by 5 feet, reduce the width of the cupola by 10 feet and move it 5 feet back of the original line.

Peck was not satisfied and renewed his protest with greater force.

It is not enough. Not nearly enough. They are still compromising the view.

It's too late to make any more changes.

If that's the case, they should take their building down.

You must make do with the accommodation they have agreed to.

The tense argument went on for some time.

When Peck threatened to withdraw from the Exposition altogether, several confrontational meetings were held with the Turks, the French and Peck. He steadfastly refused to budge and finally, after many acrimonious hours of negotiations, the Turkish officials agreed to reduce the height of their building to 5 feet below the top of the porch of the American building.

This would be a theme repeated before, during and after the Games and Exposition—we are the United States and we will demonstrate in our exhibitions and in our athletic performances that we are the strongest nation on earth, therefore we must be treated as such.

The Exposition was expected to attract 75 million visitors to gawk at the newest in machines, inventions, architecture and arts. Most visitors would see for the first time a giant Ferris wheel, diesel engines, talking films, escalators, moving sidewalks, magnetic audio recorders, and scores of sights in the emerging Art Nouveau style.

The athletic competitions would be folded in and around the sprawling, eclectic fair.

That was fine, but our athletic authorities, particularly those representing the Amateur Athletic Union and the Intercollegiate Association, had been at sea for some time as to just what the program at Paris would be. There were rumors, there were reports, but there was little clarification coming from Paris.

It was up to Peck to delegate someone to take charge of our participation in the games. Several politicians, including the soon-to-be corrupt mayor of Chicago, lobbied for the position, but Peck appointed Albert Spalding.

Spalding, if not always popular, had done much to promote American sports. He had been one of the best-known baseball players, one of the best-known baseball executives, and one of the best-known sporting goods magnates. He was a member of several prominent clubs and had helped to organize athletic events at the Chicago World's Fair of 1893. He was president of the National Cycle Board of Trade and the American Bicycle Company.

Figure 4 Albert Spalding

Spalding, no foe of alliteration, claimed he was an exponent of, "American Courage, Confidence, Combativeness; American Dash, Discipline, Determination; American Energy, Eagerness, Enthusiasm; American Pluck, Persistency, Performance; American Spirit, Sagacity, Success; American Vim, Vigor, Virility."

Who could argue with that?

A flamboyant personality possessed of insatiable ego, A. G., or Big Al as he was most often called, was professional baseball's first recorded 200 game-winner pitcher. He moved up the baseball ranks from player to captain to manager to president of the club to owner of the club and one of the principals in establishing the National League.

In 1876, with his brother, $800 and his reputation as a ballplayer, he opened a sporting goods store in Chicago that eventually made him a millionaire. Big Al had clearly become the most recognizable man in American sports.

Born in a small farming village in Illinois he was sent to a boarding school when he was young which left him so lonesome and homesick that the memories of it haunted him all his life. He was so bashful that he was almost afraid to go out of doors, afraid he would meet and be spoken to by someone not a member of his family.

Baseball alone provided him with relief from such anxiety and despair.

In the 1870s baseball was rapidly changing from a simple pastime to a systematic business and Spalding calculated his place in it. By the time he was in his early 20s he was ready to leave the confines of rural Illinois in pursuit of his version of the American dream.

In short order he became the top pitcher in professional ball, leading the National League in victories every year he pitched. In 1876, he won 47 games for the Chicago White Stockings and led them to the first ever National League pennant.

Players in those days always played bare-handed. But when Spalding appeared on the field wearing a glove to protect his catching hand, the idea caught on. Big Al was motivated by more than a sore hand, however. By then he had opened a sporting goods store, and not coincidentally, they sold the Spalding glove. Now, if the best pitcher in the game wears a glove …

He retired at 27, became president and part owner of the White Stockings and a prominent figure in National League governance.

In 1874 he got his first taste of international sport when he was sent to England to arrange for the visit of American baseball players.

By 1887 he claimed to be producing over 1 million bats a year and had developed a national web of specialized factories producing all types of sporting goods. The Spalding line out sold all others combined.

When Peck offered the founder of the largest sporting goods house in the world the opportunity to head up the athletic programs in Paris, Spalding jumped at the chance. Of course he did. The exposure would offer his company great publicity.

He would not only lead his charges in quest of victories but he would also supervise his company's massive display of athletic goods and apparel.

But as with so many other decisions connected with these games, not everyone was overjoyed to hear that the sporting goods impresario would be in charge.

Spalding is interested in Spalding and only Spalding.

The Spalding discus is the official discus; the Spalding basketball is the official ball; the Spalding football is the official ball for intercollegiate contests. Spalding published the first official rules guide for baseball. In it he stated that only Spalding balls could be used.

When an athlete in Michigan set a world record with a discus not of the Spalding manufacture the record was not allowed.

Nevertheless, he was Peck's choice and so immediately took the train from Chicago to New York to meet with James Sullivan.

Figure 5 James Sullivan

Sullivan, the son of Irish immigrants, had worked his way into a leadership position in American athletics by championing the playground movement in New York City. He became the all-powerful, autocratic, domineering head of the Amateur Athletic Union which controlled all non-university amateur sports, and president of the Metropolitan Association of the Amateur Athletic

Union of New York. He was shrewd, efficient, always let everyone know he was in charge, loudly proclaimed his America first Yankee pride and was an adamant defender of all things amateur in sports.

In his younger days he had been a good runner and then turned to sports publishing. He created *The Athletic News* and would become the editor of *Spalding's Official Almanac,* the country's most influential sports publication.

Spalding knew he needed Sullivan's influence to attract the country's best athletes for the Paris Games and Sullivan needed the games to promote his own Olympic ambitions.

It took little to convince Sullivan to serve as Assistant Director of Sports for the United States.

This, too, brought criticism:

Spalding and Sullivan are in bed with each other to the detriment of amateur sports throughout the United States.

Sullivan is so brash and opinionated he'll alienate everyone in the Olympic movement.

JAMES SULLIVAN Americans excel in athletics because we go heart and soul into the contests. We use in sports the same vim which characterizes the success of the American business man. Our system of training is better than that of any other country. I have been closely watching athletes of various nations in international sports, and, after careful comparison, I am confident that our men show the benefit of superior training. Our training system is superior because we are not tied down to old-fashioned rules, and whenever we see something worth adopting we use it. Also we have been practicing many forms of athletics longer than other nations, and yet we will learn anything to our advantage from them. Our athletes think only of national honors, and that spirit helps them greatly.

Sullivan, in close personal contact with all prominent athletes, both professional and amateur, knew that the first order of business would be to get the word out about the games to attract our top athletes.

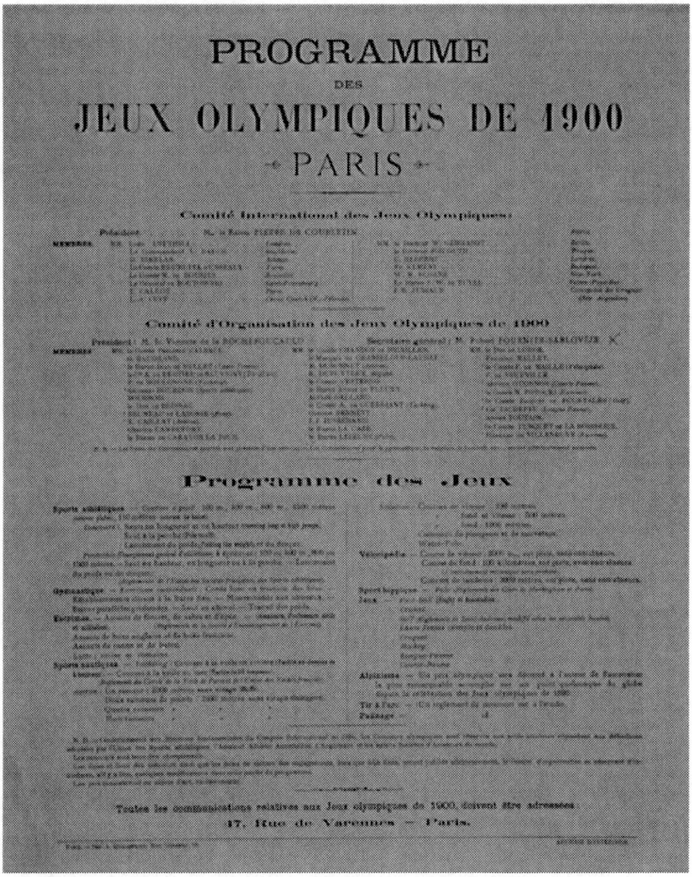
PROGRAMME
DES
JEUX OLYMPIQUES DE 1900
PARIS

Comité International des Jeux Olympiques

Comité d'Organisation des Jeux Olympiques de 1900

Programme des Jeux

Toutes les communications relatives aux Jeux olympiques de 1900, doivent être adressées :
17, Rue de Varennes — Paris.

Figure 6 Official program

Naturally the official program of Athletics of the Exposition was printed in French. Spalding had it translated, printed in English and distributed 5,000 copies. The interest in the games, which up to that time had been undetermined, rapidly took active form. Commitments came in from several universities and athletic clubs to send their best athletes to Paris.

Leaving Sullivan in charge in New York, Spalding set sail for Paris on the *Kaiser Wilhelm der Grosse*. He spent the last two weeks of May in Paris checking on the preparations for the events and inspecting the venues.

As he learned, the games would be divided into 10 sections.

Section 1: Athletic games, including track and field events, rugby football, cricket, baseball, lawn tennis, croquet, longue-paume and golf.

Section 2: Gymnastics.

Section 3: Fencing: Foil, sword and sabre.

Section 4: Shooting: Rifle, revolver and shot gun.

Section 5: Sports: Hippique, and polo.

Section 6: Bicycle races.

Section 7: Automobilism.

Section 8: Nautical sport: Rowing, sailing, steam launch races, swimming races, angling.

Section 9: Lifesaving on land and sea.

Section 10: Aerostation, ballooning, air ships, carrier pigeons.

Naturally, when the announcement of the Olympic events was made, objections arose.

What, no Alpine Climbing?

Where's the skating? That's an exciting competitive sport but lifesaving isn't a sport.

Balloons and the dubious art of guiding them is still in its infancy. These aren't supposed to be experimental games, are they?

Maybe Sweden should organize the next games and then we could include tobogganing, snowshoes and skiing,

And dump cricket and football?

Maybe if we had the games in St. Moritz up in the Swiss Engadine we could include everything. Up there the sun and snow agree all winter so well that men skate in flannel slippers and women open parasols while sleigh riding.

While in Paris Spalding also met with a similarly named Spalding de Garmendia, a prominent athlete on both sides of the Atlantic. He was well-known as a racquets player, having been the U.S. champion in that sport for many years. He was also an excellent golfer and polo player. Although he was from a wealthy family in Baltimore, he had spent most of his life in France so was fluent in French and knew his way around Paris like a native.

Spalding offered de Garmendia the position as Second Assistant Director of Sports.

Garmendia said he would accept so long as it didn't interfere with his competing in the tennis event. Spalding agreed and the administrative troika for the United States participation in the games was complete: Spalding, Sullivan, de Garmendia.

Spalding and de Garmendia held several meetings with French officials. It quickly became evident that the French wanted, needed America's full commitment to the games and the Exposition but, just as evidently, on French terms.

At first Spalding proposed organizing the events under the auspices of the United States Commission. There would be playing fields, and competitions to "teach other countries what real sport was like."

Nothing could have been more misplaced than such a move, responded the French.

Some of Spalding's requests were politely agreed to; some weren't.

Spalding asked if a marathon road race could be included in the schedule to give our long-distance runners a chance to compete against the world.

Agreed, said the French officials. We'll schedule a marathon on July 19 and offer a valuable prize to the winner.

And we'd like you to add a standing high jump and standing long jump.

Agreed, said the French. We'll schedule both for July 16.

We need to know the height of the hurdles and the number of hurdles.

Agreed, said the French. We'll supply that information.

We need to know what the obstacles are and how many there will be in the steeplechase.

Agreed, said the French. We'll supply that information, too.

We need to know what kind of hammer will be allowed in the throwing competition.

Agreed, said the French.

Several other details were discussed and agreed to. Then …

We'll need to move all the events scheduled for Sunday, July 15. We are a Christian nation and some … many of our athletes won't compete on Sundays.

Ah, that we cannot do, said the French officials.

But you must.

But we can't.

Spalding, knowing this would be at issue, presented letters from the Intercollegiate Association and several universities appealing for a change.

What is the concern? Asked the French.

No first-class American club or team holds meets on a Sunday was Spalding's reply.

Our Christian athletes compete on Sundays, the French officials said. So too, do they from other countries. We cannot change just because one country out of the many wants to.

But we are the United States.

And we are France.

If I go home, said Spalding, and tell our universities there will be track and field events on Sunday, some … maybe all of them may decide not to participate. Surely you want America's participation.

Yes, of course we do, but understand you are not the only participating country and you are not setting the rules for these games.

Then we will have to see if we will participate at all.

By the time Spalding was set to sail home, the French officials with whom he met agreed they would look into the matter more, talk with representatives of other countries, and let Spalding know in a few weeks. But absolutely no promises were made.

Our participation was seriously in doubt. Could the Olympics be staged without America? They could. Would they be as important? They wouldn't.

Spalding sailed home, depressed, a little angry, anxious. However, when he arrived in New York a cable from de Garmendia was waiting for him. The French had agreed to change the schedule to avoid Sunday competitions.

Obviously Spalding was relieved and passed the information on to the Intercollegiate Association.

Just as obviously the universities were relieved and passed the information on to their athletes.

Spalding issued a circular for the benefit of the athletes in which he outlined details for the events.

In the 110-meter hurdle race there would be 10 hurdles, 9 meters between each hurdle, 15 meters between the first hurdle and the starting point, and 11 meters from the last hurdle to the finish. The height of the hurdles would be 1.06 meters. In the 200-meter hurdle race there would be 10 hurdles over the course, 15 meters between each hurdle, 35 meters from start to the first hurdle, and 30 meters from the last hurdle to the finish.

The height of the hurdles would be 90 centimeters. In the 400 meter hurdles race there would be 10 hurdles, 90 centimeters in height, 35 meters between each hurdle, 45 meters from the start to the first hurdle, and 30 meters from the last hurdle to the finish.

Spalding distributed copies of the rules under which the athletic races were to be contested. They were largely framed after the rules of the English Athletic Association.

He also recommended that when American golfers visit Paris they bring their own golf equipment, as very good golf could be had at Compiegne, near Paris. It is a very beautiful spot, he assured would-be golfers, set in a 36,000-acre forest, with18 holes for men and nine holes for women.

Despite Spalding's positive report, criticism was levelled at him for using the games to promote himself and his company.

In response, Spalding insisted that administrative expenses were kept to an absolute minimum. He contributed all his personal services and all traveling and incidental expenses attached to his position as Director of Sports.

ALBERT SPALDING   The only expense I claimed was the steamship fare from New York to Paris and return for the special trip I made in May to examine the preparations—$200. Mr. Sullivan also generously gave his services without remuneration, claiming only his traveling expenses from New York to Paris and return—$527.54. The only other expenses were to the American Sports Publishing Company, printing, etc. $499.29; the salary of Miss Vilas, stenographer, $267.38; Mr. de Garmendia's salary as

Assistant Director of Sports, $335.38; and extras attached to the Paris office—postage, cabs, car fare, etc., about $6.00. This little extra was occasioned by Mr. de Garmendia making daily use of his bicycle without charge.

No money was spent on the athletes for housing, food or travel and nothing went to the participating universities and clubs.

There is no doubt, however that Spalding Sporting Goods stood to profit from the exposure it would generate at the Exhibition.

O O O O O

Since the Sunday issue appeared to be resolved—appeared to be—the universities went about selecting their athletes.

In 1900 there was no formal selection process to participate in the games. There were no qualifying times, distances or heights. Rather it was up to any university or club to send whomever they felt would best represent them and for whom they could marshal the resources for the trip. Spalding would head up the contingent but he would not be involved in the selection of athletes nor in their training. He would represent the Americans to the French and to whichever other countries sent competitors. The athletes would either handle themselves or they were under the care of their trainers (we would later call them coaches) from their respective schools or clubs.

At the University of Pennsylvania, the school which would send the most athletes, that meant Mike Murphy.

O O O O O

Murphy was a real-life cliché—a little smiling leprechaun of a man with sparkling eyes and a ready wit that let everyone know he was Irish. Well, his parents, James and the former Mary O'Brien, were anyway. They had emigrated from Ireland. Mike was born in Massachusetts—either Southboro or Westboro. Or if not there, in Natick. He never bothered to set the record straight. He was 40 and already at the top of his field. "A man of humble birth and scant education," as one paper called him, was our trainer at the University of Pennsylvania, one of the country's elite universities where the brightest of the bright went to become doctors and lawyers.

A formal man in many respects, he could usually be seen dressed in a neat dark suit, vest with gold fob holding his all-important watch, and derby hat. Like everything else about him, his full mustache was neat and trim. He was a precise and deliberate man—everything calculated, planned with a cat-like love of personal cleanliness. There was nothing extraneous about him, nothing sloppy or unconsidered.

Figure 7 Mike Murphy

He would become known as the "father of American track athletes." In 1900 he was known as the best coach, maybe anywhere. It was said he could spot athletic potential in a young man like

Sherlock Holmes spots clues in the ashes.

We athletes respected him for the knowledgeable, detailed man he was and so we were fiercely loyal to him. Why not? If we wanted to be the best runners/throwers/jumpers we could be, who better to train us?

Figure 8 Murphy addressing crowd before meet

WALTER TEWKSBURY   Not a man ever trained under Mike Murphy who wouldn't go to the end of the world for the veteran trainer if he desired it.

Murphy's father, like so many men in Southboro, worked in a shoe manufacturing plant for most of his life before he went to work in a wood mill. Southboro was home to many small manufacturing mills that tapped the river running through the town. Mostly they manufactured things like straw bonnets, plasters, boots and shoes. That is, until a dam was constructed in 1898 to produce a reservoir to supply a growing Boston with water. After that manufacturing began to peter out.

Mike grew up in a big house with his family and up to seven others all living close together and all supported by the shoe business. Several could neither read nor write but the Murphys made sure all their children could. There was plenty of time for play, but school came first.

The family was athletic. His father was known around New England as a fine athlete. He wanted his sons to be the same. There were five boys in the family and three girls. Mike had an older brother, Dennis and three younger brothers, with whom he roughhoused and played all the games boys engaged in—baseball, football, soccer, boxing.

William Henry, his younger brother by nine years, played with Mike when he was big enough. William all of 5' 3" and maybe 125 pounds, may have been the smallest in the family, but he was a good athlete. Better than Mike probably. Even at his diminutive size he went on to play several seasons as a shortstop/second baseman with the New York Giants. In his best season, 1894, he hit .272. Not surprisingly, his nickname was "Tot."

Mike, only slightly bigger than Tot, played a lot of baseball and football. He particularly loved baseball and even had a short stint as a minor league player, but that was as far as he got.

He boxed, and ran … and ran … and ran. He had stamina. He had determination. He had ambition. So he entered the six-day races then very much in vogue. Most competitors were Irish immigrants. Daniel O'Leary, a farmer from County Cork, Ireland, was one of the best. These six-day races became known as "go-as-you-please" races, where the competitors ran as long as they could, walked when they couldn't, slept when they could no longer move. And there was a lot of money for the winners. Charles Rowell, a Scot, earned $50,000 after winning two races in 1879. This was about equal to one hundred years of the average salary of the day—and this was in only 12 days' work. Even with the astonishingly high salaries earned by some of later days' top athletes, none made one hundred years of salary in 12 days.

Mike was reasonably fast, had good lung power and stamina. That, he could turn into money.

Amateurs?

Heck no.

You'd have to be crazy to run for nothing but glory.

They kept no records and the fellow who won the race was simply handed all the money that went with the victory.

In the years just before the Civil War, professional running (known as "pedestrianism") was one of the most important and popular spectator sports. Only horse racing could compare in spectator interest

Mike's ambition was to stand out prominently as a six-day pedestrian. By 18 he was out in the world trying to find fame and fortune on what was then termed the "tan bark track."

For decades pedestrianism events continued as a mishmash of locally promoted events with a wide range of distances, rules and prizes. Many athletes claimed to be champions or record holders at various distances, but since there was no central organization, records and results lack legitimacy and are often conflicted.

Pedestrianism was given over to working-class competitors watched by working-class spectators. After all, the higher classes couldn't possibly demean themselves by competing for money. Some events even allowed women to compete.

Mike traveled to six-day races running after those huge paydays. He never hit it big, but there was another kind of racing that caught his attention—hose racing.

In the late 1870s and 1880s, young men in New England worked in hay fields for weeks to establish a residency in some small town where hose races with rival fire companies were the leading attraction to the sport loving natives.

Figure 9 Natick Hook-and-Ladder Company

By the time Mike was 20 he had become a regular on the professional hose racing circuit, competing for various "hook-and-ladder teams," most notably the Natick team, organized by Keene Fitzpatrick. Besides Keene and Murphy, the team included Piper Donovan, who at the time was billed as "the world champion sprinter," and Steve Farrell who competed in races from 100 yards to 1 mile and was crowned by one newspaper "the greatest professional foot racer the country has ever known." Maybe that was because he joined the Barnum and Bailey Circus and for several years raced against horses. He claimed never to have been beaten.

Several members of the Natick Hook and Ladder Company— Mike Murphy principal among them—became trainers at American universities, leading Massachusetts to being dubbed the "mother of athletic mentors." Fitzpatrick became the track coach, athletic trainer, professor of physical training and gymnasium director at Yale and Princeton; Farrell at Yale, and the University of Michigan, among others.

Mike watched the best runners, watched how they prepared, or didn't prepare. A runner couldn't run faster by just trying to run faster or farther he reasoned. He needed to learn how to run faster or farther. Mike looked closely at the techniques used by the better runners. He took it all in, took mental notes, thought that most athletes, if only they trained scientifically, could become better in their chosen sporting activity.

Given the number of trainers to come from that little group, one can easily picture them sitting in a local watering hole discussing issues of athletic preparation.

How long, how far, how often should a sprinter train? A long-distance runner?

How many throws for the weight men? Should they lift weights or exercise particular muscles in particular ways?

Naturally, they didn't have the medical and scientific knowledge or evaluation devices of available to athletes later, but they had each other and they had their own experiences.

One of Murphy's friends on the Natick Hook and Ladder Company was Michael J. Finn, a big, genial, good-natured, and excitable man with a prominent red handlebar mustache. He could be gruff and blustery but he was fond of flashing his Irish wit. A devout Catholic, he didn't drink, curse or smoke, but garnered the trust of others and became an organizer, handicapper and backer of sporting events. He apparently organized the event in 1888 when the Natick Ladder Company set a world hook-and-ladder race record of 38 seconds with his team of 20 men, 15 of whom had to sprint 200 yards, meeting the other five who then all returned with a truck carrying a ladder while one man climbed to the top, some 28 feet above the ground. They would become known as the "Natick Immortals."

Maybe he wasn't good enough to be a top athlete, but Mike had ideas about what it would take if someone was talented enough, and he had ideas on how to spot the talent.

When he was 26 he set up a training camp in Westboro and invited athletes to come to prepare for whatever sport they were interested in whether that was track and field, football, boxing or any other athletic competition. Young athletes began to train with him and tell others that he was knowledgeable, and his reputation spread. Perhaps this was an activity in which he could excel. Another Irish immigrant, John L. Sullivan, the world champion boxer, even came by for training. Murphy worked with him and scoured around looking for opponents for the champ.

JOHN L. SULLIVAN I had been closely connected with Mike Murphy and he was from the very day he entered the coaching business, not only a national character, but an international character, and I really believe the coaching system of his day was due to the work of Mike Murphy. He brought entirely new ideas into the work.

A year after opening his training center Mike Finn contacted him. Would he be interested in the position of trainer at Yale? Would he? Finn explained that he had received a letter from the prestigious college asking him to become the trainer. But Finn was still at the top of his game as a sprinter and didn't see himself working with young men at any college. So he would recommend Murphy in his stead. When Finn mentioned this to a group of fellow runners, he received only a round of jeers in response. Never mind that Murphy wasn't the best of runners. Finn assured them that Mike a head on him that would get them more someday than their legs would.

Murphy agreed with that assessment and jumped at the chance to take the job.

At Yale he was an immediate success—liked and respected. So much so that he came to the attention of the Detroit Athletic Club.

The DAC had recently been created by Frank Eddy, a respected businessman/athlete, and a zealot for amateur athletics. They quickly recruited Detroit area athletes and formed a competitive track team.

In the days before professional teams provided constant mass entertainment, amateur athletics was the only game in town. The DAC almost immediately became an important force in amateur sporting competitions. They hosted the Amateur Athletic Union's first major track and field meet in 1888. Eddy, a sprinter who seldom missed his daily jog around the club's new cinder track had also been a key figure in the organization of the Amateur Athletic Union which would govern the sport for over a century.

Impressed that their local club had been given the honor of hosting the meet, Detroiters turned out in the thousands to watch 129 athletes from clubs and colleges as far away as Ireland. Of the 61 points on offer to the competing clubs and colleges, the DAC garnered two.

That's an embarrassment!

Something has to be done.

Let's hire a top trainer someone suggested.

And who might that be?

Why, Mike Murphy over at Yale suggested DAC co-founder Nate Williams. He was a graduate of Yale, a former manager of its baseball and football teams, and he knew Murphy.

So Murphy was lured away from New Haven to take up the reins of the new track and field team where Murphy brought unbridled energy, deft skills, and precise planning to the job.

His commitment bordered on the fanatical. He drove the team with a whirlwind schedule of events that bordered on full-time jobs and the DAC quickly became an accepted power in amateur track and field circles.

Under his watchful eye, several young Detroit businessmen were transformed into elite amateur athletes. Chief among them was John Owen, Jr. The same age as Murphy he had been born in Detroit, the son of a bank president. He had no formal training, didn't begin running until he was 28, didn't see himself as a track man at all— until the afternoon Murphy watched him play tennis. Murphy, in his usual methodical way of analyzing the athletic movements of players in all sports, thought he picked up something promising. Leaning over the fence near Owen while the players were wiping away the perspiration between sets, he asked Owen if he might consider sprinting.

Me? returned Owen. I can't run a lick.

Murphy persisted. After all he knew potential, didn't he? He had been a sprinter. He knew lots of other sprinters. He knew how to get the best out of a man.

Eventually Owen acquiesced and said if Murphy was that confident he'd give it a try.

MIKE MURPHY Owen was about 5 feet 7 inches and only about 128 pounds. He had never worn a running shoe, but the minute I saw him move over the cinders I knew that I had found a wonder. He had the bounding stride that covered great distance. Had I begun training Owen when he was 18, he would have set records for the 100-, 220- and 440-yard dashes where no man would ever touch them again.

33

Figure 10 John Owen, Jr.

Murphy worked with Owen over the course of months, working on his technique and the psychology of adopting a winning attitude.

Incredible things were about to happen. Owen beat all comers. Often easily.

Owen's crowning achievement came in an 1890 race that included Luther Carey of Princeton, then the country's fastest collegian, and Fred Westing of the New York Athletic Club, the fastest club sprinter.

Owen's style was to run the first and last 20 yards faster than anyone, but slack off some in the middle.

The starter pistol rang out. With Murphy watching, Owen sped out to an early lead over Carey. When Carey closed ground, Owen kicked in his great closing push and beat Carey by a foot. The four official times checked their watches.

Nine and 8/10 seconds!

Is that even possible?

Well, all four watches had the same time.

For the first time ever, a runner had clocked an official time of under 10 seconds for the 100-yard dash.

Murphy beamed his I-told-you-so Irish grin.

The Associated Press reported that the large crowd went dead quiet. Then the momentary pause of incredulity was punctured by prolonged applause and Owen was carried off on thrilled shoulders.

He was the first of the Murphy-trained athletes to establish a world record. He wouldn't be the last. Not by a long shot.

They remeasured the track to make sure it was a full 100 yards. It was actually an inch longer. They checked to make sure it was a level track. It was.

The press hailed the race as the finest sprinting ever seen in an amateur contest.

When Owen's train arrived back at the Michigan Central Depot he was greeted by a throng at least a thousand strong and carried in a torchlight procession to the DAC.

A modest man, he constantly deflected praise by crediting luck and Mike Murphy for all his track accomplishments.

Murphy wasn't done developing great sprinters for the DAC. At a meet at the University of Michigan Murphy watched as Harry Jewett sprinted for Notre Dame. Murphy and club directors wooed him for some time before he agreed to join the club. He proved to be a great all-around athlete. He could sprint, broad and high jump.

In the summer of 1890, Jewett bested Owen in a 100-yard dash on the DAC field in a spectacular upset in front of 2,500 spectators.

King Owen Is Deposed, ran the headlines.

Murphy had another outstanding runner.

The young trainer's reputation was spreading.

The Athletic Association at the University of Michigan instructed their football manager, Royal Farrand, to see if he could get Murphy to work with their players for a few days before turning them over to a football coach. They had yet to land a coach even though Yale's coach, Walter Camp, offered to coach the team by mail. They turned down the Camp offer but got Murphy to come for three days to help the team.

Murphy, without being paid, worked the players hard.

Nobody takes a deeper interest in their success. His knowledge of the game and tactics make him a very desirable personage, the student paper claimed.

Murphy returned to Yale the next year and immediately turned them into a dominant track and field power. Then in 1896 when he moved to the University of Pennsylvania, they became the dominant power. In his first season at Penn they won the intercollegiate track championship by defeating … Yale.

His teams were usually the best in the country, winning 15 of the 21 indoor and outdoor championships they contested during his tenure at these two schools, earning him "the father of American track athletes," approbation.

At Penn, besides serving as head track coach, he was also trainer for the football team and took a two-year course in medicine and surgery. He learned all he could about muscles, lungs, and hearts and he knew as much as most physicians anywhere.

During the summer months, Michael Murphy, trainer extraordinaire, coached many of the country's elite athletes at the New York Athletic Club's summer facilities on Travers Island in the

Long Island sound.

The *Washington Post* deemed him the greatest coach of track men and trainer of men in other branches of sport that America had ever known.

No surprise then that he was chosen to coach the American athletes at the Paris Olympics.

O O O O O

As a recruiting officer in the army of young athletes, Murphy was unrivaled. Material, partially molded, was turned over to him annually because athletes wanted him to put on the finishing touches.

What everybody mentions when asked about Murphy is how well he got to know his athletes, how well he listened to them.

He'd sit on a bench and play chess with an athlete for hours. He'd play long games with the jumper, Irv Baxter, secretary of Penn's chess club and a patient and skillful player. But Mike's interest in the game was secondary to his interest in the athlete. He probed like the expert psychologist he was. He wanted to know how best to motivate each athlete. One formula doesn't fit all. He was a con man and his con was getting each athlete to believe he could succeed where doubt pervades.

Murphy abandoned the old school of thought that said the best way to prepare athletes is to work them till they drop and then work them more while shouting at them the whole time.

The drill-sergeant mentality so popular with some coaches was never a fit for Murphy.

What's the matter with you?

Is that the best you can do?

C'mon, push, run. More, harder, faster.

He believed that a clean body and mind had as big a part in success as muscle and sweat. He treated his men as gentlemen and personally set an example for clean living.

And his connections with the professionals?

Forget that.

But you were a professional runner.

That was another time, another place. I don't want you to have dealings any more with the professional element.

Mike understood the need for physical conditioning to keep the body and mind in top shape. The irony is that he was not a robust man himself, and throughout his life he suffered extended bouts of ill-health.

He read a lot including, but not exclusively, what his athletes read in their classes. The novels of Balzac were his favorites.

There was much for the driven coach to admire in the driven novelist.

Balzac's work habits were legendary. So were Murphy's.

Balzac toiled with incredible focus and dedication. So did Murphy.

Balzac often worked 15 hours or more at a stretch. Murphy was known to work more.

Casually, subtly, while playing chess or eating or just passing the time of day, he plants ideas. He emphasized positive self-talk to overcome fatigue and control emotions. Autosuggestion he called it. He promoted what later might be called healthy lifestyle choices.

He was more than just a coach to his boys, he was a mentor, but also a friend.

Oh yes, he listened to them for hours on end.

Except that he was almost deaf.

You had to raise your voice … almost shout if you wanted to be sure he understood you.

He admitted he was not one to tell a secret to.

He communicated much with hand and face gestures, with a shrug or a frown, a smile or a grimace. He'd demonstrate when he could, write down instructions when he needed to. He never talked about his deafness. It was there, a part of who he was, and it would only get in the way if you let it. He didn't.

Listening/watching Murphy was a lesson in running, throwing, jumping that may not exist elsewhere. At least in this country. But what about in Europe? Nobody knew for sure.

The USA athletes defeated the Europeans fairly decisively four years ago in Athens, but did that only motivate them more?

Did they copy our training methods?

Different countries emphasized different events and that specialization might have taken them above us.

Mike Murphy didn't know. His job was to work with the Americans. He insisted that what the other countries did was not his concern and shouldn't be the concern of his athletes.

Years later, George Murphy, Mike's youngest son who was then a U.S. Senator and had been a successful actor and a famous a song-and-dance man, reminisced about his father.

GEORGE MURPHY My childhood memories of Dad are mostly that he was a natural born philosopher. Dad was hard of hearing, but since I was the youngest in the family and my voice was high-pitched, he could hear me better than the rest of us Murphys, so he talked to me a lot.

Dad was a wizard at looking at a man and deciding instantly on his physical ability. He could shoot a glance at a man 200 yards away and tell by the way he was walking or running whether he was in good physical condition.

I distinctly remember Dad saying, "The most important thing in my life is my self–respect, even if maintaining it means that if I'm lucky, I may end with only four or five good friends. I've been an honest man for 50 years. I plan to die an honest man."

He wanted no strings tied about him. I am sure the important issue was to look every man in the eye and tell him to go to hell if he felt like it and the occasion warranted such instructions.

He was also a real coiner of immortal phrases. He took one look at the fighter Jim Jefferies just before his Reno fight with the champion, Jack Johnson, and stated the sad but inescapable truth, "they never come back." Another of his famous phrases was, "you can't lick a team that won't be licked."

It's my guess that he was the quietest, yet the best–liked character connected with track and field sports in America. His ideas and customs were all his own. He was peculiar and always had his own way, and he was generally right.

For some reason, he had no faith in athletes with red hair. He claimed that they lacked the nerve necessary to make them first-class competitors. His idea of very large man was just the same, although he admitted that John L. Sullivan was an exception to this rule.

My dad originated as many innovations for track as D. W. Griffith did for motion pictures. I ought to know. Until I tangled with politics my life was deeply involved with running and the entertainment business.

It was Dad who invented the crouching start used by track men ever since. Dad also had a shoemaker friend make the first spiked running shoes ever made. Dad even invented indoor track shoes with short spikes, and he had a steel ankle brace built into the sides of football shoes. It was his boast that no Penn football player ever had a bad ankle during his time there.

Dad even told one of his track teams to use the first sweatpants and sweatshirts.

Simply put: Dad knew the game.

Despite his considerable accomplishments, Mike Murphy was a modest man. However, while he seldom offered up his accomplishments without being prompted, he was not shy about discussing them when asked.

Some years back someone wrote Mike that there was a great big schoolboy up in Lawrence named Bernie Wefers whom Murphy should take a look at. As soon as Mike saw him limber up he declared that he could make that man the greatest runner in the world.

It was largely due to Murphy's work in keeping the football candidates in proper physical condition that the Pennsylvania team occupied such a prominent position in the football world.

He had succeeded in so many areas that he had been accused of trickery.

Trickery no, but he always had his athletes take advantage of everything in the rules and he stuck with them and encouraged them.

He was set to do the same with America's Olympic athletes.

O O O O O

The plan was to send the chosen athletes first to London for a warmup dual meet against the British before heading to Paris.

The American Olympic Committee would be nominally in charge of the American team, even if it wouldn't select the competitors. Nevertheless, all the athletes making the trip would have to remain in good standing with the Amateur Athletic Union.

There were no qualification events. The only criteria: selection by a university or club and the funds to make the trip. That, or just the desire to go and the funds to make the trip.

Since there was no national funding to send anyone, it would be up to the clubs and universities or the individual competitors to come up with the money. Not an easy task.

For a while it was unclear which teams would send athletes.

The University of Pennsylvania was the first to commit.

For us, the journey to the games had begun in early April when we assembled to learn who among us had been chosen to make the trip.

O O O O O

I remember that morning with great clarity because it changed my life and led to my first publication when some years later I turned my observations into a short article that *The Century Illustrated Monthly Magazine* saw fit to publish:

> By late morning, blue sky began to show through shifting gaps in the cloud cover. As the streets of Philadelphia slowly dried, wisps of steam hovered low. Horse car lines were busy delivering workers to offices and shops while pedestrians and bicyclists poured across the Schuylkill Bridge. On the campus of the University of Pennsylvania surrounding the quad, the slanting rays of sunlight warmed the faces of the men lounging on the central grass quadrangle in front of the university's massive

College Hall. They pour over books, chat idly. High above the Gothic spires, birds fly lazy loops against the slowly bluing sky.

The men wear dark suits or blazers with slacks with turned-up cuffs and sharp creases front and back made by the new trouser press. Their shoes are freshly shined. Most wear hats. A few smoke Duck of Durham Cigarettes. They are studying to be doctors, lawyers, bankers and teachers. Whether they know it or not, they are the fortunate ones. Only about 160,000 men and women (or less than 0.2 percent of the population) were enrolled in colleges across the country but, relatively few at the prestigious colleges such as Harvard, Yale, Princeton or The University of Pennsylvania.

Founded by Benjamin Franklin in 1749 Penn was an alternative to the other four colleges then in existence in the colonies all of which primarily trained students to enter the clergy. In short order nine signers of the Declaration of Independence and 11 signers of the Constitution became associated with Penn. It became one of the first colleges to accept women and students of color but their numbers were sill minuscule compared with white men.

Casual conversations floated around the quad.

Was Nap Lajoie the greatest second baseman in the game? If not who else? You don't really believe it's Bid McPhee, do you?

Our Phillies have a chance this year. Definitely. Yeah, the Brooklyn Superbas took it last year and the Boston Beaneaters will be tough again this year with Fred Tenney and Chick Stahl, but with Lajoie …

Plans are laid to get over to the Baker Bowl for a game sometime soon. Maybe the opener with Boston.

Did you hear what Carrie Nation is up to?

Read about that genius over at Johns Hopkins who came up with a new theory about the cause of the earth's magnetism? Strange.

A small knot of women in unfussy tailored shirtwaist suits sit in a shady nook out of sight and earshot of the conversing men. Their hair is carefully sculptured. Like the men, they talk about classes, but they seldom talk to the men. That wouldn't have done at all.

By late morning the sun had completely broken through, unleashing a warm golden glow across the sprawling campus.

Three young men left the quad dormitory and loped across the grassy sward and onto the walkway past College Hall and Logan Hall. They were roommates: Irving Knot Baxter, Alvin Christian Kraenzlein and John Walter Beardsley Tewksbury, known to their friends as Kraenz, Tewks and Bax. Three bright young student, three fine athletes with similar dreams. Three friends.

Bax is sinewy and lithe, his light brown

hair parted straight down the middle. His well-scrubbed face is thin and sharp-featured with penetrating, ever-alert eyes.

Figure 11 Irving Baxter

Kraenz is more tautly built and darker complected with dense curly dark brown hair parted above his left eye. Tall, thin-limbed, at 6 feet he weighs 165 pounds. He is supple and active and nervously energetic, but phlegmatic even when excited. It is this quality of steady nerves that has won him many a close race.

45

Figure 12 Alvin Kraenzlein

Tewks is whippet thin, his 140 pounds
stretched over a 6' frame. His studious,
angular face suggests the serious young man
he is.

Figure 13 John Tewksbury

All three are 24. Bax is in the Law School; Tewks and Kraenz, the Dental School. They are stars on the track team at the school *The New York Times* claims "at present has the best college athletes in the world" but that didn't guarantee them a boat ticket to Europe that summer. They would have to be selected by a school committee that really meant selected by Mike Murphy. The boys didn't doubt that whatever he said would persuade any committee. And so it should.

The young men crossed the campus three abreast in long flowing confident strides drawing not so covert glances from the young ladies as they pass. The lithe threesome looked and walked like the trained athletes they were. They rounded a corner of the Library, skirted the new Dental Hall continued past the Dining Hall and then cut diagonally across Spruce Street.

Their destination was Franklin Field. Now 5 years old, it was dedicated for the first running of the Penn Relays. It was used by the track team and football teams and boasted the nation's first scoreboard. People are still talking about the successes of the football team, particularly the trouncing of Harvard before 24,000 people two years earlier. Hopes are high for this fall, but Yale? Well …

Franklin Field with its cinder track and grandstand along one side was one of the best athletic facilities in the country and the college men who trained and competed there were perhaps the strongest track and field team representing any college, which likely made them the strongest team anywhere. Maybe the New York or Detroit Athletic Clubs, but probably not even them. Compared to England, compared to France and the other European countries? They couldn't know, but they were willing and eager to find out.

When they arrived at the field, they waited until the entire team showed up and then took seats in the grandstand. Mike Murphy would tell them who was selected. He has about 150 athletes in training this year from which to choose.

Mike Murphy, already recognized as a good track and field coach, will soon be recognized as a great coach and eventually recognized as a legendary coach.

The young men sit on the bleachers in front of coach Murphy— "Mike" to them—the warm spring sun on their faces is welcome after days of rain, days when they were forced to train inside. That was never a good thing, never the same as outside. Mike made sure they knew that.

"I don't have to tell you what's at stake here," Mike said in the high-pitched, Irish-tinged voice they were all so used to. "It's an honor to represent your university and your country. I wish we could take all of you. You are the best track and field team in the world. I know that. You do, too. But I can't."

That's Mike. Straight to the point and direct. No embroidery.

He tells them there are funds enough to take up to 15 athletes plus the manager, Frank Ellis.

From the inside pocket of his suit jacket he pulls out a sheet of paper and reads out the names.

To absolutely no one's surprise, Kraenz, Tewks and Bax are the first named. They are among the best runners, jumpers, throwers in the country and if their world's records mean anything, they are among the best in the world. Combined, the roommates would enter 12 of the 23 track and field events on the schedule, and probably be favored in all of them.

Kraenz was something of a one-man team—an absolute phenomenon. By this time in his storied athletic career he already held seven world records—broad jump; 50 yard hurdles indoor; 120 yard hurdles indoors, outdoors and on turf; 220 and 300 yard hurdles outdoors. He had also high jumped over 6 feet; thrown the hammer 110 feet, the discus 122 feet, and the shot 30 feet; and run competitive times at 100, 220 and 440 yards.

Tewks was a great sprinter, having won the Intercollegiate Association of Amateur Athletic titles in each of the last two years in both the 110 and 220 yard sprints.

Bax held the world record for the high jump and had never been beaten in that event. Never. He was also a world-class pole vaulter.

After these three, the rest of the team wasn't as clear cut, but Mike called out the names of 10 others.

Most of his list was about as surprising as the sun coming up in the morning. It included their two big throwers, Josiah McCracken and Truxtun Hare (known to teammates as Jos and Trux); the runners, Alex Grant, Ed Mechling, George Washington Orton, Walter Drumheller, William Remington, Thaddeus McClain, the vaulter, Meredith Colket.

Oh, and finally me. I wasn't one of the stars, but I was going to the Olympics in Paris, reportedly the most wonderful of cities where I would attempt to record everything about our experiences.

O O O O O

A strong team to be sure, but mostly, we had no idea who would represent the European countries. Oh, we knew a little about some athletes from Great Britain, but what about those coming from France, Germany, Italy, Sweden, Australia, Norway, Austria, India, Bohemia, Greece, Hungary, Luxembourg? All were said to be sending competitors about whom we knew absolutely nothing.

"Gentlemen, go change for practice," said Mike after announcing the team. That was it, the way Mike did things. Not a lot of hoopla or fanfare.

After we had changed and returned to the field, someone suggested taking a few pictures.

Figure 14 The University of Pennsylvania 1900 Olympic track and field team

We practiced that day, but admittedly there was a little extra energy and some apprehension mixed in with our elation. We would represent the United States and that meant we would have a lot to account for over there.

O O O O O

The jingoistic American writer, Caspar Whitney, writing in *Outside Magazine* assured his readers that Penn alone could whip the rest of the world in track and field.

Perhaps no one was more influential in fanning the flames of American hegemony than Whitney. During the Spanish–American

War he reported from the front in Cuba, romanticizing the Rough Riders and gaining considerable reputation as a journalist. After the war he became arguably the most read national sports columnist, writing frequently about intercollegiate sports, always vehemently defending amateurism.

Figure 15 Caspar Whitney

He was opinionated—some said dogmatic and narrow-minded—often excessively chauvinistic, but his essays were widely distributed and persuasive. His was a voice of considerable influence in the world of athletics.

CASPAR WHITNEY   Except in the quarter mile and distance runs, there seems to be no one wearing spiked shoes in Europe that can beat a Pennsylvania entry. There will be no athlete of English or other nationality who can beat Tewksbury in the sprints, Cregan in the half-mile, Orton in the mile, Kraenzlein in the hurdles and broad jump, McCracken in the weights or Baxter in the high jump.

After Pennsylvania and then Princeton announced they were participating, other colleges and clubs followed suit.

The New York Athletic Club had ignored the 1896 Games and wasn't convinced it would send anyone to Paris.

That would be a big disappointment. They had some of the country's best athletes, Ray Ewry among them. He alone would be counted on for several golds.

Charles Sherrill, the captain of the New York Athletic Club appeared at a meeting of the Board of Governors and argued that they needed to be represented.

Penn and Princeton are going. We don't want them to show us up, do we?

However, Caspar Whitney, ever the cheerleader for amateurism, wrote an editorial in which he hoped that the New York Athletic Club would appreciate the impropriety of including on its team one man whose amateur status needs clearing (Ewry), and another (Flanagan), who, having landed in America from the Emerald Isle only two years ago, was hardly qualified to now represent the country of his adoption against the country of his birth. None but native born athletes should be eligible for international teams.

At their next board meeting the NYAC selected six athletes to represent the club including Ewry and Flanagan.

The team representing the University of Chicago was decided upon after several trials at Ravenswood in northeast Chicago where the maroon candidates were put through the tests. Their four-man team would be led by their already-famous coach, Alonzo Stagg, who would become a pivotal figure in the biggest controversy of the Paris Games.

Stagg was convinced his men would carry away honors both in London and in Paris, (even if they had to pay their own way) no matter whom the home meets selected.

Stagg ended up barrowing $2,500 from friends to pay for transportation to Europe.

With the impetus coming from these squads, other programs agreed to send athletes … if the money could be found.

Georgetown determined that it would send the best athletes if the alumni, student body and Washington friends provided the necessary funds.

A committee was set up under the direction of the Alumni Association to raise money and arrange for the trip. These plans contemplated the collection of a large part of the sum needed through subscriptions from the alumni and others.

Their Alumni Association sent out an appeal:

> We venture to address you to ask for assistance for an enterprise in behalf of Georgetown University which calls for the support and aid of all her friends who are able to give it, and which, in some respects, is one of the most important ever undertaken in her interest. We beg to submit the following facts:
>
> In July there is to be held at the Paris Exposition a series of athletic events, to extend over two weeks, in which amateur athletes from all parts of the country, and from various parts of the world, are to compete. These Olympian Games, as they are designated, will, on account of the occasion in connection with which they are to be held, as well as because of the tremendous enthusiasm which has been aroused in the collegiate circles of France, the

United States and England, constitute the most important athletic carnival ever held in modern times. Most of the large universities of the country have already arranged for sending over representative teams of athletes to compete.

Georgetown has achieved a position in athletics among the foremost of the largest and richest universities of the country. We have this past year won more first and second prizes in the winter indoor meets than any other college or university. Besides this, we have won the indoor championship for relay races by defeating the fast Harvard team. We have on our track team one man, Arthur Duffey, who is acknowledged to be the fastest known amateur in the world for distances up to 150 yards. In addition to this world champion, we have four other men who are among the fastest in the country for the various distances up to and including the quarter mile. With this team in competition with the best-known runners in the world, Georgetown has the prospect of winning a few world championship races and of scoring more points than any other American college, with the possible exception of one (Penn) in the track events.

This will not only bring great and conspicuous honor upon Georgetown, and incidentally upon Washington, but it will help the American boys to wrest the palm from

France and England, our chief competitors. We must not miss this opportunity given to us to spread the fame of our Washington college practically the world over, and we must send our men to help win points for America.

To raise the funds necessary to send our team to Paris we must appeal to the friends of Georgetown, to those who would wish to aid in the advancement of our amateur sports and who would wish to see America's team triumph over those of her rivals.

On the evening of Wednesday, April 18, a select concert and dramatic entertainment will be given at the New National Theater, the proceeds to be devoted to the fund. We respectfully ask you to help our cause along by patronizing this affair, which will be one of the most elaborate and noteworthy, from a social and artistic point of view, ever undertaken by the college.

They raised enough to send their three top athletes.

The University of Michigan solicited funds from faculty, students, alumni and Ann Arbor businessmen. They collected enough to send four athletes and a coach.

Syracuse University planned to send four athletes, including their star long jumper, Meyer Prinstein but could not raise the funds.

That the competition between Prinstein and Kraenzlein might not happen was disappointing. But the university had a wealthy supporter who worked for the Standard Oil Company which owned a fleet of transatlantic steamers. They agreed to offer free transportation to and from Europe on one. It wouldn't quite be up to the level of comfort offered by the steamships used by the other competitors but the price was right.

Some athletes including James Connolly, who in 1896 became the first modern Olympic champion, and Princeton's captain, Robert Garrett, paid their own ways. (Garrett was from a wealthy family.)

Cornell planned to send a team of seven men to the games. An expense budget of $2,280 was prepared and an effort made to raise the required amount. However, they could not raise enough and sent no one.

A marathon race was organized in New York to select an entrant … if the money could be raised.

Twenty-five athletes started the race. It was run on a 15-mile course that led along Thompson Avenue for 6 ¼ miles to Maple Grove Cemetery, near Jamaica on Long Island. Macadamized for the entire length, it included a half dozen hills on the way to the turning point which brought out the cross-country skills of the runners and caused six runners to quit and wait for a race when the company was a little less swift.

Fortunately, for the first time in a week, the mid-June sun was not beating down strong and a cooling breeze made it a good day to run a long way.

The first half of the race found Kennedy and Schell of the Star Athletic Club the pacemakers, with Arthur Newton, representing the New York Athletic Club in close pursuit. Then around the 10-mile mark Newton, the little 17-year old hat factory worker from Massachusetts, moved to the front. He entered the quarter mile cinder path at Celtic Park where he was met by a cheering crowd, which never quit yelling for the speedy little New Englander until after he had finished an easy winner by a quarter of a mile.

Now, if all the money could be raised through subscription he would be on his way to Paris.

The only other club-sponsored team would be the Vesper Boat Club of Philadelphia. They would send eight men to compete in the coxed eights event. Since they couldn't raise the funds to send an alternate in case one of them became ill or injured and could not participate, a member of the Harlem Rowing Association agreed to go along as a substitute at his own expense.

O O O O O

There would be no official USA team per se, no national uniform, no standard policies about who would compete in which events. That would be up to the schools and clubs.

Mostly, the universities realized that athletics were desirable and perhaps necessary for the full development of the student. Since not every faculty member agreed with this, some friction remained between teachers and students, but in many schools, coaches and athletic trainers had become regular officers of the universities.

William Curtis, known as "the father of American amateur athletics" and a founder of the U.S. Olympic Committee, loudly trumpeted the feeling that the Americans would fare well in Europe.

WILLIAM CURTIS   During the past 20 years many parties of American athletes have visited Europe, but no one of these expeditions ever approached, in dignity or strength, the American army of athletic invasion heading to Paris. The party includes the athletic strength of the country, and if they are beaten, the United States will be beaten.

As it entered the 20ᵗʰ century, the United States was imbued by an inveterate optimism about its future. The widely held belief was that the coming century would be "the American century."

By 1900 the American West had been won and the continent settled from coast to coast. The U.S. was by far the world's largest agricultural and steel producer. Henry Ford had built his first gasoline engine car and the age of the automobile was underway. Telephones were in wide use, cities were being electrified, moving pictures were a curiosity, skyscrapers were going up in big cities.

The American people felt exhilarated by the possibilities of America. Cynicism and self-pity were out of style. If any single word characterized the spirit at the turn of the new century, it was "confidence."

With the nation established as a world power it was flexing its muscles on the world's stage. Its athletes were America's athletic missionaries expected to demonstrate their superiority and by dominating the games, prove we were the strongest, boldest people in the world.

Show 'em what Americans are made of.

Didn't our success at the Athens Games prove our athletic preeminence?

Rev. Thomas Wentworth Higginson, the celebrated Unitarian minister, author, abolitionist, and soldier preached a creed called "muscular Christianity." He proffered physical activity was essential for moral well-being.

Modern urban life may have created soft men, but exercise and sport can restore manhood.

Sport builds character and teaches moral principles.

Sport's discipline and values turn boys into men.

Physical training is an important factor in the regeneration of the human race.

We were heading to Paris to preach to the world our gospel of national greatness, of the special providence of the American civilization.

While the Olympics were supposed to represent not conquering but fighting well, we had other ideas. Fighting well only counts if you also conquer. Winning is not everything; it is the only thing.

If we are the strongest nation on earth, then by God, our athletes must demonstrate that.

Olympic triumphs will confirm the divine providence of American civilization and echo America's vision of itself. Our victories will be evidence of the special qualities that make our nation great.

So, go ahead boys, and demonstrate that democracy builds winners.

Muscular Christianity would be on display to the world. Anything less than domination at the Olympic Games would be unacceptable. The pressure was on.

O O O O O

There is no question about who was expected to lead the team. Alvin Christian Kraenzlein was considered the greatest track and field athlete in the world—maybe one of the greatest athletes in the world, period.

The press was never shy about extolling his achievements:

"The greatest athlete the world has ever seen."

"Probably the greatest all-around athlete in the world."

"One of the most expert athletes in the history of America."

"His equal has never existed."

"The peer of all athletes of all the world."

"Probably the greatest all-around athlete ever seen on the college field of sport."

"Undoubtedly the best of all-around track athlete yet produced in the American universities or in the general field of amateur sport, either here or abroad."

"The most marvelous athletic phenomenon that has ever competed in public."

"In a class by himself."

"The king of college athletes."

"One of the finest specimens of manhood that ever wore spiked shoes."

"He forged the most remarkable athletic career the world has ever known."

"His record on the cinder path and in field sports makes him the most marvelous athletic phenomenon that has ever competed in public."

"The most wonderful hurdler that ever strided the sticks."

As he was among the most celebrated, written about, talked about athletes of his day, he was on a par with boxers such as James Jeffries, James Corbett and John L. Sullivan; baseball players, Wee Willie Keeler, Christy Mathewson, Napoleon Lajoie, Honus Wagner and Cy Young. Among College athletes only a few All-American football players such as Columbia University's halfback Bill Marley or his Penn teammate, Truxtun Hare received as much attention.

Such was the interest in Kraenzlein that several newspapers published his vital dimensions.

Height: 6 feet

Weight: 165 pounds

Calf: 14 ½ inches

Biceps: 11 ½ inches

Biceps expanded: 13 ¾ inches

Thigh: 23 inches

Chest: 30 ½ inches

Chest expanded: 38 ¼ inches

Forearm: 11 ½ inches

Length of leg inside: 35 ½ inches

Length of stride: 8 feet

Figure 16 Alvin Kraenzlein

He is a phenomenon, variously called, "The Man O' War of the Cinderpaths," "The Pennsylvania Flash," "The Kangaroo," "The Flying Dutchman."

He was the unquestioned leader of the American team, the spokesman, the star.

Kraenz didn't look particularly athletic. He was tall, somewhat ungainly when not running and walked with a slight slouching gait, but when he put on his spikes … well, he not only regularly beat all comers, he beat them easily. "Walk-overs," the press called them.

In Paris it was expected that he would win the 110 and 200 meter hurdles, probably easily, most likely the 60 meters and the broad jump.

What got the attention of the sporting world was that he excelled in so many branches of track athletics. He was not only several seconds faster than the next fastest hurdler in the world, but he was also probably the best broad jumper on earth and intended to prove that when he faced Meyer Prinstein in Paris.

Meyer Prinstein of Syracuse was good. Very good. So anticipation was high that their confrontation in the broad jump would be a (maybe THE) highlight of the games.

Prinstein was an aggressive, focused jumper, as competitive as any athlete on the American team. He wouldn't have as many opportunities for medals as Kraenzlein because he didn't run the hurdles but in the broad jump he would be a force.

OK, let Kraenzlein have his fun in the hurdles, but in the broad jump he'll find his match.

Maybe.

If the phlegmatic Kraenzlein was worried, he didn't show it. As always, he carried himself with a quiet self-confidence. Some onlookers took it to be laziness, but he had always worked hard without making it look like hard work. Some gifted athletes simply made effort look effortless. He was one of those athletes.

He ran the hurdles within his stride and loped over the cinders in the flat races like a greyhound. Unlike many runners, he was never sick after a race.

His natural athletic gifts outweighed his ambition. The only time his teammates saw him punish himself was once when Mike Murphy made him run a quarter mile on the mile relay team. Kraenz was as sore as a hornet. The idea of exerting himself for as long as 50 seconds was too much.

His perpetually relaxed demeanor could be taken for an arrogance that frequently annoyed competitors—particularly the more fiery Prinstein. There was never any love lost between the two, but the Paris Olympics would take their hostilities to another level.

Kraenzlein was born in Minneapolis, Minnesota in 1876. His father, Johann, a big, bearded, dark-haired malster in the beer brewing business was from Bavaria, Germany. His mother, Augusta, was from Selesia in Prussia. He had two older sisters, Rosa and Maria, and an older brother, Hugo, in the real estate business.

After his family moved to Milwaukee he attended East Side High School where he learned to clear hurdles in an improvised gym set up in the school basement. In 1895, the school formed a track team to do battle with West Side High School. Kraenzlein won the 100-yard dash and then went on to take six more events—both dashes, the two hurdle events, both jumps and the shot put. This was his first meet.

In the summers, he spent many days jumping over fences in the Wisconsin woods and fields.

In 1895 he entered the University of Wisconsin where he studied engineering and later represented the Chicago Athletic Club.

In 1896, at the freshman-sophomore track and field meet he won the 220-yard low hurdles and the high jump and placed second in the 100-yard dash and shot put. During the 1897 Intercollegiate Athletic Conference Championship, he won the 220-yard low hurdles and the high jump and led Wisconsin to the team title. The next year he set an indoor world record of 36.6 seconds in the 300-yard low hurdles.

Mike Murphy didn't have to see any more of this magnificent hurdler to know he wanted him on his University of Pennsylvania track team. He convinced Kraenzlein to transfer after his initial year at Wisconsin. Murphy knew as good as Kraenzlein was, he could make him better. Sure he had natural talents, but the coach could teach the lanky youngster the proper techniques of hurdling, jumping and sprinting.

So Kraenzlein entered the University of Pennsylvania to study dentistry and to learn from the master.

Kraenzlein's presence and efforts made the University of Pennsylvania supreme on the track at the turn of the century. Starting in 1898 he set six world and three intercollegiate records. He set world records for the long jump, the 120-meter-high hurdles and the 220 meter low hurdles, the last standing for quarter of a century.

Spectators often commented on how it looked as if he were stepping rather than jumping over the hurdle.

And he doesn't even look like he's trying.

Never seen anything like it.

And you won't again.

He had that rare coordination of eye, mind and muscle which, as Mike Murphy put it, "marks the perfect athlete."

Despite all the accolades thrown his way, he remained a most modest athlete— "an affable and genial gentleman."

One paper described how he once fooled a teammate while on the train from Philadelphia to New York. The train stopped at a station, and his teammate heard someone apparently on the platform of the station calling him by his name. He looked out at the platform but could see no one he knew and before he could figure out what was happening the train had moved on. At the next station the same thing happened. Someone else on the platform called "George," and again he looked anxiously around for the person who knew him. And again the train moved off, leaving him curious. But the third time, he noticed Kraenzlein's lips moving, and then he knew that he had fallen a victim to a clever ventriloquist.

The world of athletics knew boasters and self-promoters. But Kraenzlein wasn't one of them. He could become as reticent as a bashful teenage girl when questioned about his success.

He claims that his brother, Hugo, a cricket bowler, was a better athlete than he was.

After the 1899 meets were completed Kraenz made a trip to the University of Wisconsin where he was warmly greeted by his old teammates. He was by then famous, but they found him the same old modest lad. As much as they prodded, they couldn't get him to talk about his accomplishments.

He was the star of the team but he did not set himself apart from the others.

He is just as fine a man as he is a fine athlete.

Nothing seems to ruffle him.

Even tempered.

Confident but not cocky.

When interviewed he comes across as authentic and sincere.

ALVIN KRAENZLEIN   How do I train? Well that would be hard to explain. It is much like the training of any athlete. I never use liquor of any kind, anyway, so there is no 'lushing' to guard against. I use tobacco to some extent and do not stop it when I am training. I tried to at first, but I found that upset me worse than to use it. So Mike Murphy told me not to quit, and I have used it during all my training and cannot see that it interferes with my work.

Figure 17 Kraenz practices hurdles

The fact is, he trained far less than his teammates because he simply didn't have to.

In practice, Kraenz frequently pulled off broad jumps over 25 feet, ran the quarter mile in 49 seconds, high jumped 6 feet, put the shot 41 feet and pole vaulted 11 feet. No one else in the world could do that. Mike Murphy insisted that had he tried for all-around honors he would have established a record that would have defied the athletic world for years to come. He was that unique.

TWO

A S A RESULT of massive technological advancements, the second half of the 19th century saw a tremendous sports boom. Communication innovations in telegraphy and telephony allowed newspapers to report on events from locations all over the country. Some daily newspapers even included dedicated sports sections and numerous sports only weeklies sprung up.

New railroads enabled athletes to compete in distant events and cheap urban transport like electric streetcars brought more spectators to sporting contests. Edison's light bulb greatly improved the visibility of indoor events. Vulcanized rubber for balls and tires and new bicycle designs led to mass-produced sporting goods, all of which Spalding used to his advantage.

Elite colleges offered intercollegiate competition beginning with rowing in 1852, baseball in 1859, football in 1869 and track and field in 1873.

Of course, 19th century sport was primarily a male exclusive sphere, but women were eventually taking up sports like croquet, archery, golf and tennis.

It is not entirely clear when track contests arrived on college campuses. Foot racing was known in colonial times. Ben Franklin's College of Philadelphia which became the University of Pennsylvania had a foot racing championship in 1770. However, it was not until the mid-19th century when serious interest in track and field arose. Princeton was evidently the first college to develop a strong track and field program, followed shortly by Yale, Cornell, Williams College and the University of Pennsylvania.

Upon an invitation from the presidents of the Harvard and Yale athletic associations, 10 colleges met in 1875 to create the IC4A—Intercollegiate Association of Amateur Athletics of America. They laid out strict rules for its athletes.

The amateur athlete could not accept monetary awards for athletic contests, could not receive compensation for coaching, officiating or scoring, and could not receive payment for any occupation related to track and field or any other form of athletics. The definition stopped short of the English concept of an amateur which barred competition to "mechanics, artisans and laborers," who could not be considered "gentlemen amateurs." Nevertheless, most of them were exactly that.

When newspapers criticized the practice of offering cash prizes, colleges offered prizes worth a certain value. To pay for the prizes they charged entry fees, sometimes as much as 50 cents which was about double the cost of a baseball ticket.

Yes, it was hypocritical but it met the standards of upper class amateurism.

Tradition, however, obstructed this as it had other athletic movements, and many conservative leaders in American colleges remained apathetic if not hostile to the intercollegiate sport. President Buckham of the University of Vermont was among them.

MATHEW BUCKHAM Neither the character of our community nor the traditions of the college are such as to encourage sporting habits. A large proportion of its students, large enough to determine the prevailing tone of the institution, are sons of farmers and would regard it as beneath the dignity of free born Vermonters to expose their muscle in public like gladiators in the amphitheater.

With the increase in the sporting activities came the rise of the professional athlete. By the 1860s baseball was already hiring paid players and by 1871 the first professional league was in business.

Track and field contests were characterized by informality, lack of organization, variations in rules and chaotic scheduling. Athletes could compete where and when they wanted and against whom they chose. Although few athletes could make a living from competitions the better ones could supplement their incomes from the cash prizes on offer.

Athletes competed against others in an open and unregulated environment. The better ones roamed the country seeking challenge races or exhibitions and were among the first professional sports stars in the country.

By the late 1860s a different philosophy had emerged. It came not from working-class participants or organizers but rather from the wealthier segments of society. They espoused pure amateurism in which true athletes would never compete for monetary gain, but more honorably, for the love of sport. Any form of financial reward for athletic accomplishments was contrary to the ideals of good sportsmanship and gentlemanly behavior. Anything other than honor which resulted from athletic success contaminated competitions and rendered the outcomes illegitimate.

Beginning in 1868 supporters of amateurism formed sports clubs which replaced the distasteful professional running competitions with amateur events now organized, standardized and controlled by them.

The New York Athletic Club, formed in 1866 by William Curtis and two other New York City sports enthusiasts emerged as the most important regulator of track and field events. Club members based their philosophy on the London Athletic Club's constitution which banned athletic competition for compensation. Their membership was limited to "gentlemen amateurs." Now track and field was being controlled by middle and upper class gentlemen doing their best to exclude the working classes.

The rules were strict, if difficult to enforce.

Once an athlete accepted money it was impossible to regain his amateur status.

Amateurism prohibits any profession related to athletic careers including coaching.

Amateur athletes cannot compete against professionals even in competitions not offering prize money.

This meant that even one professional athlete at any meet contaminated all other athletes in the meet. So every person who had ever competed in a pedestrian race that awarded any cash prize was considered a professional athlete.

The New York Athletic Club abhorred not only professionalism but also track and field as a working-class sport.

To protect their ideas of amateurism, in 1888 they came together with eight other clubs to form the Amateur Athletic Union of the United States (AAU) with the expressed aim of regulating all competitive amateur sport in the United States, including track and field. James Sullivan ran the organization with an iron fist.

By the mid-1890s the AAU dominated American track and field. Any athlete who competed for money, coached for money, wrote articles about his sport for money, or allowed his image to be used for advertising purposes was banned for life from all AAU competitions. By the end of the century AAU affiliated bodies controlled almost all the best facilities, meets and coaches.

A. G. Spalding and Company was granted the right to keep lists of all the official national records. It excluded professional records and any results obtained in unsanctioned meets.

Any athlete wishing to compete in track and field had to go through organized amateur athletic clubs affiliated with the AAU. This included college athletes.

O O O O O

By the 1890s with the AAU leading the way, America was itching to demonstrate its athletic prowess.

Who better to compete against than the Brits? Ever since the Revolutionary War we have measured ourselves against the British model. Yeah, we may dislike the mother country, but against their culture we judge ourselves.

So, on July 16, 1894, the first collegiate international track and field meet took place in London.

It was, as English summer days are wont to be, wet and chilly. Nevertheless, nearly 10,000 spectators turned up to watch. Wet and chilly was nothing new to them. The outcome wasn't decided until the final half-mile run in which an Oxford runner came in first.

What went wrong asked the American sporting press?

We weren't prepared answered observers. We didn't even send a trainer along and once in England the boys trained little.

We can and will do better next time.

And they did.

The following year, led by Bernie Wefers' world record in the 220-yard dash, the Americans swept all 11 events on the program.

For the first time the Americans didn't have to look up to the British. The British, however, were wont to look down on the brash Americans.

There is doubt as to the amateur status of certain of the American athletes, the British press claimed. They are in the habit of seducing away members on other teams by offers of employment. We are pure amateurs; they are not.

O O O O O

At the University of Pennsylvania ever since the class of 1875 created an Association for the Promotion of Track and Field whose motto was "a sound mind in a sound body," there had been a close alliance between the academic authorities and those especially interested in athletics. By the early 1880s the university was supporting teams in track athletics, cricket, football, baseball and rowing. Gradually plans to secure an athletic field, coaches for the teams and a gymnasium took shape.

When the Track and Field Committee spiced up their spring handicap meet in 1893, they added a relay race, a relatively new concept. So that spring in a meet against Princeton University they held a race comprising four men each running a quarter of a mile one after another. Thus was born the most long-lived and most successful track meet ever—the Penn Relays.

In 1895 the University built Franklin Field for $100,000 and it was used for the first official running of the Penn Relays. It was a huge success, attracting nearly 5,000 spectators and competitors from Penn, Harvard, Cornell, Columbia, Lafayette, Lehigh, Rutgers, Swarthmore, College of the City of New York and New York University. Nine relay races were run with Harvard defeating Penn in the championship race.

In the second year of the Relays the number of entries quadrupled. Eventually they added the high jump, pole vault, long jump, shot put and hammer throw.

The University of Pennsylvania was at the center of American track and field.

In 1895 Pennsylvania was third in the intercollegiate championships for the first time; in 1896, second, in 1897, first. This was merely the beginning of the University's success. The championship cup returned to our trophy room in 1898 and 1899.

In the spring of 1900 with the Olympics looming, we were eager to strut our stuff at the annual Penn Carnival. We were pretty sure we had the best team, but very sure we had the best athlete in Kraenz.

O O O O O

Saturday, April 28, broke fair. The sky was cloudless, the sun warm enough for the spectators but not too hot for the athletes. Until early in the afternoon only the faintest southwest breeze swept across Franklin Field for the Intercollegiates of 1900. This was an opportunity to see some of the elite athletes who would represent the United States at the Paris Games.

Around 8000 spectators were on hand to watch. A fluttering mass of multicolored flags and streamers of the universities flew everywhere. Athletes warming up jogged around the track—500 from some of the top university programs in the country—Yale, Harvard, Princeton, Columbia, Cornell, Brown, Chicago, Michigan, Minnesota, Nebraska, the University of California, and others.

Our Penn athletes were out in full force and appeared to be in top spring form. No university in the United States had the indoor track facilities to match ours. It was a 220-yard cinder track with a 100-yard straightaway. Murphy says it gives us the advantage of regular winter training. Other universities have their men work on wooden gymnasium tracks which Murphy claims does more harm than good. Because we could work out all winter on this track, we were probably in better shape than ever before.

Figure 18 Orton running on Franklin Field track

The only concern: Kraenzlein's fitness. He had a touch of malaria. Probably this wouldn't make a difference in the hurdles where he holds a large edge over anyone else. He could probably win in a walkover even if not at full strength, but the broad jump was a different story. If he was to beat his archrival, Syracuse's Myer Prinstein, he would likely have to jump 25 feet.

Kraenz had been working daily in the heat of the sun to boil the malaria out of his body. He had been avoiding damp and chilly weather and had spent his Sundays out of town. He seemed to be on his way, but complained that he couldn't get his arms into play as he wanted.

After a slow warmup lap he said his chest muscles were weak. If Murphy was worried about his star, he didn't show it.

Before the meet it was feared that Princeton was about to dethrone us from the championship pinnacle we had held for three successive years. In response Murphy entered Kraenz in four events, adding the 100-yard dash to his specialties—the two hurdles and the broad jump. Hitherto Kraenz had never been thought of as a **pure** sprinter and most of our local writers were sure Murphy was risking his great star by this combination, particularly since Princeton had a 10-second man in Frank Jarvis. Kraenz himself wasn't at all convinced he should run that race.

Princeton's Jarvis is in that race.

He is.

He's one of the best sprinters in the world.

He is.

I haven't trained for that.

We need every point we can get.

If you think …

I do.

Consider what this program meant for Kraenz. Besides competing in the preliminary round in the broad jump, he had to run heats in the sprint and in both hurdles Friday, and then to go through the semifinals and finals in the three track events on the following day. It required him to be almost continually engaged on both afternoons.

He took just one leap in the broad jump Friday and then confined himself to his other events. He ran all the heats of the 100 including the final and all the heats in both hurdles. And to top it off, rain began falling late Saturday afternoon making for a soggy track which meant the athletes had to work that much harder. Still, Kraenz took the 100 beating Jarvis on the muddy track and took both hurdles as expected.

His suppleness and agility made the difference.

Still, when he won the 120-yard-high hurdles in 15 2/5 seconds he looked dissatisfied and a little tired. Not Kraenz-like at all. Still, he received the unprejudiced applause of the spectators. They know.

While he was engaged in this strenuous competition, Prinstein improved on Kraenz's single attempt of the day before in the broad jump.

Every one of Prinstein's jumps were over 23 feet. On his final attempt, he got off a truly astounding leap of 24 feet 7 1/2 inches. The crowd erupted. It was a world record jump.

Mike says in practice Kraenz once jumped 25 feet 8 inches and frequently 25 feet 6 inches.

Kraenz wanted to take another jump hoping to win four firsts, but because of the rain and the fear of injuring him for the Olympic Games Murphy refused permission, so Kraenz had to live with his results in his early jumps where a rested Prinstein set the best mark.

The spectators understood due to the malaria, he wasn't at his best. Anyway Prinstein's record was made with a slight wind at his back.

Anticipation was rife for the matchup of these two at the Paris Games.

But it left Kraenz itching to get his record back from Prinstein.

As it was, Kraenz won three firsts and a second, totaling 18 points. His individual score was within seven points of Princeton's total.

I came second in the two-mile to Alex Grant. I knew in Paris I would also be up against Princeton's John Cregan, but I ought to beat anyone else in the event.

Both McCracken and Hare unleashed long discus throws. The results were less important than the condition of the athletes. But they, too, looked satisfied with their efforts.

Tewks wasn't there to compete in the sprints but expectations were high that when he, Jarvis and Duffey line up in Paris, it ought to be one heck of a competition. Could the U.S. sweep? Possibly. Quite possibly.

THREE

THE ADVANCE GUARD from the colleges and clubs set off in mid-June. First to leave were the Princeton athletes aboard the steamer *St. Louis* led by John Cregan, their captain. Accompanied by their manager, J.W. Jameson, they headed directly for Brighton in England where they would spend several days practicing before the England meet. It would take them a week to 10 days to cross the Atlantic.

Three days later the team of the New York Athletic Club sailed on the *Patricia*. That same day the team representing the University of Chicago departed on the *Cunarda Servia* in the charge of Alonzo Stagg who had left for New York a day earlier to arrange for the trip across the Atlantic.

In the coming days other teams followed. In all, 42 track and field athletes representing 14 institutions sailed for Europe.

Pennsylvania	13
Yale	4
Chicago	4
Princeton	4
Georgetown	3
Michigan	3
Syracuse	3
NY Athletic	2
Williams	1
Columbia	1
Harvard	1
Purdue	1
Harvard	1
Brown	1

An additional 32 competitors would represent the United States in other events, some of whom were already in Europe. Among them would be seven women.

Athletes Representing America in London and Paris.

Figure 19 Nine of America's 42 athletes

We left Philadelphia for our country training quarters in Haverford, Pennsylvania, remaining there until taking the Pennsylvania Railroad to New York. There on June 20 we boarded the steamship *Southwark* for a sailing directly to Liverpool, passing the Statue of Liberty on the way out to sea.

The *Southwark* was a grand ship. The interiors were graced with statues, mirrors, gilding and various portraits of important-looking people. The first-class salon was adorned with elaborate tapestries, plush blue seats and Oriental carpets. The smoking room, as always a male preserve, had been made to look like a typical German inn. The huge dining room, rising several decks and crowned with a dome could hold all the passengers in one sitting.

Figure 20 Steamship Southwark

The elegant *Southwark* did its work beautifully, rolling and swaying just to make it interesting. Mr. Ellis sat at the head of the long table for our first luncheon.

Eat hearty lads. When we get to England you'll regret it if you don't.

We are just finishing the second course when a message arrived that a large shark was swimming lazily along the side of the boat waiting for his midday meal. Drumheller left immediately, looking rather pale. Moments later he gave up everything he had just eaten.

McClain soon followed thinking the shark had not been satisfied by all Drummie had shared with him.

We all enjoyed a good laugh.

At breakfast the next morning, noticing three vacant chairs, I went reconnoitering and found McClain, Drumheller, and Grant on deck carefully devouring milk toast.

Drumheller explained they found it far more pleasant to take their meals on deck while watching the waves and fish.

Are you going to do this for every meal every day?

Probably.

Our meals were everything that could be desired by an athlete. At first Murphy thought it advisable to eat big meals as a preventive for seasickness. We all agreed with that, especially when extra portions of the excellent pastries come out. The quantity we consumed was enormous and the effect on the waiter, who had never served athletes before, was amusing. But then Murphy changed his mind and put us on a regular training diet. Our faces dropped, but despite our disappointment, no one challenged Mike.

After Murphy and Ellis consulted with the captain for a place to train we were given space on the lower deck. Murphy assured us a gently rocking track was better than no track.

Every afternoon a large crowd gathered to watch us work, many with cameras in hand. Our work consisted mostly of short sprints for the short distance men and half-mile jogs around the deck for the rest of us, usually winding up with a salt water bath and an alcoholic rubdown.

Afterward Mike talked about what he had expressed often,

but Mike Murphy was a careful communicator and careful communicators make sure their messages get through. He wanted nothing that could be controlled to be left to chance. Chance can take care of itself.

The best man doesn't always win he reminds us. No, sir. He doesn't.

We had all heard the speech before. Knew what was coming. Knew we couldn't act as if we had. Mike Murphy demands attention and he got it.

"So, here's the reality," he says. "Control. That's what it's about. You need to be in perfect control. What does that mean? Well, for one it means you can't worry about the competition. Let him worry about himself. The moment you forget this you reduce your chances of victory. So what do you do if you're the nervous type and can't get the competition out of your mind no matter how hard you try? Yeah, I know that happens sometimes. You do, too, probably. Well, the only thing you can do is to keep as busy as you can leading up to the competition. Do something, do anything, but keep busy. Keep your mind busy. Play cards, play chess, read a book. Something. But not work. I've told you before, no work for at least two days before your event. OK, maybe a little jog or light weight work for the throwers. Particularly for those of you who have said you have sore shins or muscles. This is a good rule. It's proven. You know I never let you work the last five dates before an intercollegiate meet. This is no different. Treat it like an ordinary meet even if we have to go a few thousand miles first. Don't lose the good habits I've taught you."

"And the food?" Tewks prompts. "What about the French food, whatever the hell that is?"

"Thanks for reminding me," Mike says. "The 24 hours before

your event are critical. Nothing hard to digest. On the night before, eat your normal, hearty meal. Don't worry, the French know how to cook. You'll be well served. Eat anything that is easily digestible. Let's say you're racing in the afternoon. Eat a moderately good breakfast—toast, a medium-cooked egg if you can get one. Cereal, potatoes are OK. If your race is, say, scheduled for 3 o'clock, eat a midday lunch by 11:30. A light meal. Maybe a soft-boiled egg, a little tea, but absolutely no dessert of any kind. No French pastry. You hear that Bax? You want your stomach and bowels in good condition. Constipation. That's the cause of nearly all the illness and out-of-sorts feelings athletes get. Understand."

We all nod in agreement as we always did after a Murphy this-is-what-to-eat speech.

When not training, our amusements consisted mostly of playing quoits and shuffleboard. Tewks decided to organize competitions. The finals in quoits were won by Hare and Kraenz, with me and Tewks a close second. At shuffleboard Remington and Orton showed their superiority.

The social side of the trip was also very pleasant, the favorite girls having three and four admirers, all doing their best to get the upper hand. The outcome of these shall go unrecorded by this scrivener. The evenings were generally spent at cards, table games and dancing. Mandolins furnished nightly music. There were many collisions due to the swaying of the boat, but no serious accidents.

The stokers' games supplied considerable amusement. Every evening after dinner they engaged in sack racing, feeding each other with porridge while blindfolded. Bax and Tewks decided it would be fun to join in but with very humiliating results—especially the porridge deal.

On Thursday evening, Mr. Ellis arranged a farewell entertainment.

The feature of the evening was the news read by Orton. He had been busy all day in the radio room receiving word of the presidential convention at Philadelphia, to the Boar war, the affairs in China, and, most importantly, the intercollegiate boat race at Poughkeepsie. The Penn team won, he announces, with Wisconsin second. We let loose a long yell for our winning crew, which greatly amused the audience.

At the conclusion of the program, Rev. Harris, a passenger on his was to Italy, made a short address in which he offered great praise for how we conducted ourselves and hoped we would win in all our undertakings. This created great enthusiasm and long applause, followed by another of our yells.

Everyone on the team seemed in perfect health so the expectation of a good showing in England and France was high. McCracken had gotten over his poison ivy and seemed as strong as ever. Kraenz's thigh, which he had strained slightly before sailing, was improving rapidly, but as Mike suggested, he had to be very careful with it on board as the rolling deck had the potential to stress it further.

On our last day aboard I gathered most of the lads together to take photographs. Photography was a burgeoning interest of mine so I thought I would try my hand at a group sitting. Not everyone was around at the time, but those who were posed for a nice shot.

Figure 21 Back row left to right: McClain, Baxter, Mechling, Colket.
Front row left to right: Tewksbury, Kraenzlein, McCracken, Grant, Hare.

We docked at Liverpool at an early hour and although yawning and yearning for more sleep, we all agreed that the last 10 days were among the most pleasant we had ever spent. Spirits were high and we felt like a true team. The divisive elements that we would come to face in Paris were completely unsuspected by us then.

After a hurried goodbye to the friends we had formed on shipboard, we are off to do our first training on British soil.

O O O O O

After arriving in Southampton, Mike took us immediately to Brighton on the English Channel, where we set up headquarters at the Hotel Metropole. For several days under the watchful eye of Murphy we trained on the local cricket grounds, where a year earlier the Harvard and Yale teams had practiced.

The Princeton men worked out in the suburbs near London. Other athletes trained in parks or fields where they could find them. It would be years before any ideas of a unified team living and training together come about.

We all draw hearty applause from the English spectators.

After watching the Americans, the British sporting press expressed amazement over what was referred to as "Americans cleverness and agility" and commented specifically on the outstanding work of Kraenzlein.

We were preparing to meet all the best athletes from the universities of England, Ireland, Scotland and Wales together with some of the best amateurs of Australia and India.

The thinking among those who followed such things went something like this: Though the change of climate and excitement of sightseeing must be considered, America's athletes ought to win most events they enter. The quarter and half are the dubious events if England is as strong as usual, but Americans should win the sprints, hurdles, jumps and with Cregan, the 1-mile, although there are good English runners at that distance. Usually an Irishman or two of great strength and skill in the weights shows up, and perhaps these also should be reckoned among the losses but Sheldon may have something to say about that. The English Championships also include a 4-mile run and a 2-mile steeplechase, in which Grant and Orton will have a chance—Grant especially.

O O O O O

Earlier in the year, Secretary Herbert of the London Athletic Club, which claimed to be the oldest independent track and field club in the world, dating its inception to 1863, had written to us saying that the Penn athletes would be made honorary members of their club during our stay in England and would have the use of the club's Stamford Bridge grounds, otherwise known as the "bridge at the sandy ford."

Jolly good they were, too.

On Saturday, July 7, we arrived for what was billed as the "English Championship Meet." Most of us anyway. The athletes from Syracuse had intended to compete, but the boat they took up the Thames to Stamford Bridge had not arrived by the time the events got under way. If they didn't show up, the anticipated Kraenzlein-Prinstein confrontation would have to be postponed until Paris.

The meet would contest 13 events including the 4-mile walk, in which we had no entrant.

Let the Brits have their funny little stroll.

The day was cool and damp. Not good for running.

Unless you're British.

ALEX GRANT   Ah, yes, the English weather. The less said, the better. All I know is the climate affected me … and not in a good way.

GEORGE ORTON   The grounds were equal to anything we had in America. Maybe better. The track, one of the best I had ever seen, was one-third of a mile in circumference. The turf was magnificent, and for the hurdle race almost as fast as cinders. The circle for the hammer was 16 feet in diameter. In comparison with the American 7-foot circle, the 16 foot one looked like a miniature track marked out on the grass.

Although the competitors included the best of England's athletes and the cream of America's colleges and clubs, our Penn men carried off the greatest honors.

Baxter took the pole vault with Colket second. McCracken took third in the shot and fourth in the hammer. Tewksbury came third in the 100-yard dash behind Jarvis and Pritchard in a close finish setting up the expected showdown in Paris.

The distance runners, handicapped by the English climate, didn't perform as well as in America. However, Grant and I come third and fourth in the mile run and Drumheller fourth in the half-mile.

Kraenzlein set a world record on grass for the 120 yard hurdles and won the broad jump from a very poor takeoff.

Figure 22 London 60-yard sprint won by Duffey (right) over Tewksbury (4) Rowley (16) and Jarvis (21).

ALONZO STAGG   At the Stamford Bridge meeting in London we captured eight of the 12 contests in which we competed. This was the most remarkable performance in the history of athletics. We were beaten only in the distance runs and walks, specialties in which the modern American athlete had little interest. The Englishmen knew they were safe in the distance running, and expected to break at least even on the field events. When they failed to capture a single event on the green they were nearly dumbfounded.

From the standpoint of running and field form, the Britishers were not in it. Their runners did not carry themselves with grace, whether as regards position of body, use of arms or swing of gait. Over the hurdles they were awkward. Their methods reminded me of the style of hurdling so common in the '80s. They cleared the hurdles high in the air, making a strained leap over each, while Kraenzlein treated each barrier simply as an incident in his run. With the pole they were also far behind. Their method of jumping was antique. They lost several inches as a result of keeping their bodies too upright.

The mediocre work done by our distance runners was only to be accounted for by the change of climate. Our trainers feared this would be the case before we left America. Consequently, they were not altogether surprised when such men as Cregan, of Princeton, and Grant, of Pennsylvania, were defeated.

In the other events we swept everything before us, and astonished the Londoners by the ease with which we defeated the Englishmen. I have to say, though, the games were excellently managed, and every contest was run off with remarkable precision. In the management of track and field games the Englishmen are ahead of us.

There were no cash prizes but valuable trophies were handed out. The challenge cup, valued at $300 for the 100-yard run, went to Arthur Duffey. One nearly as valuable, given by Lord Southall for the 120-yard hurdles went to Kraenzlein. The K.T. Digby cup worth $225, for the quarter mile, was won by Columbia's Maxie Long.

The Syracuse athletes arrived just as the day's events were coming to a close so the anticipated Kraenzlein-Prinstein confrontation never came about.

The English people marveled at the ease with which Kraenz did things. One report said "he set the followers of the game to wondering what he was made of, for he cleared everything he took part in."

As usual, his style was perfect in everything he did. I punished myself much harder than Kraenz ever did, running the half and 1-mile runs. He never pushed himself because he never had to.

I can't exactly say I was jealous but it would have been nice to have had his natural abilities.

In the few instances we were defeated the result might have been otherwise under a more liberal division of drawings. This was particularly true in the hurdles where Moloney would have taken a second place had he not been barred from the finals because of having to race Kraenz in a heat.

Other than that, though, we were well treated by the English and our stay was most pleasant. There were a few complaints that we were treated unfairly by officials from the British Amateur Athletic Association when they disallowed two American foul claims. A few Americans spectators complained about what they considered substandard conditions for fans.

I guess you can't please everyone.

We ended our stay by being feted with a lavish banquet.

O O O O O

While in London, the American officials held discussions with their British counterpart. At issue was the question of where the Olympics would be held next. Since it was planned to hold them every four years, London was expected to be the next host city. However, the British were not keen to serve as the next host and suggested that the United States take on that responsibility.

The American triumvirate on the Olympic Committee, Sullivan, professor Sloane and Caspar Whitney saw the Olympic Games as an opportunity to not only promote their ideas of American social, cultural, and athletic preeminence but also to solidify their positions of power in the strategic locations they held in American sporting institutions. They each expressed the desire to bring the games to the University of Pennsylvania in 1904.

No place better suited for the sports could be found than the Penn grounds. The track was exceptionally fast, the field large enough to accommodate all contesting athletes, and seating capacity could be arranged for fully 25,000 spectators.

O O O O O

The meet with us was to serve as the selection process for the British team heading to Paris. The British Amateur Athletic Association had set aside £100 to send a team.

That wasn't a lot of money, but then again few of their athletes shined against us.

After being soundly drubbed, the Brits looked for reasons, and they came up with many.

It had to be more than just "an off year," because in several events they had champions defending their titles. And the Americans were already at a disadvantage since they weren't acclimated to the climate.

A writer calling himself, "Old Blue" writing in *The Sporting Life,* had a few ideas:

> No, nothing can excuse the defeat of our cracks by the Yankees. The fact remains that the best of America has beaten the best of the British Empire, and that, too, in all-around fashion. Why is this? Does the United States produce better athletes? I do not think so, nor

are the real reasons far to seek. First, athletics outside universities and a few leading centers has inexplicably fallen out of favor in England during the last decade. The fact is, latter day athletic sports lack that essential to increase popularity—party spirit and party feeling.

Another reason for the current superiority of American athletes is we play at sport; they work at it. We in England have raw material just as good as theirs, but they handle it better.

Our Yankee friends have reduced athletic sport almost to the level of fine art. Egad! As one watched Mr. Kraenzlein skimming over the hurdles last Saturday it made one think of perfect music! Then one couldn't help noticing the precision with which their vaulters handled the pole, or the way all the Americans took immense pains down to the minutest detail, to insure success.

Those who have visited America will corroborate my statement that athletic proficiency is most seriously cultivated at all the clubs, and that no stone is left unturned to make sure that the men have the most thorough preparation for every meeting. A careful study is made of the idiosyncrasies of each individual, and his daily work is arranged for him accordingly. Such a system thoroughly carried out cannot fail in time to produce some remarkable performances—such as those on Saturday last.

Caspar Whitney, ever the flag-waving jingoist defended his countrymen from the English charge that U.S. victories stemmed from the American penchant to make "a business" out of athletic games. Whitney was convinced that England's system was corrupted by wagering and professionalism.

CASPAR WHITNEY There was, perhaps, no professional in the world filled with so many dirty tricks as the English professional.

Among the professionals of England, from the racing of whippets to the racing of yachts, the tendency to "beat the game" was apparent—and recognized.

This desperate struggle for existence among professionals in competitive English sport had touched with a corrupting hand nearly every game in Great Britain, save cricket—and even that honored relic showed evidence of evil association.

True, the American team, with such performers as Kraenzlein, Tewksbury, Duffey, Jarvis, Long, Boardman, Prinstein, Baxter and Johnson, was one of exceptional strength—such a one as is not to be gathered every year, even in the United States. But even with men of lesser prowess, America would have demonstrated its preeminence in track games. England's poor showing, in plain fact, was a revelation, and it looked as if the low ethical status which had prevailed in club athletics for so long, were finally sapping its vitality. Oxford and Cambridge represent the best of English athletics in performance and in amateur status. Club athletics are neither prosperous nor entirely wholesome.

I resent, as utterly unjust and in most offensive taste, a very sly but perfectly obvious insinuation in the English journal, *Land and Water,* against the amateur status of the American team. When it came to viewing the conquerors of English athletes, the editors disclosed an astigmatic eye.

Outside of the universities, English athletes were especially poor in field events. If it were not for Ireland, British field athletes would have been but little above mediocrity. Their sprinters were barely first class, and although they had one or two good middle distance men, the average was far below that of America. In distance running, England was pre-eminent. This is largely explained by the popularity of cross-country clubs.

America's superiority could not be accounted for by the usual English assertion that "Americans make a business of their preparation for sporting contests." As comparing English and American university athletics that explanation was true; but as between American and English club athletics it is not sound. On the contrary, English club athletes, often, made athletics so much of a business that they were managed by bookmakers. No, it is not that America made a "business" of her athletic preparation, but it is that England did not know how. Now, ignoring incidentals and details, and cutting straight to the heart of the question, the basic reasons for this are two: 1. Englishmen are inherently slow. 2. They are sure they "know it all."

They are strong, persistent, thorough, courageous—qualities that long kept them the superior race across the Atlantic, but in the American they encountered an opponent who not only has all of these qualities, but had in addition, alertness, finesse, mobility. Splendid courage and dogged plugging are not of themselves sufficient to scoring on either the athletic or the battlefield.

ALBERT SPALDING   I am convinced that athletic sport has had its influence in developing the physical nature of the English speaking countries. I am not sufficiently familiar with the Italian character to make an intelligent estimate whether any athletic sport will ever take there. When we traveled to England though, we found interest in outdoor sports even though they did not look favorably upon our American game. It is not natural for Englishmen to look with much favor on anything new.

ARTHUR CONAN DOYLE We know that we have the material. There is no falling off there. I think the human machine is at its best in these islands. But we have a way of doing things rather less thoroughly than they might be done, and that needs strengthening. It is deplorable that we could not raise the money which would have made athletics more democratic, and put the means of practicing them within the reach of the bulk of the people. We tried hard and failed. The result is that we built on a much narrower base than the United States, which had 20 athletic clubs to our one, and widespread facilities by which every man had a chance of finding out his own capacities. This country is full of great sprinters and shot putters who never dreamed of their own powers, and have no possible chance of developing them. We sorely needed also some methodical inspection of our public school athletes, to put them on the right lines and save wasted or misapplied effort.

As athletes, we took little note of the assertion of some British writers that we take the matter too seriously and lay too great stress on winning. We were winning, that was all we cared about. Let others try to figure out why.

After thoroughly defeating the British we were exceedingly confident. We were on our way to Paris to show the world that through our Yankee determination we would do well whatever we undertook to do at all.

Bring on the Europeans. The Americans are ready.

FOUR.

AFTER THE LONDON meet we headed across the channel to Paris. Compared with the events that would unfold in France, our problems in England would seem minuscule.

O O O O O

Most of the team was together when we took a train to the English coast where we boarded a screw-driven ferry to cross the English Channel to France. The crossing was choppy causing some to spend time again near the rails. Still, it was the first time most of us would set foot on the continent so excitement trumped queasy feelings.

We chatted among ourselves.

I never thought I'd see Paris.

You think we should drink the water? I heard we shouldn't drink the water.

The French girls, ooh la la!

What do you know about French girls?

I know they're French.

You nervous?

A little maybe.

When we landed in France the train was right there to take us into Paris. Already France seemed warmer than England. As soon as the great city came into view we could see the big tower dominating the skyline.

Paris, lads! She's yours for the taking.

GEORGE ORTON   I had left London a little ahead of the rest of the team and so arrived in Paris before them. I had felt a little over trained and wanted an extra day of light exercise out on the track— or should I say, what they passed off as a track.

Feeling the effects of the dank English climate I reasoned that a few days in the Paris sun would remedy that. It was hot, though, and that proved to be an energy sapper.

In later games athletes all stayed in one Olympic village. Not so in Paris. Many athletes from other schools were left to their own devices to come up with accommodations. They were all over the map of Paris and vicinity. The Princeton team stayed out in Neuilly, a tony suburb 4 1/2 miles outside of the center of Paris. We stayed away from the bustle of the big city and the temptations of the Exposition by setting up camp in Versailles near the great palatial symbol of the *Ancien Régime* absolute monarchy.

The Germans were so upset with their housing arrangements that they claimed the French were deliberately trying to humiliate them, perhaps because the French president had opposed German participation in the first place.

Another big difference in Paris is that the we all wore whatever we felt comfortable in—mostly school or club uniforms. We had a big block "P" on our chests. Some runners sported a shamrock or a green maple leaf. There were no such things as national uniforms.

By the time we had left London we were feeling very good about ourselves and eager to show off in the Olympics. However, soon after arriving in Paris we realized that the great athletic games had been somewhat sloppily shoehorned into a sideshow of the International Exposition. We could find no place where the word "Olympic" was used in reference to the games— not even on the posters advertising the event!

They were being referred to as "the Paris Championships" or "The Great Exhibition meeting of 1900," or the formal name: "*Concours internationaux d'exercices physiques et de sports.*" Some men openly expressed their displeasure at this, but what was there to do other than to compete to the best of our abilities?

It seems the French would go just so far in accommodating the games.

Use our park for the track and field events, sure, but we will not make a mess of our beautiful Paris. We're not going to chew up our fresh green turf just for a bunch of runners. This is Paris after all, not New York, London or Rome. This is the most beautiful city in the world and we mean to keep it that way.

On Thursday, most of us made the trip out to the Racing Club at the Bois de Boulogne to check out the venue for the track and field events and to get in some light practice.

We were informed that the Racing Club de France dates to 1882 and was France's premier omnisport club. Their rugby team was apparently particularly successful and well-known throughout Europe.

ARTHUR DUFFEY When I got to Paris and saw the track for the first time I was rather taken aback. It was green. It was grass. It was lumpy! I had always run on dirt or cinders. We all had. I knew right away this would take some getting used to. Did the Europeans always run on turf I wondered? I asked around and found out that no, they didn't, but for whatever reason the French couldn't be bothered to lay down cinders. Maybe they thought turf would give their runners an advantage, I don't know. All I knew to do was to see how much practice time I could get on the somewhat knobby grass before Saturday. It wasn't much. I was worried. Doing something I had never done before and doing it at the Olympic Games wasn't a good idea. I was also fighting off a cold.

The Bois was huge, covering many tree-laden acres, winding paths, beautiful glades and a multifingered lake. The area they called the Pré Catalan, where the athletic competitions would be held, was in the center. It would have been a fabulous place to take your girl for a sunny spring Sunday picnic. As a place to run it wasn't so fabulous.

Figure 23 Bois de Boulogne

The French somewhat grudgingly had created a 500-meter track oval by sketching it lightly on the slanted, undulating grass surface. We could see how uneven it was. One section of the 100-meter straightaway sloped. The turf was not only uneven but it had been excessively watered and so in places was spongy—not like the flat, groomed, dry cinder paths we knew at home.

There was even an overhanging Giant Sequoia on the edge of

the track.

Bois De Boulogne

Figure 24 Bois de Boulogne

Now I can understand (maybe) that they didn't want to tear out the trees, but couldn't they at least have trimmed the branches? What real damage could that have caused? Branches grow back, don't they?

So many trees lined the track that the spectators would get only occasional views of the runners as they flitted past the overhanging branches on their way to the finish line.

It will keep the runners shaded ... cool said an official.

And for the throwers?

There's a clearing between rows of trees. They can throw into that.

But they're likely to catch their implements up in overhanging branches.

They should learn to throw more accurately.

The running hurdles are bent and broken telephone poles and

some have shrubs and weeds growing around them.

They're supposed to jump over them, not through them.

The takeoff position for the jumps is loose and on a slight decline.

It will be the same for all competitors.

Surrounding the area was a rickety fence through and around which spectators could enter such that they were virtually on the track itself.

And it was at least a mile away from any tramway and far from any railroad station. It didn't seem to be a place to attract large crowds—not like the thousands who crowded the stadium in Athens four years earlier.

Even the French press commented on how difficult it was to get to the venue for the track and field events.

If you had a bicycle or an automobile … but the athletes didn't.

That is why the crowds will be small.

Why couldn't they have held the events at the new municipal Velodrome? Wouldn't spectators rather go there than all the way out to Bois de Boulogne? And for the water based events … The Seine may conjure romantic images, but it was muddy and dirty with all sorts of unsavory things floating on it.

Swim with your mouth closed was the response.

ALBERT SPALDING   The grounds where the championships were held were pretty grounds, indeed, but not laid out as our grounds in America, to accommodate thousands of people. It was what we would call a country club. The track was of grass, and that to a certain extent would handicap our boys. The jumping places were fairly good, even if they were slightly inclined. The boxes for the discus and hammer were good, the earth being packed solid, and in some respects it was superior to the average American grounds from which our boys were used to throwing.

Complaints about the grounds notwithstanding, all day long during the practice day the grounds of the Racing Club were alive with athletes. The Princeton men were out early. They seemed to be in the best of spirits and condition and practiced hard before the intense heat of the day.

We arrived a little later when the temperature was already uncomfortable. Unless a storm should make the grounds wet and break the summer heat we knew we were in for a sticky day.

Workmen were busy arranging the track and hurdles and softening the jumping spots, the hardness of which caused some complaint. Others were busy setting up the grandstand.

Kraenz checked out the broad jump area. It had a slight incline which naturally concerned him. He mentioned it to one of the French officials and got nothing more than a shrug in response. He also had issues with hurdles which were about 6 inches higher than he was used to.

Mike worked with him a little on adjusting his final stride accordingly.

He would also have to take off from turf rather than the cinders.

So despite being favored to win his events, there was concern.

The Michigan men spent the day taking light exercise early in the morning and then again in the afternoon. The Georgetown athletes were the last to leave the grounds.

O O O O O

The day next day—the day before the events were set to begin—was a hot, sticky Friday presaging a hotter, stickier week to come.

We stayed out in Versailles, not taking the train into Paris at all.

We spent the day in lounging and taking short walks at Neuilly. The Princeton men did the same while most members of the other teams, which were in the city hotels, kept indoors, avoiding the intense heat.

Mike knew we had trained all we could. We were ready. A workout in those conditions could do nothing but sap our energies, maybe dehydrate us.

Were there nerves? Sure. There always were before big meets, but we were excited, too. Besides us and the nine competitors from Great Britain against whom we had already competed and shown our strength, there were European competitors from Austria, Sweden, Bohemia, Norway, Denmark, Luxembourg, Germany, Italy, Hungary, Greece and of course, France. There were also representatives from Australia, India and Canada. So this would be a truly international competition.

O O O O O

The American sporting pundits predicted that the Americans would dominate in Paris which only added to the pressure. We were expected to uphold America's position as the world's leader in … just about everything.

Four years earlier this wasn't the case. When Greece hosted the 1896 Games in Athens we sent some of our best athletes, but it was widely felt that the long journey and the change in conditions would make it out of the question for them to win. Still they performed well but much more is expected this time around.

Yes, the measurements in use there would be metric meaning they won't agree with what we are used to. Nevertheless, we should be able to adapt.

According to the press the American's will:

Win the 100-meter dash, the 400 flat, the 800 and 1500 meters.

Likely win the 200 and 60 meters.

Have a chance in the 400 meter hurdles.

Will take the high jump and pole vault.

Need to find someone to enter the steeplechase.

Kraenzlein will take the high hurdles, the low hurdles and, as one writer opined "whatever Jack game hurdles there may be lying around loose." In the broad jump he'll be challenged by Prinstein but has a good chance to take that, too.

Both McCracken and Hare were entered in the shot. One paper wrote, "McCracken is a young giant who toys with ponderous hammers, heavy shot, and huge dumbbells merely to gratify his idea of pleasure." Even so, pundits were of the opinion that Richard Sheldon, of the New York Athletic Club held this contest at his mercy.

Maxie Long of Columbia and Dixon Boardman of Yale are probably the sweetest of the Americans who will try for the 400.

Our big men figured to do well in the discus but there would be stiff challenges from some of the Europeans.

In the distance races … well, those weren't among our strengths. The argument went that given the American public's fondness for quick results that was to be expected. In American meets the sprints always trumped slower distance races. It is the American way. Still, Grant, Orton and Newton were ready to give the long runs a go.

While the American press was predicting great things for our team, much of it came with harsh words for the French.

CASPAR WHITNEY   The Frenchman is not a lover of sports as the Americans and English are. He takes his pleasures cheerfully enough but goes just so far in sports as pleasure and fashion allow. Deep in his heart I believe he really curses the Anglo-Saxon sporting wave that has swept over his country in recent years. The national prejudice against anything not of French origin is pervasive.

The real Frenchman lacks the Anglo-Saxon appreciation of sport for its own sake. The youth of France have never indulged in sports like the youth of England or America. There is no development of athletic skills in the schools. Only a few even have a gymnasium. There is no intercollegiate competition. There are no sports in the army. Schoolmasters don't encourage healthy outdoor activities. If anything school officials and the French government have exerted influence in the opposite direction.

Not surprisingly, they found organizing the games a daunting task. They had to overcome their national disposition, opposition of parents, of schoolmasters and of university faculties. They also had to struggle with imperfect knowledge of training, improper standards and ignorant officials. Track athletes are not yet nearly so well understood in France as in England or America.

French amateur track records showed that their performances were but little above mediocrity, and sometimes even below it. They wouldn't even compare favorably with American interscholastic records. They were accomplished running on grass, but still they are not impressive.

BARON de COUBERTIN   Anglo Saxons have trouble in getting used to the idea that other nations can devote themselves to athleticism.

CASPAR WHITNEY The oldest game in France—the only one native to the country—is court tennis which, while never popular, has always had enough devotees to keep it alive. Football has shown more real activity than any other of these sports, and its progress in recent years is notable. Rowing is one of the oldest sports in France, but to many oarsmen, the word "amateur" had no significance. Rowing in France is neither prosperous nor clean. Bicycle racing was killed in France by masquerading professionals just as it was in America. A great deal of polo activity is due to the winter residence of Americans and Englishmen. The Frenchmen apparently do not take to it. Perhaps this is because they do not ride well.

Simply put, France is just not a very accomplished sporting nation.

O O O O O

Great sportsmen or not, the French had created a city of considerable charm and interest. Walking around the city before the athletic events were to get under way I quickly learned to get my bearings by finding the big tower.

Figure 25 Eiffel Tower

The Eiffel Tower on the Champ de Mars could be seen from just about everywhere in Paris. It commands the city like no other structure in any city in the world. It is either an iron-latticed work of genius or a monstrosity defiling the city's artistic integrity. Opinions were varied.

Erected for the entrance to the last world's fair in Paris 11 years earlier, it was described by its designer, Gustave Eiffel, as symbolizing "not only the art of the modern engineer, but also the century of Industry and Science in which we are living, and for which the way was prepared by the great scientific movement of the 18th century and by the Revolution of 1789, to which this monument will be built as an expression of France's gratitude."

Almost immediately a "Committee of Three Hundred" (apparently one for each meter of the tower's height) was formed and was headed by prominent figures in the world of arts and letters in Paris including Charlies Garnier, Guy de Maupassant, Charles Gounod and Jules Massenet. They came up with a petition:

> We, writers, painters, sculptors, architects and passionate devotees of the hitherto untouched beauty of Paris, protest with all our strength, with all-out indignation in the name of the slighted French taste, against the erection ... of this useless monstrous Eiffel Tower. To bring our arguments home, imagine for a moment a giddy, ridiculous tower dominating Paris like a gigantic black smokestack, crushing under its barbaric bulk Notre Dame, the Tour Saint-Jacques, the Louvre, the Dome of Les Invalides, the Arc de Triumphe. All of our humiliated monuments will disappear in this ghastly dream. And for 20 years ... we shall see stretching like a blot of ink the hateful shadow of the hateful column of bolted sheet

metal.

Critics called it a "factory chimney—gigantic and hideous." Looking more like something from a railroad bridge design, it positively defied the scale of the city and didn't seem to go along with the mansards, stately edifices and grand boulevards of the great city. Rather it was a gigantic advertisement for the accomplishments of the industrial revolution.

Eiffel responded to these criticisms by comparing his tower to the Egyptian pyramids. "My tower will be the tallest edifice ever erected by man. Will it not be grandiose in its own way? And why should something admirable in Egypt become hideous and ridiculous in Paris?"

It would come to be one of the most recognized structures in the world, if not the most recognized, but for us athletes at these games it served as a handy reference point while wending our ways through the winding Paris streets. And the sparkling lights at night were spectacular.

FIVE

A MODERN OLYMPIAD modeled after those of ancient Greece came from the mind of one Frenchman.

Pierre de Frédy, Baron de Coubertin was a French aristocrat and as such was never expected to work for a living. He could have become an officer in the French army, a priest, a member of the government. He could adopt and support a charity. He could remain a man of leisure. He could travel. He could dabble in the sciences, or maybe the arts. But no matter what he did it would always be as an amateur. French noblemen did not accept money for such things. Even if he were to win an athletic event he would accept a metal, never cash.

His father was an artist whose work adorned many churches, but any fees he received were donated to charity. His mother inherited an estate in Normandy, which is where Coubertin spent his childhood years. He had two brothers, one a poet, the other an army officer and a sister raised to be a lady with social standing.

When he was eight, France was defeated in a war against Prussia. German troops moved into Paris. Pierre, like so many of the French, saw a weak French army. They were ashamed. Why were the Germans stronger than the French? They were more fit the French press wrote. They emphasized physical training.

When he was 11 Coubertin was sent to a school run by Jesuit priests expecting he would someday enter the priesthood. He studied Greek and Latin, mathematics and history, but the school offered no physical activities.

It was only during the summers that he could ride horses, fence, row, box, run.

He was an excellent student, an avid reader, an original thinker. He learned about how the English had beaten Napoleon at the Battle of Waterloo and how in the British schools the students strengthened their bodies through sport and so became soldiers capable of beating the French.

He became enamored of all things English. He read English novels, wore English clothing and grew an "English" mustache.

When he was in his twenties he crossed the channel to England, where, since he was a French aristocrat, he met important upper class Englishman. He had read and loved *Tom Brown's School Days* about life in a boarding school called Rugby, so when he could, he visited the school. There he saw the boys regularly play sports—cricket, soccer, rugby. Games were part of the daily curriculum and they were helping develop the English youth in ways the French did not match.

Figure 26 Young Baron de Coubertin

He learned about a man named Captain Robert Dover who, to irritate the Puritan government and their dislike of amusements, organized what he called the Cotswold Olympics with competitions in various events. And he learned about Dr. W.P. Brookes and his Shropshire Olympics. Coubertin met with Dr. Brookes and was made an honorary member of Brookes' Olympic Society.

He hadn't yet thought about an international Olympic competition. The French tended to be against anything international, believing it would make them less French. Coubertin felt quite the opposite— that unless France became more international it would be left far behind the more advanced European countries.

When he tried to explain this to his father his father was outraged.

We are the French; we have nothing to apologize for.

But other countries are stronger.

But they are not French.

We need to look at how other countries are strengthening their youths.

Other countries look up to us, we don't look up to them.

Pierre began seeing a future for himself as a reformer, as a proponent of change to bring France up to the standards of other European countries.

He wrote articles supporting his ideas. He gave speeches about the need to reform French education. He stressed the need for athletics and games. He traveled throughout France visiting schools, comparing various methods of education and concluded that when physical education was part of the curriculum, students' performances in the classroom improved.

He picked up the favorite Latin motto of one headmaster: *Citius, Altius, Fortius*—faster, higher, stronger. His sentiments exactly.

Coubertin had found his calling. He would dedicate himself to improving education in France by including physical training in the curriculum. But how to commit people to change? He still didn't know. He traveled to the United States and Canada looking at public and private schools and how they organized sports. He met Theodore Roosevelt and admired how he had developed both his intellect and his physical capabilities. Roosevelt a rather sickly child, grew up a nervous and shy adolescent, indecisive and lacking in audacity. He resolved to overcome it by cultivating his physical strength.

Coubertin thought about ways in which people from different countries might come together to participate in physical activities, exchange ideas and styles of training and playing games and to achieve goals of peace and unity while doing so. But it wouldn't be easy. Games differed from country to country, languages were different, communications between countries were difficult.

From his studies of Greek language and culture he knew something about the ancient Olympics in Greece. They were held every four years with prizes and laurel wreathes given to the winners. The athletes trained for many months before the contests, supported by wealthy citizens hoping their names would be linked with the names of victors.

Coubertin held an idealized version of the ancient Olympics in his mind. A vision where bonds would be formed among athletes and leaders of many nations, where artists would come to paint and sculpt the athletes, where poems and songs would be composed about them, where threats to war would be diminished.

This was the catalyst he had been looking for.

He developed his plan, but he would not go through the French government. Rather he would use the more efficient means of a committee of private citizens. He met with influential men, formed the Union of the French Athletic Sporting Clubs and worked tirelessly in recruiting advocates to his plan.

Some people mocked him for advocating that athletes compete in the nude as they did in ancient Greece. Some were aghast when he suggested that Europeans compete with Asians and Africans. Even his family thought he was a lunatic. How could he turn his back on the French upper class?

Undaunted, he arranged for the first international meet. He invited an English rowing team to come to France for a boat race. He was delighted when the French won but even happier about the idea that an international event between athletes from different countries could succeed. He arranged more sporting events in Paris and accompanied them with parades and banners just as the Greeks had done with their games.

Amateurism was always essential to his plans. After all, an athlete's motives were critical to the ideals of sportsmanship. Any athlete motivated by money certainly did not have the same love of sport as those who played simply for the joy of competing.

Coubertin's philosophy of sport combined his ideas of the Greek's pursuit of excellence, the medieval knight's chivalric code of honor, the English gentleman's sense of fair play, and the modern man's need to lead a more robust life.

BARON de COUBERTIN   Above all things it was important to preserve the noble and chivalrous qualities in athletics that characterized it in the past, in order that it would continue to play the part in modern education that the ancient Greeks attributed to it. Imperfect humanity always transforms the athlete into the paid gladiator. These two formulae are not compatible so we must choose between them. As a protection against the lore of money and professionalism that threatens to engulf them, amateurs all over the world have drawn up complicated rules full of compromise and contradictions; too frequently the letter rather than the spirit of the law is followed. Reform must come.

Because his motivation for the Olympics came from a nationalistic desire for revenge, patriotism and the Olympics idea go hand in hand. But there was more to it than that. The Baron also wanted to restore the cultural superiority of the destroyed aristocracy of which he was very much a part. He wanted the Olympics to help restore and protect the cultural ideas of monarchists, which he saw as under attack by the policies of the Third Republic. The noblemen of France had become men of leisure who had abandoned physical exercise so were no longer capable of meeting their potential as they had in former years. To Coubertin, the idealized French knight and the idealized Greek Olympian shared common ideals including an athletic spirit and a commitment to physical fitness.

Coubertin, when he began his call for a revival of the Olympic Games, never imagined the hostility he would encounter. Even his own French Athletic Association defied him at every opportunity. Their ill will ran deep. Petty power-politics and irrational envy trumped reason.

Maybe the French weren't particularly interested in sports, but if he could get other countries to agree, perhaps he could get his Olympic idea off the ground anyway.

So, in 1894 he sent invitations to influential sports men in numerous countries inviting them to a conference at the Sorbonne to discuss his ideas. All were from the upper classes, and none were women.

Not everyone was as enthusiastic as the Baron.

What a crazy idea. It won't happen because national politics will get in the way.

We have more important issues to attend to in our country.

French gymnastics delegates refused to attend if Germans were invited. Then one German finally agreed to come as an observer. So since he wasn't an official delegate the French gymnastics delegates agreed to attend.

Other countries had issues about who would be invited … who should be invited.

After much cajoling, 79 delegates from 12 countries agreed to attend the Sorbonne Congress. Most were connected with sports. Others were lawyers, educators, and members of various peace organizations. They attracted 2,000 people for the opening banquet, including the 79 official delegates. Coubertin explained his ideas and had them listen to poems and a performance of the "Delphic Him to Apollo."

BARON de COUBERTIN   A sort of subtle emotion flowed as the ancient eurhythmy sounded across the distance of the ages. Hellenism thus infiltrated the vast enclosure. In these first hours, the Congress had to come to a head. Henceforth I knew, consciously or not, that no one would vote against the restoration of the Olympic Games.

Coubertin proved to be a master salesman. For several days he kept the delegates wined and dined, while musicians played and sang. This was very expensive, but the Baron paid for everything out of his own deep pocket and let everyone know so. He would buy their support.

BARON de COUBERTIN   One might feel that when the elite of Greece gathered on the banks of the Alpheus—artists to show their work, poets and historians to read their literary compositions, diplomats to conduct their negotiations—the sport was but a pretext, in reality but a secondary consideration.

But no, these others came only to pay homage to the athletes. The predominance of the athlete was evident everywhere. It is he whose statue was erected in the avenues, he whose name was inscribed upon the marbles.

One can explain these things only by two inspirations–civic pride and art. We must admire in the athlete ambition and will, the ambition to do more than his rivals and the will to do his best.

The Greeks, who idealized their entire national existence, idealized athletics. So athletics, in their minds, had an origin in a divine legend. Olympia, they said, had been consecrated by the gods. Jupiter there had wrestled Saturn. Apollo there had vanquished Hermes in a race.

The Olympic Games were born in Greece because the feature of athletic accomplishment existed there by some strange law of physiology or some peculiar principle of heredity—and because of this germ the games were born.

Sport is not natural to man. We must not confuse sport with muscular perfection. They are very different. All animals have a certain vigor, suppleness and agility, but in sport there is something else again—something more. It presupposes combat and consequently willing, thoughtful training, the ardent desire for victory, and the resulting moral acceleration.

The Sorbonne Congress split into two committees—one concerning itself with amateurism, and the other the creation of the Olympics. There was never an actual vote on whether to create the Olympics. Rather they just moved forward with plans on how best to organize the games. This was Coubertin at his charming, manipulative best.

The games, said Coubertin, should be held every four years as they were in ancient Greece. They should comprise modern sports and only adults should compete. Athletes should not be paid or rewarded with money, and each set of games should be held in a different country, so they would be truly international. The first games would be held in Paris in 1900. At least that's what Coubertin proposed.

Others at that meeting, however, were more impatient to get the Olympic ball rolling and argued for the games to begin in 1896 in their original home—Greece. Greece deserved the honor to host the first revival, they argued, in recognition of their having been the originators of the Olympian ideals. For the first, but hardly the last time, Coubertin gave in and so Athens was selected to stage the first modern games.

The committee renamed themselves the International Olympic Committee. Initially there were five members of the committee, one each from Greece, Sweden, England, United States and Coubertin from France. They decided that each would take the presidency for four years ending with a meeting of the Olympic Games and that the president of the committee should be from the country where the next games were to be played. So the Greek, Demetrios Bikelas, was selected as the first president, Coubertin as secretary and William Milligan Sloane from the United States as vice president. The plan was for the presidency to pass to Coubertin for 1900, to Sloane for 1904, and so on.

With this structure in place it was then up to Greece to organize the first games four years earlier than Coubertin had planned. Nevertheless, he immediately got busy. It was, after all, his dream, his idea. He met with the heads of various sports, determining how long each race should be, what equipment was necessary, and how disagreements would be settled. He was doing what he did best—organizing and influencing.

Coubertin was hands on, up to his neck in details. He drew up the official invitations, he found plans for a velodrome and sent them on to Athens. He secured designs for medals and diplomas. He did what he could to whip up interest in the games.

But it wasn't easy. In France, the French Shooting Federation refused to participate. In Great Britain calls were made to hold "Pan-Britannic Games" instead. The Germans issued an official announcement that they would not participate. Despite these and other problems Coubertin was resolved that nothing could kill his enthusiasm for the games. He remained in constant communication with sports figures throughout Europe and America.

But soon bad news came from Greece. The games were in danger of collapsing. Money was the issue. Coubertin sailed for Greece at once. He found the government unwilling or unable to accomplish much of anything. Neither for the first nor last time, Greece was embroiled in seething political turmoil, so while there was some level of public support for the games, there was little official government support.

If anything would save the games, Coubertin knew, it would be Greek pride. His contagious enthusiasm and refusal to let anything stand in his way stood him in good stead. His singularity of purpose and dogged determinism, were more than any other single cause, the reason the modern Olympic Games came into existence.

Coubertin recruited the aid of the one man in Greece whom everyone would respect: the crown prince. Constantine jumped at the chance. The Greek people could now watch him, their future king, accomplish the impossible. With his two brothers he took over the job of raising money to save the games.

Meanwhile Coubertin rallied the Athenian public. He talked to everyone he could. He talked to cab drivers and told them about how many visitors would be in the city. He talked to merchants about how the visitors would spend money in their establishments.

Before he returned to Paris he made a pilgrimage to the site of ancient Olympia. There he imagined famous Greeks going about their business of philosophy, democracy, arts and sport. By the time he left Greece, he thought his troubles were behind him.

They were not.

He was barely back on French soil before things began to crumble again. Coubertin's estimates of expenses were far short of what the games would actually cost and the government staunchly refused to pick up the difference. The prince's reputation was now at stake. He had told his people he would raise the necessary funds. Eventually, from the sale of special postage stamps, and large donations from wealthy Greeks living outside their country, and from thousands of small donations, they had enough—barely.

The king and queen eventually became enthusiastic supporters.

We'll host the games now and always they declared.

Coubertin had other ideas. They need to rotate every four years to a different country.

The Olympics are Greek. They're ours.

They belong to the world.

Then let the world come to us.

They will for the first games.

The Olympics are a local festival.

No matter where they're held, they will always honor Greece.

Eventually the Greek royal family gave in. We'll host the first games in Olympia and we'll see after that. Olympia is the perfect place to revive the ancient tradition.

Except it's too far away from the populace. It needs to be in Athens.

But there was one problem: no money for a stadium. Finally, a Greek financier named Averoff came to the rescue and agreed to finance a magnificent new stadium in Athens.

Then when they announced the games to the world they mostly got a yawn.

The British argued that competitive sports originated with them.

The Germans were only really interested in football, the Americans in baseball.

Even the French were noncommittal. Coubertin was French. Why didn't he bring the games to France?

Constantine was now firmly in charge. Coubertin was brushed

aside. He became bitter, unable to understand how his Greek friends could turn against him.

BARON de COUBERTIN Sure of success, they had no more need of me. I was no more than an intruder, recalling by my presence, the foreign initiative. From this moment on, not only was my name no longer mentioned but each appeared to make it his business to help wipe away the memory of the part played by France in the restoration of the Olympiads. Most of those whom, the year before I had gathered around the newborn work, avoided meeting me or pretended not to recognize me.

Not everyone was disappointed to see Coubertin's influence limited.

CASPAR WHITNEY Coubertin was a well-meaning, fussy and incompetent little Frenchman, who stirred up the athletic feeling in France, but that's no reason to permit the International Olympic Committee to be a fad of his. What was desperately needed was a complete reorganization of the whole IOC in personnel and in method of conduct. The IOC is a clumsy affair, composed largely of inexperienced men, chosen after the fashion that obtains in nominating patronesses to smart garden parties by the well-meaning, if capricious gentleman, who appear to view the *Comité Athletique* as a kind of social boardwalk.

With the games ready to begin, Coubertin arrived in Athens early in April 1896. On the official documents he was simply referred to as a, "journalist."

Bitter, yes, but he would show only unbridled enthusiasm to the public. He wrote a letter from Athens on the eve of the games:

> The sun shines, and the Olympic Games are here. The fears and ironies of the past year have disappeared. The skeptics have been eliminated. The Olympic Games have not a single enemy.
>
> The flags of France, Russia, America, Germany, Sweden, and England fly in the soft breezes of Attica. Preparations are comprehensive. Everywhere people are shining up the marble, applying new plaster and fresh paint. They are paving, cleaning, decorating.
>
> The surroundings of the stadium produce an impression heightened by reflection. Here we have a tableau that the ancestral Greeks so often witnessed. There is room for about 50,000 spectators. Portions of the seats are in wood, time having been lacking to cut and place all the marble. After the Games this work will be completed, bronze work, trophies, and the columns will break up the severe monotony of its lines. The track is no longer dusty as before. A cinder track has replaced it, built by an expert brought from England for the purpose.

O O O O O

It was up to professor Sloane, the American representative on the International Olympic Committee, to gather a team of athletes to represent the United States.

Figure 27 William Milligan Sloane

Sloane, an historian and academic, had received a doctorate from the University of Leipzig and was a professor of Latin and History at Princeton University.

Putting together an Olympic team was no easy task when almost no one had even heard of "Olympic Games." The American papers hadn't covered the events at the Sorbonne Congress and showed little interest in some unknown French Baron's ideas of internationalism.

Sloane contacted everyone he knew in the sports world. A football coach knew some athletes from the Boston Athletic Association who might like to go to Greece. The coach came up with eight men who could run, shoot or jump. Sloane contacted other colleges and eventually rounded up 13 men to represent the United States.

Finding the money to travel to Greece proved difficult. Few athletes could afford tickets on their own. At the last moment, a former governor of Massachusetts helped find the money for all but two tickets. Dr. Sloane and his wife who had saved up everything they could for their tickets, gave the tickets to the last two athletes and stayed home in New Jersey, where they searched mostly in vain for newspaper accounts of the games.

Figure 28 James Connolly

JAMES CONNOLLY   When I heard they would stage modern Olympian Games in Athens, I knew I couldn't pass up the opportunity to participate. I was a pretty decent jumper so I figured I'd try my hand against some of the world's best. Whether I could win or not I didn't know but I knew I wanted to try. The problem was, though, I had just entered Harvard to study classics. I didn't want to lose my tenuous place in the college.

My parents were poor Irish immigrants from the Aran Islands where my father eked out what living he could as a fisherman. We had no tradition of higher education in my family. I never even attended high school but I passed the Harvard entrance exam and felt lucky to be studying there. The only thing I could think to do was to request a leave of absence. They turned me down flat saying that the only thing I could do would be to resign and apply again when I returned from my foolish junket. My Irish temper got the best of me and I replied, "I'm not resigning and I'm not making an application to re-enter. I'm through with Harvard right now. Good day." That was rash on my part and I immediately regretted it, but it was done and I had to live with it. I never went back to Harvard. Many years later, they offered me an honorary doctorate. I turned them down flat.

Anyway I had to get to Greece. I had been competing as a member of the Suffolk Athletic Club and they came up with some funds. I appealed to members of my church who arranged for cake sales. The rest I had to scrape up myself which was anything but easy, but I managed.

I sailed for Greece on the German freighter, the *Barbarossa*. But when we arrived in Naples, I was in some difficulty because I didn't know the language. I located the train station and bought a ticket to Athens. Then while waiting on the platform for the train, some kid came running by and grabbed the ticket out of my hand. Given my meager finances to begin with, I knew I certainly couldn't afford to lose that, so I took chase. Being a track athlete has its advantages. I caught the kid as he was rounding the station and retrieved my ticket. He got away but I didn't care, I had what I needed. I took the next train to Athens arriving just in time for the competitions to begin.

Most of the rest of the American team sailed for Naples on March 21, 1896, aboard the *Steamship Fulda* and then took a series of trains, finally arriving in Athens the day before the events were to begin.

Despite the relative apathy, the games opened with a huge crowd in the stadium as the Queen and the King of Greece decked out in full military uniform presided as a choir of hundreds sang the new Olympic Hymn.

Figure 29 The 1896 Olympic Stadium

There were all of 241 athletes and 164 of them were Greek. Most of the non-Greek athletes were tourists who happened to be in Athens and entered on a lark. Forty-three events were staged in 10 sports before large crowds.

The Americans won nine out of 12 track and field events. The Germans and the Greeks won the gymnastics and wrestling. The French cyclists and fencers took top honors. The Hungarians and Austrians won most of the swimming events. In weightlifting the Britons and Danes took the laurels.

James Connolly took the hop, skip and jump by more than a meter, making him, the first American Olympic champion. He received a silver medal for that because in those days that's what they gave the winners. After that he took second in the high jump, and third in the long jump.

Probably the most important American competitor, though, was

Robert Garrett, whose widowed mother was a member of a wealthy Baltimore banking family who also owned the Baltimore and Ohio Railroad. She financed not only her son but three Princeton students as well. Garrett won both the shot put and the discus and came in second in the long jump and high jump.

Spyridon Louis of Greece, the first winner of the marathon, received a silver medal and a laurel wreath, as well as free shaves for life from a patriotic Greek barber. Unfortunately, the barber died after giving Louis only two shaves and his sons, who took over the business, refused to honor their late father's pledge.

SENATOR HENRY CABOT LODGE   Here was one more symbol of the growing belief of our superiority. It is the spirit of victory which subordinates the individual to the group, and which enables members of that group whether it be a college or a nation, to achieve great results and attain high ideals.

Some Americans opined that our athletes demonstrated Anglo-Saxon superiority and the quest for world domination as Lodge and other imperialists claimed.

JAMES CONNOLLY As I understand it, the Athens Games had the largest international participation in a sporting event ever held until that time and the magnificent Panathinaiko Stadium held the largest crowd ever to see a sporting event. Why would they ever think about holding the games any other place? Athens was perfect and it was the birthplace of Olympianism. When we heard that they wanted to hold the next games elsewhere, all of us American athletes wrote up a petition and signed it.

To his Royal Highness, Constantine, Crown Prince of Greece:

137

We, the American participants in the international Olympic Games at Athens, wish to express to you, and through you to the committee and to the people of Greece, our heartfelt appreciation of the great kindness and warm hospitality of which we have been continually the recipients during our stay here.

We also desire to acknowledge our entire satisfaction with all the arrangements for the conduct of the games. The existence of the Stadium as a structure so uniquely adapted to its purpose; the proved ability of Greece to competently administer the games, and above all, that Greece is the original home of the Olympic Games; all these considerations force upon us the conviction that these games should never be removed from their native soil.

Coubertin was not moved to change his mind and certainly not persuaded by American athletes.

On the final day of the games, which had run for 10 days the King of Greece hosted a banquet. He thanked all those who made the games possible and announced that he wanted Athens to be the permanent home of all future Olympic Games. He did not mention Pierre de Coubertin.

Numerous American papers chided the absurdity of holding the Olympic Games anywhere outside of Greece.

"I hope that we should never think of giving the name Olympic Games to contests held in the United States," wrote *The New York Times.*

So successful were those first games that the Greeks again claimed it their birthright to become the permanent home for all future Olympic festivals. Even the king of Greece got involved in lobbying Coubertin and the newly formed International Olympic Committee on behalf of Greece's claim to be the permanent host. Coubertin strenuously objected. The games ought to belong to all the people, not just the Greeks. The Greeks became angry at the Baron's obstinacy accusing him of being a thief, trying to strip Greece of one of the historic jewels of her raiment. The King responded that Coubertin ought to approve of Greece's proposal or immediately resign.

Coubertin refused. He was distraught. He argued that every major city in the world should have a chance of hosting the games. How else would they be truly international? If Greece was the permanent home the games would always be a local festival. He argued again and again that the 1900 Games should be held in Paris.

The Greeks could not be deterred. They were determined that even if games were organized in Paris, they would have to compete with their games in Athens.

Eventually, after much arguing, numerous meetings and considerable hostility, the Greeks softened their demand. Not because of Coubertin's persuasiveness, but because of the financial contingencies brought on by their war with Turkey.

But if not Athens, where? When Coubertin again proposed that Paris host the next Olympics the Union des Sociétés Francaises de Sports Athlétiques opposed the plan even though Coubertin was its secretary-general. The lack of French enthusiasm was discouraging but Coubertin was determined.

Still, it was one thing to stage successful games in Athens, the birthplace of the Olympics, but serious questions remained:

Was Athens a one-off event?

Would there be interest in more games? Will interest die out?

Can the idea of modern Olympics be sustained? And if it can, can it survive outside Greece?

Yes, yes and yes, proclaimed Coubertin. Everyone was waiting for something spectacular, said Coubertin, something to crown everything else in modern sports. That will come in Paris in 1900.

At the dawn of the new millennium France was struggling with a diminished reputation in the world but hopeful that the Olympic Games and the great Exhibition would serve as transformational events to a brave new French world.

O O O O O

The Games of 1900 had a very difficult birth.

The ancient Greeks who invented the Olympics would have shaken their heads at the traveling-circus idea of the modern games. They had no interest in holding Olympics one year in Sparta, the next in Corinth, then in Delphi. No, for more than a thousand years, they successfully took place in the same wooded sanctuary of Olympia. That only ended because in the fourth century A.D. the Roman Emperor Theodosius, a Christian, was appalled at the thought of anything celebrating the old pagan gods.

Coubertin had left Athens a dispirited man. Although for the press he said he wasn't, he was deeply hurt by the way he was treated in Athens. Still, he went ahead with his plans for the games to go on in Paris in 1900.

To The Union of French Societies for Athletic Sports fell the task of organizing the games. They arranged for most competitions to be held outside of Paris in a beautiful private manor setting. At the last minute though, after imagining the mess the athletes would make of his property, the lord of the manor reneged on his agreement.

It looked once again as if the games would have to be canceled.

But wait! Maybe they could be folded into the *L'Exposition Universelle Internationale de 1900 a Paris* which was already well into the planning stage. Yes, it was to be a trade and industry fair, but that meant there would be plenty of people around that summer when many Parisians usually abandoned the hot city for country retreats. They approached the organizing powers that be.

With more than a little uncertainty they eventually agreed to shoehorn the Olympics into their much grander scheme for the Exposition.

Because of the agreement, Coubertin was pushed aside. He would have little influence on how the games would be run. Not on their promotion, scheduling, choice of venues or even selection of judges. All of this would be left to commissioner of the Exposition.

The problem was that Paris had committed so much to the spectacle of the Exposition that there was little left for the games. Facilities were scarce. There was no stadium, no swimming pool. Runners would have to use the city streets and a big wooded park. Swimmers would be left to cope with the currents of the murky Seine.

Coubertin had envisioned a fabulous reconstruction of ancient Olympia complete with statues, temples, artworks representing the entire history of sport, gymnasia, and classical stadia reminding visitors and athletes of the glory that was ancient Greece.

But Alfred Picard, General Director of the Exhibition had a very different vision that had little room for sport, at best a useless and absurd activity, and he bitterly resented Coubertin's attempted intrusion into his Exposition plans.

BARON de COUBERTIN   How could anyone, in 1900, refuse for an undertaking anything like the revival of Olympism after its success in Athens and the interest it had met with in the press? But Mr. Alfred Picard was averse to "taking over" somebody else's idea. Right from the start, he disliked including the second Olympiad within the Paris Universal Exhibition, nor was he any more enthusiastic about having a separate sports section.

The 56-year old Alfred Picard was trained as an engineer. A graduate of the Ecole Polytechnique and the School of Roads and Bridges, he engineered several French canals, railroads and highways. After a stint in the army, he was promoted to the Chief of Staff of the Ministry of Public Works.

Figure 30 Alfred Picard

An ultraconservative politician he, like many others at the time, positively loathed sport. They were a complete waste of time, they took time away from more important activities, they were without redeeming values.

Picard argued that including sports in his Exposition would be an "absurd anachronism." So when Coubertin submitted a draft plan to him, with Greek-inspired stadia, temples and statues, Picard dismissed them without hesitation.

This is France, not ancient Greece.

But it will be good for France, Coubertin insisted.

The Exposition will be good for France, not … meaningless games.

Sport is a wonderful means to widen horizons.

Nothing will widen horizons more than a Universal Exposition showcasing the latest inventions, the newest scientific ideas, the greatest arts in the world.

Sports are not only beneficial to the body, but to the mind as well.

Coubertin, pushed, prodded, begged until Picard grudgingly agreed to allow silly sports into his grand fair, but no new stadia, temples or statues. They would have to be tucked into and around the 16 sections of the Exhibition—like a carnival sideshow.

Some of Picard's tentative organizational plans were beyond absurd, Coubertin argued. Rowing coming under lifesaving? Fencing under cutlery?

It's a universal exposition, not a sports exhibition.

It can be both.

What could runners and jumpers do that would add glory to France?

The rift between Coubertin and Picard was immense and fundamental to the principles each espoused.

Picard was a resolutely determined Republican entirely dedicated to modernity and the future while the young Baron was attempting to restore ancient games.

BARON de COUBERTIN   My whole plan was doomed from the start. In view of the site chosen, the multitude of committees and subcommittees, and the enormity of the program (they were planning to include billiards, fishing and chess), would be nothing more than a vulgar glorified fair, exactly the opposite of what we wanted the Olympic Games to be. For the athletes we wanted to provide what they could not find elsewhere. In Athens they had come in contact with antiquity in its purest form. Paris should have showed them the Old France with all its traditions and finest settings.

One man's gaze was forward, the other's rearward. No wonder they didn't get along. Picard wanted everything to be based on the republican ideals of France and to be open to the masses. Coubertin wanted everything to be based on a pre-Republican elitism.

Picard wanted to open events to as many competitors as possible. Coubertin wanted to reserve the games for his idea of the elite.

BARON de COUBERTIN   The masses will have their competitions and the fairs of the Exposition, and we will make games for the elite: elite competitors, not numerous, but including the best champions in the world; elite spectators, aristocrats, diplomats, professors, generals, members of the Institute.

ALFRED PICARD   The Universal Exposition of 1900 must reflect the philosophy and synthesis of the century; it must have grandeur, grace and beauty; it must reflect the evident genius of France and show us on the forefront of progress; it must honor the country and the Republic.

What annoyed Coubertin most was that the games would lose their ancient splendor when replaced by Picard's patina of republicanism. The elite Olympians alongside working-class athletes! That would never do.

Coubertin wanted the games to be contained either in the aristocratic seventh *arrondissment* or at a luxurious garden of a chateau outside of Paris.

Picard wanted to spread the competition across Paris.

Since Picard was in charge, his arguments carried the day.

How could Coubertin have allowed his baby to be wrapped in such a commercial blanket? Was he simply naive? Or did he fully embrace the idea that with the coming of the new century, displays of progress would prove irresistible to the public and that attaching the games to that train of progress would prove beneficial to the Olympic movement? Either way, combining Picard's commercial sense with his dreams for the games made for strange bedfellows.

Still, Coubertin marched on with his organizational efforts. Then personal tragedy struck. His new young baby, left out in the sun too long, suffered severe brain damage and could never master more than simple skills. Coubertin coped with the tragedy by keeping himself busy with organizing the games.

He set up a new Olympic Organizing Committee specifically for the Paris Games, and filled it with his young, aristocratic friends—mostly counts, barons and titled gentry. The Vicomte de la Rochefoucauld was chosen as president. Given the general mistrust of aristocracy among the average French citizens, this may not have been Coubertin's wisest decision.

The new committee set out to organize the games according to

Coubertin's plans. Eighteen committee members took over planning. There would be all the events that made up the 1896 Games, plus football, polo and archery. Venues were found for cycling, horseback events and water polo.

Realistic plans were finally underway, but serious trouble was brewing. Paris officials declared that under no circumstances would they approve a program created by a committee dominated by the despised aristocracy. *Liberte, equality, fraternity*, still rang true. Coubertin resigned only to comment later that he made a mistake in doing so. When the Vicomte de la Rochefoucauld also resigned the committee dissolved itself. Coubertin and the IOC were excluded from further planning.

Coubertin's dream of bringing the games to the country of his birth housed in a grand Olympic complex modeled on the stadia of ancient Greece was dead.

BARON de COUBERTIN   Meanwhile Mr. Rochefoucauld became the subject of subversive attacks, which I never tried to get to the bottom of because I was afraid I might discover the work of a friend who would be diminished in my eyes as a result. Certain social rivalries are sometimes excusable although far from glorious.

A new organizing committee was formed. Instead of letting Coubertin organize the games, Picard put a 48-year-old gymnast and head of the French Shooting Association, Daniel Mérillon, in charge with two immediate consequences: Coubertin was reduced to a figurehead and since the gymnast wasn't much of an organizer, chaos resulted.

Mérillon was a controversial choice. Many considered him a most distinguished, agreeable and competent man. Others questioned his competency. He was an arrogant man whose high-handed, dictatorial approach rubbed many people the wrong way. He was committed to maintaining as low a profile for the athletic contests as he could, one that would not interfere with the main attraction—the Exposition.

Figure 31 Daniel Merrillon

The athletic program, as he designed it was a mess. Events were scheduled to be spread throughout the summer, and all over Paris at a time when transportation from venue to venue was difficult.

The French officials spared no effort to belittle the role of the games to make sure that the attention of the public would not distracted away from the glories of their Exposition.

WILLIAM MILLIGAN SLOANE   The French organizing committee was an organization of incompetents.

CASPAR WHITNEY   The Paris Games were jointly the enterprise of the Paris Exposition Company and the French government—neither of whom had any previous experience in athletic management. What the French organizers did not know about sports would fill volumes.

Some idea of the capability of that management might be gathered from the fact that within days of the first athletic competitions work had yet to begin on the running path.

The elaborate programs recently distributed were instructive, too, as to the ethical standard likely to prevail. For example, the gymnastic contests would be open to all except "professionals who have exhibited in public circuses or in theaters!" Elaborate plans were in place for an amateur rowing regatta even though about 90 percent of the French oarsman believed in racing only for money prizes.

So far as he was permitted to do so, Baron Pierre de Coubertin, chairman of the set–aside Olympian Games International Committee, may have been counted upon to guide the Exposition people, but his voice was frequently drowned out by the ignorant babble of Exposition and Government committeemen. As a huge picnic, the affair would no doubt have its uses, but given the French ineptitude, I could see there were certain to be poor tracks, unreliable measurements, questionable amateurs, and much subsequent confusion of status.

BARON de COUBERTIN   When I met with Mérillon he complained about the other countries, whose committees set up for the Exhibition could be of no help and that it was only our colleagues who could save the day. He asked me to send them a circular, which I did immediately.

I proposed a journey to Central and Northern Europe to speed up the efforts of members of the IOC. I assured Mérillon that wherever I went I would serve his cause all the more fervently as it was also my own. The fact is, I wasn't pleased that we were having to make do with "the Competitions of the Exhibition" instead of the Olympic Games, a poor and clumsy title we had to accept for the time being for want of something more elegant and appropriate.

My first stop was Berlin. During my fairly long visit I was able to observe the state of mind of German sports officials. It was not exactly excellent, due to friction with the French. A meeting was held in the Palast arranged by the German General Commissioner, who invited me to lunch afterward. The meeting had been somewhat strained; the lunch was rather "cold." Not that there was any deliberate ill will, but fears had been expressed regarding the moral security of the German athletes who would come to Paris and "might risk being insulted." I naturally protested and, of course, did not suggest a German withdrawal, but it was obvious that their participation would lack enthusiasm.

In 1900 it was still only among real sportsmen that the true sporting spirit existed instinctively. The general public did not understand it. In addition, while these gentlemen were lacking in sporting spirit, they were equally deficient in efficiency. Various circulars were sent off occasionally, devoid of any real useful information. Complaints kept coming in. On October 11–six months before the opening date—Caspar Whitney expressed Americans' dissatisfaction with plans. On the 23rd I received a message announcing that everyone in Prague was discouraged, not knowing what was going on or what to do. Shortly afterward came the same reproaches from Copenhagen. On all sides came expressions of mistrust regarding the games. Whitney naïvely asked his Embassy in Paris to persuade the Exhibition to give up the official plan and simply hand over "the money and the freedom to act" to those chosen by the IOC. And on April 14 the Austrians demanded there should be an Austrian member of the IOC and the Canadians made the same demand.

Meanwhile the days continued to pass. Nothing concrete was being achieved, not even the acquisition of any offices except those of the new subcommittees and, of course, the issuing of endless regulations. No money, no stadium, no grounds. Just as members of the IOC were being asked to make up juries, the clubs were asked as a last resort to give direct support and lend us their grounds—in particular the Racing Club for the athletic sports. And to think that in 1898 my plan had been rejected out of hand as being "mean and unworthy of the nation."

I refrained however from informing Mérillon of the real state of affairs, as he seemed so unaware of the whole matter. Most politicians of the time shared the opinion that sport was a superfluous, eccentric neologism.

The German IOC member, Willibald Gebhardt, when meeting with the French Prime Minister, Faure, was told that members of the IOC were expected to speak French. Gebhardt, who didn't, was offended and left.

Word was getting around that the Olympic Games, (under whatever name) might be canceled. Coubertin, a man of indomitable will and perseverance, although no longer in charge, responded as he so often did when faced with any crisis. He went on the offensive. He promised that the Exposition officials were wonderfully competent and that Paris was a spectacular venue for the games with pleasures and accommodations "such as never seen in the New World," and the games themselves would prove to be "exceptionally wonderful."

BARON de COUBERTIN   Paris was a perfect city to host the games. We had not been drawn into the error of constructing a cardboard stadium to reproduce that of Pericles. With the hill of Montmartre in the background to replace the Acropolis on its rock, this would have been ridiculous and paltry. We began by considering with good reason that there was no need to trouble ourselves about preparing amusements and special activities. Because the Exposition would constitute a permanent festival full of attractions the committee need only be concerned with the technical part of the sports. At Athens this point had been rather neglected, because the committee was also engaged with the interests of the spectators and had to take measures for their amusement, for the decoration of the sites and monuments, and for preparing attractions of all kinds in order to bring large numbers of spectators and to detain them. Now this issue does not exist, and the interests of the athletes would predominate above all else.

The Paris Games were to include all the sports contested in 1896 as well as a few others such as football, croquet, cricket, lawn tennis, golf and bowls. There were others, such as baseball which was to be an exhibition.

Gymnastics were to be open to foreign gymnasts as individuals. Gymnastic societies were to be invited to compete in groups, but only to send their best gymnasts to participate in the international championship, which would be individual. This was a prudent decision because in adhering to it, no attempt had been made to exclude certain nations while admitting others, but the aim had been to avoid trouble and dispute. Gymnastic societies of all countries always behave in a more or less martial fashion. They march in military order preceded by their national flag.

Fencing would include matches with foils, with sabres and with swords. I could foresee a fine contest in which the French and Italian schools would be opposed in a sensational manner.

Equestrian and Aquatic sports including polo, rowing, sailing and swimming matches would follow. There was some question of having an equestrian competition in the real sense of the term, but the difficulties of transporting real horses were so great that the idea was abandoned. There would be target shooting, pigeon shooting, archery, and shooting with various firearms. For cyclists, there was to be a whole week of track-racing, preceded by a sensational twenty-four-hour race. Also to be included were motor-car races, and competitions of firemen.

Unfortunately, the competitions were to be spread out all throughout the summer. I had no doubt this would be too long a period. It would have been better for everything to have taken place in the space of six weeks, but the officials of the Exposition insisted on prolonging things as much as possible and I lost the argument.

One sticky point was the issue of amateurism. Different countries had different definitions of that term, so I understood that the conditions would not be the same for all sports. The gentlemen who shoot pigeons or who participate in yacht races would expect cash prizes and so such arrangements were made. In fencing there were no professionals strictly speaking, but on the other hand, professionals fence with amateurs but generally no prizes are given. They fight for honor alone. Personally, convinced as I am that amateurism is one of the first conditions of the progress and prosperity of sport, I proposed to revive the Olympian Games, with the idea they would always be reserved for amateurs alone. For the Paris Games, however, a slightly different theory prevailed. It was decided that it was necessary to reserve the first rank for pure amateurs, and in all cases to guard against any person suspected of the slightest taint of professionalism slipping in amongst them. There were to be special competitions for professionals, but the line of demarcation between amateurs and professionals would be strictly laid down and closely adhered to.

Given my oft-stated objection to professionalism, it's a reasonable question to ask why I agreed to this. Well, we were at the beginning of a new century, and the Paris Exposition would represent an exceptional occasion for attracting and bringing together representatives of foreign nations of all classes. So it was a matter of importance to establish records which would be a sort of athletic starting point for the 20th century. The amateurs and professionals, without intermingling, could see each other at work, and comparisons advantageous to sport would be the result. Now I do not say I was a convert to this way of thinking. It is not my own, and I vowed to do everything in my power that the following Olympian Games would revert to the true theory of amateurism, which declares in the strongest way the uselessness of the professional and desires his disappearance. But for the Paris Games, at least we would maintain an absolute separation between amateurs and professionals, thereby preventing the former from losing their quality as amateurs by comingling with professionals. The direct and personal interests of amateurs would thus be protected and safeguarded in 1900, and that is the important point.

Despite the Baron's unbridled public optimism, everywhere he turned there were problems.

France's prestige in the world was extremely fragile. The English were annoyed that France sided with the Afrikaners in the Boer war. The Americans were annoyed that they sided with the Spanish in their war. The Germans were annoyed over their position on Alsace-Lorraine. The Italians were just generally annoyed.

The political situation in France itself was becoming increasingly unstable. The cabinet kept turning over, the president died mysteriously. National angst was rising.

The call went out: Boycott here, boycott there, boycott everywhere. That was the hope of some foreign journalists.

Unite to punish France!

France is on the precipice of a Civil War.

Do not participate in the Exposition of 1900.

Stay away from the Olympic Games.

And, hanging over everything like the sword of Damocles was the Dreyfus affair.

Capt. Dreyfus had been arrested in October 1894 and accused of treason for passing documents to a foreign power. Dreyfus, a Jew, and an unpopular officer, was found guilty by a military court, publicly degraded and sent to Devil's Island to live out his years.

In January 1898 Emile Zola published his famous open letter "*J'accuse*," charging scores of French politicians and military officers with obstructing justice. The affair, painting France as unjust, corrupt and unraveling, became the central crisis in French political and intellectual life.

With most of the world convinced Dreyfus was innocent, the French attempted to stem the tide of anger by convening a second court-martial. But the military judges upheld the guilty verdict.

The foreign reaction was swift and virtually unanimous.

France is wrong.

France is corrupt.

France is unjust.

France must suffer the consequences.

In London 40,000 protesters marched on Hyde Park.

In the United States crowds burned the tricolor.

In Italy, police were sent to guard the French consulate against threats of violence.

In Belgium and Germany the press responded with invective and insults.

Switzerland urged "fury against anything connected with France."

The idea of a boycott was gaining traction.

The organizers of the Exposition were thrown into near panic. The very concept of the Exposition was to showcase France and the French as the beacon of enlightened progress at the dawn of a new century. They had hoped it would be nothing less than the greatest world's fair of all time, showcasing France in the way it wished to be viewed.

By the time the Exposition was getting close to opening, the Dreyfus affair was overshadowing everything in France. France was seen as an international criminal—a pariah on the world's stage.

What could be done? How can we save the Exposition and the Olympic Games?

Perhaps a pardon for Dreyfus.

So the Exposition organizers approached President Loubet. He, however, wanted a cooling off period.

Surely the Exposition would be ruined unless Loubet took action. In desperation, the Exposition organizers turned to influential politicians and businessmen and asked them to pressure Loubet. Eventually the president signed the pardon and the foreign calls for a boycott subsided.

France's integrity may not have been completely restored, but at least the Exposition and Olympic Games could now go forward.

The games were on, albeit with reservations.

JAMES SULLIVAN   I think it is a fair statement to say that the French were remarkably indifferent when it came to the games. Their interest was squarely centered on the Exposition and, frankly, their antipathy toward the Olympics was hardly disguised. The French officials were afraid that any success the games might have would negatively affect the success of their Exposition, and they made life as difficult as they could for the organizers. If they could have stopped it all together, they would have.

I know for a fact that Hungarians, Brits, Danes, and Swedes all complained that they even found it difficult to get any kind of reply from the French about any of the arrangements. Two-way communication was hard to come by.

The whole spread-out affair seemed a bit impromptu and more than a bit odd.

CASPAR WHITNEY   I was an American member of the International Olympic Committee heading into the Paris Games and I have to say I found so many things wrong about the French preparations. I even wrote to Coubertin about the American dissatisfaction but failed to receive a satisfactory response. My complaints were not so much directed toward Coubertin himself, (although I held plenty of those, too) but toward the inept French organizers who failed to keep us informed about the preparations. This at the expense of the true American amateurs who are significantly better than anyone else.

So many important details had been left to the last moment, so our Gallic neighbors had to rush at them in hysterical haste with results that could hardly have failed to be confusing.

A columnist for several journals including *Outing, Harper's Weekly* and *Colliers,* Whitney persistently trumpeted the value of pure amateurism over professionalism, often using astringent language and confrontational techniques. He had a great deal of disdain for French sporting life, which he portrayed as antithetical to the traditions and prowess of American sport. He saw the French athletic practice as mirroring the corruption and decay in France's bankrupt version of republicanism.

CASPAR WHITNEY   The statistics and parliamentary reports published by the French government, supplemented by the results of careful observation by able and impartial writers (many of them French), left no room for doubt as to the causes of the decline of the French race. Generations of free indulgence of the dictates of an inordinate sensuality, combined with malthusian practices and a long abuse of absinthe and other adulterated alcoholic stimulants, had resulted not only in a most alarming decrease in the birth rate, but in a decided physical deterioration of the French race in general. That the population of the country at large remained stationary, instead of decreasing, was due to the very considerable immigration of foreigners–Belgians, Italians and Germans–who were supplanting the rapidly diminishing native grace of France.

The leaders of the new Nationalist Party hoped to arrest the decay of their race and to rescue it from threatened extinction by instituting a series of measures. They called for a heavy tax on bachelors and a gradual but decided lessening of taxation in proportion to the number of children in a family, thus encouraging an increase in the birth rate. They wanted heavy penalties for any adulteration of wines, beers and spirits, together with a severe tax on absinthe and other liquors. They advocated the encouragement of physical exercise and athletic training in the private and public schools of France, thus rendering the rising generation stronger and more robust than the present one. They proposed the enactment of a rigorous law, compelling all employers of labor to hire native French rather than foreigners. They recommended an amendment of the naturalization laws rendering it difficult for foreigners to become French citizens.

Perhaps there were good grounds for the claim of a Montréal editor that the French Canadians are more pure blooded French than the citizens of France itself, because their ancestors left France some

200 years ago, before the depopulation of the native race and the influx of foreigners had commenced.

JAMES SULLIVAN   Without any reservation whatsoever, I can say that Caspar Whitney had a profoundly positive effect on the American Olympic movement. His staunch commitment to pure amateurism was admirable, if bullheaded. He was a superb journalist, with a clear and engaging style. But he was unbelievably dogmatic and lacked even the slightest pretense to broadmindedness.

So, despite the problems and the attitudes of some toward games organized by the French, we were committed to participating. But there was one very sticky issue we had yet to confront and it resulted in quite an upheaval for us.

SIX

LET ME SEE if I can characterize the uproar caused by the on-again, off-again Sunday issue.

By the time we had sailed for Europe we were assured by Mr. Spalding that he had received word from the French that no competitions would be held on Sunday.

However, doubts were raised that the telegram announcing the French decision was an official communication sanctioned by the French organizing committee.

As it turned out, it wasn't or so they claimed, and it was regrettable the sender had not verified it, as it caused real injustice and considerable confusion and anger.

When we arrived in Paris we found that the French officials had in fact set the opening of the track and field events for July 15—a Sunday.

We objected. That's not what you promised. That's our Sabbath. It can't be desecrated. It's … a religious duty to observe the Sabbath.

The French remained firm. That's when the events will open. It's been planned. It's been announced that way.

Change the announcements. The public will understand.

Not the French public.

If you don't change the schedule, we'll pull our athletes out of such an ungodly program.

In Europe Sunday is always a day for sports … and other amusements.

Well, not in the United States.

Except we're not in the United States.

Then we'll go home, back to the United States.

The French didn't want to lose the Americans if for no other reason than most of the foreign tourists there were Americans and Americans spend money. We suggested rescheduling the Sunday events to Saturday.

Ridiculous, said the French officials.

Why is that?

Because that day is sacred to us. July 14, the anniversary of the fall of the Bastille.

That's not the same as a sacred religious day.

We would have no spectators at the games. Do you really want that?

A holiday is a great day for sporting events.

Everyone in Paris will be on the boulevards watching the military parades and listening to the marshal music of Bastille Day from vantage points along the boulevards. It would be most inconvenient for the French officials and athletes to be at the Racing Club when they should be viewing, reviewing or even participating in the military parades on the boulevards.

Our officials were resolute. We will not participate in any event held on the Sabbath. We want no finals run on a Sunday. If you insist on Sunday events, we want the finals to be held over to the following Monday. That way our Sabbath observers will still have a chance to win those events.

The bewildered French needed the Americans which meant making some concession to keep the puritanical athletes in Paris. Yes, there were English athletes there, there were local French heroes ready to go, there were a few athletes—mostly weight men—from other European countries, but as much as they were loath to admit it, the American were the star attractions. We had just soundly beaten the Englishmen in London, we had the lion's share of athletes in Paris, and we had the brightest stars headed up by Kraenzlein. So at an open meeting at the Racing Club Wednesday preceding the scheduled first events, Spalding and de Garmendia made heated pleas/demands. The French relented.

OK, we'll (grudgingly) rearrange the schedule to accommodate the Americans distaste for Sunday athletics.

CASPAR WHITNEY   It was very gratifying to American sportsmen that the Paris Exposition authorities finally abandoned Sunday athletic fixtures. No doubt the firm stand taken by Mr. Spalding was quite the most persuasive influence which fell upon the Frenchman—who were fully alive to the *éclat* that would be given the games by the attendance of American university athletes. Whatever they may do in France, there was no section of the United States where clubs of the first class held organized sports of any kind – track athletics, baseball, football, golf or rowing–on Sunday.

But … on the evening before the first day of the second Olympic Games, the French called a meeting in the rooms of the Racing Club in the Bois de Boulogne. They invited representatives from all the countries represented at the games—all 27 … except one: The United States. It was a single-agenda meeting: Sunday events.

The meeting the French officials claimed had been called by "unspecified" representatives of "unspecified" countries.

Said the "unspecified" representatives: Why do we have to change the change because of one country's objections? We object to their objections and want the games to go on as planned. Our athletes have arranged their training schedules to adhere to the program as announced. And it will be utterly confusing to the spectators. How are they going to know how and where to show up? And the family members, too. If the Americans don't like it, let them go home.

The French caved in and reversed their position yet again. If that's what you want, said the French officials, we'll agree to revert to the original schedule as published.

Later that evening a French official went to see Mr. Spalding and delivered the news.

I'm afraid that despite what we said earlier we won't be able to alter the schedule to suit your request. The program stands as originally scheduled.

You agreed …

Several other countries complained.

We had an agreement.

There were too many objections.

You're going back on your word?

I hope this doesn't mean you're leaving.

We'll have to see about that. It's up to the individual schools and clubs.

Mr. Spalding understood, even if the French didn't, that there wasn't such a thing as a United States team. No unified body selected the athletes. We were chosen by our schools and clubs and as such had to adhere to our organization's rules. Mr. Spalding could recommend if he so chose. He could try to influence but he could not dictate, particularly when it came to religious principles. As I understand it, Mr. Spalding himself wasn't religious. The closest he ever came was to join the Raja Yoga Theosophical Society for "the conscious exercise, regulation and concentration of thought."

Anyway, Mr. Spalding took the news in stride. He always considered himself an elegant and cultured gentleman, so he would never get into a shouting match with the French officials. No, he would do the gentlemanly thing—accept the French decision and try to make the best of a prickly situation.

Not competing was a fundamentalist Christian gesture, but he said it would be left up to each school and club to determine its course of action. Either "thou shall not compete on Sundays," or "thou shall decide for thyself whether to compete on the Sabbath or not."

Back home apparently several newspapers wrote that it was very gratifying to report that the American athletes firmly refused to take any part whatever in sporting events on Sunday and so the program had finally been altered to accommodate the Americans. Not so!

CASPAR WHITNEY   The Americans, protested to the French officials. But it was to no avail. The management of the French officials and of Mr. Ferdinand Peck, American Commissioner, was quite as miserable as expected.

O O O O O

Athletes from six schools and one club were affected by the Sunday mess: Chicago, Syracuse, Yale, Michigan, Princeton, the New York Athletic Club and Pennsylvania. Their athletes were told they mustn't compete or shouldn't compete or it was up to them to decide whether to compete or not.

At the meeting of the University of Chicago, their athletic director Alonzo Stagg, clarified his position: Christian athletes don't compete on Sundays. He had four athletes in Paris, but only one was scheduled to compete on Sunday—William Moloney in the 400-meter run. Stagg is an impassioned and persuasive man who leaves no doubt about his commitment to his faith. Strongly influenced by his Sunday school teacher and the minister of his church, Stagg attended Yale University intending to become a Presbyterian minister. Although he never went into the ministry he remained determined to spread his Christian ideals to others. He decided that if he couldn't do so as a minister, he would accomplish the goal on the athletic field as a coach. He consistently articulated his concern that his athletes integrate the physical, mental and spiritual dimensions of their life. For him, being "spiritually ready" was as essential for the successful athlete as physical preparedness. As he so often said, he placed athletes "within the eternal narrative of Christ and his church."

Mr. Moloney, thou shalt not run on Sunday.

After his qualifying race, his Olympics would be over.

ALONZO STAGG   Everybody in Paris felt this was a most contemptible trick. Not a single American university would have sent a team had it been announced that competitions would be held on Sunday. Even at that late date it seemed likely that the American teams would unitedly refused to compete if the French officials persisted in carrying out what seemed to us a very nasty piece of business.

Syracuse University's roots go back to the Genesee Wesleyan Seminary founded by the Methodist Episcopal Church. It identifies itself as nonsectarian although it maintains a relationship with the United Methodist Church.

Surely the Sunday issue won't be a problem for their best athlete. Meyer Prinstein is a Jew.

Sorry, Meyer, but our athletes will not be competing Sunday.

I honor Saturday as the Sabbath, not Sunday Prinstein responded.

But our university observes Sunday and you're a student at our university.

That's not right.

It's the way it is.

Let's get them to switch dates. Let's jump on Monday.

We'll try.

Everybody wants to see me and Kraenzlein.

We'll see what we can do.

Yale has its own Divinity School but while they recommend Sunday abstinence, they told their athletes it was up to their own conscience to decide. Dixon Boardman said he would not compete; Richard Sheldon said he would.

Although the University of Michigan counts as one of its principle founders Reverend John Monteith, a Presbyterian minister, it is officially a nonsectarian institution. Nevertheless, Charles Dvorak was urged not to compete. He said he was not sure what he would do.

Although not formally affiliated with any denomination, Princeton University has close ties to the Presbyterian Church and so told its athletes not to compete.

Georgetown University was the oldest **Catholic and Jesuit** institution of higher education in the United States, yet they stopped none of their athletes from competing on Sunday. Nor did the New York Athletic Club.

That left Pennsylvania, with the largest contingent of athletes, to decide.

O O O O O

It was a beautiful, clear night with a starry canopy overhead as we gathered on the garden grounds of our hotel. To compete or not to compete Sunday. That was the question. And it wasn't an easy one to answer. Our manager, Frank Ellis, took charge of the meeting. Mike was there, too, but he remained on the sidelines, said nothing. This was not his bailiwick.

Ellis was obviously nervous. We could all see that.

FRANK ELLIS   I had the authority to prevent our men participating. This was solely my responsibility. I told them I would leave the decision to them … and their conscience … but that I strongly advised them they should not contest.

For more than an hour we sat on the lawn discussing the situation. Some men had a lot to say, some said nothing.

It was not an enjoyable time.

Central to the drama were the roommates, Kraenz, Tewks and Bax. Each had at least one event scheduled for Sunday.

None grew up in a strict religious family.

None felt compelled to avoid Sunday competitions.

They knew several of their teammates surely would not compete and would urge them for the sake of team unity to do the same.

They knew several of their teammates would likely be disappointed in them or even angry if they competed.

Any way they looked at it, American team morale would suffer, conflicts would arise, and perhaps performances would be affected.

Tewks wanted to run the 400-meter hurdles, Kraenz wanted to enter the long jump, and Bax the high jump and maybe the pole vault.

After training so long, after raising the money for the trip, after traveling 4,000 miles and then not to compete in their specialties … what an incredible disappointment that would be.

Jos McCracken had no such concerns. He was a big man, a good athlete, a leader. All the boys looked up to him, so what he said carried weight.

He was a solid citizen, honest, straightforward, liked by everyone. The president—president of his class, president of the Christian Association, president of the Houston Club. An article in *The New York Times* called him the University of Pennsylvania's most popular student and best all-around athlete. Not surprisingly he had been elected captain of the track team.

Figure 32 Josiah McCracken

Jos was born into a highly religious family in Tennessee. His father was a scholar/minister, who after moving west to Kansas as a homesteader helped build a local community church. When he was eight, Jos formally joined the United Presbyterian church. I think it's fair to say that besides developing a profound faith in Christianity, he acquired qualities typical of those of American frontier men—a strong physique, endurance and the spirit of enterprise— all qualities that made him the strong leader he was.

Josiah was one of 11 children in the McCracken household, all of whom were prohibited from working or playing on Sunday. They didn't go shopping, play games, attend dances.

There was never any question about where he would come down on the Sabbath issue. The only question was about how much influence he would exert on everyone else.

McCracken was known to lead meetings of Penn's Christian Association where he would recite bible passages with implied references to his track teammates.

He was a persuasive speaker all right.

JOSIAH McCRACKEN   Each man must go by his own conscience according to the word of God and the Bible is the word of God and the Bible says the just shall live by faith. I am being true to what I understand God's word says. I am fully committed to Christ and I make my decisions based on faith and I want to have a good conscience before God. Yes, it's a deep faith that has moral content and it affects my life. It affects the choices I make. We worship on Sunday because that is the day Christ rose from the dead. It's the first day of a new week when we are new creatures in Christ Jesus.

Deuteronomy tells us we can labor six days a week but the seventh day is the Sabbath of Yahweh and on it "You shall do no work: you, nor your son, nor your daughter, nor your male servant, nor your female servant, nor your ox, nor your donkey, nor any of your cattle, nor a stranger who is within your gates, and your male servant and your female servant may rest as well as you."

That's good enough for me.

God promises to pour his fury out on those who pollute the Sabbath. He says in Exodus, "Six days may work be done; but in the seventh is the Sabbath of rest, holy to the LORD: whoever does any work on the Sabbath day, he shall surely be put to death."

I will never compromise. Compromise is the language of the devil. Sunday is the Lord's Day; it symbolically represents the acceptance of Christ as Messiah.

God made rules for us and one of those rules says that the Sabbath is His. And I for one intend to keep it that way. For as great as your dreams may be, the dream of God is greater.

God made me for a purpose, but he also made me an athlete, and when I compete I feel His pleasure. But it won't be on a Sunday.

Figure 33 John Walter Beardsley Tewksbury

WALTER TEWKSBURY   My response to McCracken was to remind him that Romans 14 tells us not to judge one another, to let every man be fully persuaded in his own mind and that when thou judgest another, thou condemnest thyself.

He nodded in agreement but I guess not everyone knew Romans 14. Not everyone was as agreeable, particularly some from other colleges.

The manager of the Princeton team suggested that if any of us from Penn competed, we should be indicted for treason.

Look, I was a believer. But the way I saw it, competing on Sunday sure as hell wasn't going to condemn me there in the hereafter. That's just the way I felt. So did my roomies, Kraenz and Bax. We talked about it and decided we would compete. That's why we came all the way to Europe. If the Almighty had other ideas, well, we'd just have to deal with them later.

Yeah, I know we weren't real popular with some of the other fellows, but the more enlightened among them understood that every man had a right to his personal opinions … and feelings. At least I hoped that was the case.

Anyway, doesn't the First Amendment say that ALL persons are entitled to free excise of religion, or not?

If it doesn't, it should.

IRVING BAXTER   I hadn't come several thousand miles to spend the day looking at the damn Parisian sights. Yes, they're magnificent. Yes, we should see them. Yes, I would make the time. But not during my events. I came to compete and compete I would. Look, I'm not a complete idiot. I knew damn well some of my mates would feel betrayed, but that's just the way it would have to be. That's a damn sight better than betraying myself, isn't it? All those hours and hours of practice, all those Mike Murphy lessons would have been wasted.

I talked it over with my roommates, Kraenz and Tewks, and a few others. We agreed that we would support each other if we all competed Sunday.

WALTER TEWKSBURY   We knew that any of us who competed

would have to stick tight. We'd have to support each other. We knew that some would think we were just plain stupid. How could you do that if you ever expected to get into heaven? Maybe they'd just feel sorry for us for missing out on heaven. I figured I'd take my chances. We also knew that some of the others would … well, maybe they'd be angry. Maybe they'd think we were traitors to the cause—their cause, of course.

Look, I was as religious as the next guy. I even attended Wyoming Seminary for christsake. But nobody there ever told me I'd be damned to hell if I ran on Sunday.

Anyway, the way I had it figured (rationalized) when I was scheduled to compete in Sunday in Paris, it wasn't Sunday everywhere else, so Sunday was Sunday depending only on where you were.

IRVING BAXTER   I respected the rights of the others to abstain and hoped that they would respect ours to compete. Some apparently didn't. So be it.

ALVIN KRAENZLEIN   Of course, not everybody was in the same situation. Many men were signed up to compete in events that weren't scheduled on Sunday. Most, in fact. The only track and field events with Sunday competitions were the shot, 400 meters, discus, 1,500 meters, high jump, 400 meter hurdles, pole vault, steeplechase and long jump.

Anybody not in these events was off the hook. Some, however, let their opinions be loudly known, which I didn't appreciate one bit. It's easy to criticize someone else's decisions when you don't have to make one.

I was really conflicted. My primary event was the 800, but that was safely scheduled for Monday, so no problem there. The 1500 was set for Sunday and, even though it wasn't my specialty, I considered entering primarily because I understood our best runners for that event—George Orton, Alex Grant and John Cregan—would sit out. In the end though, I decided to honor my Methodist heritage and not enter. In hindsight, maybe that was just an excuse to avoid an event in which I didn't really shine. I don't know.

I know this, though, I didn't hold it against our athletes who decided to compete. Their choice was theirs and they would have to live with it. I supported them in their decision which was not something everyone did.

By the time our meeting broke up, Kraenz, Bax, Tewks, George Orton, and Meredith Colket indicated that they would likely compete Sunday.

As soon as that became known, a loud howl of treachery rose from some of the other programs—most loudly from Princeton and Syracuse.

WALTER TEWKSBURY   Those of us from the University of Pennsylvania were accused of bad faith, but unjustly so. We were the first to protest against Sunday competitions and the last to object, but when the French authorities stated that they would be held at that day and our faculty manager, Frank Ellis, allowed us to decide for ourselves, five agreed to compete and eight stayed out either on principle (not because of faculty restriction) or because their events weren't scheduled for Sunday anyway.

As far as I was concerned, the anger directed at our team was out of line. We had a right to decide and that right should have been respected.

Some athletes and officials on other clubs took shots at us—the Pennsylvania pariahs.

What Penn did was contemptible and Georgetown and the New York Athletic Club are no better.

We are a team—America's team—and we all should have stood together to demonstrate our moral courage they said.

The defections made us look weak to the world, but we aren't weak. We should have showed our strength.

ALVIN KRAENZLEIN   If in fact we were ever a team in the strictest sense of that word we certainly weren't after the Sunday decisions. The good feelings were gone.

O O O O O

CASPAR WHITNEY   Their breach of faith was but another example of the wretched management of French Exposition officials. Add to that the-none-too-careful scrutiny of the conditions under which the games were to be held by our own sporting leaders and it's not too hard to explain the Sunday mess.

To stand with Georgetown and the New York A. C. in not forbidding Sunday competition to its athletes is a record that can provide no very gratifying reflections for Pennsylvanians.

The majority of the American athletes, including the Princeton, Chicago, Michigan and Syracuse teams and two-thirds of Pennsylvania, to their credit be it said, declined to compete on Sunday. The individual sportsmen who declined to compete on Sunday, regarding principle worthier to be cherished above mere prize–winning included Prinstein, Syracuse; McCracken, Remington,

Grant and Bushnell, Penn.; Garrett and Carroll, Princeton; Maloney, Chicago; Boardman and Johnson, Yale; Dvorak and Lee, Michigan.

Whitney may have expressed the sentiment of many, but not all. In Britain, The *Daily Express* correspondent saw the Sunday issue as nothing but a dastardly plot by the French. His reasoning was that after the French saw the domination of the American athletes in London they realized that their athletes would likely fare poorly against us, so by scheduling events on Sunday, they knew our ranks would be thinned. He wrote that "One phrase which describes this to all of us is 'unEnglish.' Unfortunately, both the literal and the sentimental meanings of it are unknown to our neighbors across the channel."

Then the French changed course again… sort of. They said they would open the games Saturday and then stage special field events Monday for any athlete who qualified but chose not to compete in the Sunday final. The understanding was that any times, distances or heights made Monday would count as if they had been made Saturday.

At least we were secure knowing that all of our athletes could fully compete in their chosen events with no concerns about Sabbath Sunday defections.

Ah, but not so fast. On the initiative of Yale, a protest was presented to Spalding. It said: "We, the undersigned, beg to protest against the change in the agreed arrangements whereby our clubs are now able to compete in field events Monday, the records to count for the championships. We do not agree to a substitution of a series of special field events to take the place of the above agreed arrangement."

That's too bad responded the French, you must live with our decision.

And we did.

SEVEN

WHEN THE EXPOSITION officially opened it was clear that most attractions wouldn't be ready for public viewing for some weeks. So the opening ceremonies that day were a strange mixture of sumptuous splendor in the Salle des Fétes combined with confusion and half-ready buildings all over the city.

Fourteen thousand guests had been invited to the function but the traffic arrangements were so inadequate that hundreds of vehicles never reached the ceremony.

Fortunately, I was on foot, so I made it just as the festivities were about to start. They were in a picturesque stage setting with gorgeous uniforms on the diplomats and soldiers, a splendid orchestra and chorus, and the magnificent effect produced by the grand staircase where President Loubet viewed the events. It was lined with some 200 picked men of the Republican Guards, decked out in jackboots, white breeches, gleaming cutlasses, and horsehair plumes streaming from shining helmets.

Figure 34 Exposition program cover

The ceremony itself was splendid. The assembly of dignitaries was unlike anything seen since maybe Victoria's Jubilee or the czar's coronation. There were turbaned chiefs, Arab sheikhs in flowing white robes, with faces muffled in linen scarves; Hungarian magnates in magnificent velvet dolmans; Chinese and other Oriental Embassy officials in characteristic silk garments; tall Cossacks in sumptuous cloaks with bandoliers slung across their chests. All these outlandish figures rubbed shoulders with the wearers of the no less splendid, but better known, European uniforms.

After numerous formal speeches the presidential party descended into the grounds emerging into the Champs de Mars at the Chateau d'Eau. The picture from this point up through the arched Eiffel Tower to the Palace Trocadero was spectacular. The splendid exhibition buildings on both sides were abundantly decorated with bunting and flowers. A double rank of infantry left a broad passage through which the procession marched. Behind these rows of red–trousered soldiers with fixed bayonets was massed the great crowd of people. The president was cheered throughout the progress to the Bridge de Jena, where luxurious upholstered river steamboats were waiting to take the party on the trip up the Seine to the Alexander Bridge.

Despite the unreadiness of most Exhibition buildings, all of this suggested wonderful things to come—assuming, of course, it ever got finished.

This was it when it came to opening ceremonies. There were no opening ceremonies per se for the athletic competitions to begin the next day—Saturday.

O O O O O

After croissants and juice, we boarded the train in Versailles just as the sun was coming up on what would be an especially warm July Saturday. It wasn't long before we could see the river Seine on our left, and shortly after that we arrived at the Gare d'Orsay—the first electrified urban rail terminal in the world. It was a magnificent structure opened just a little more than a month earlier to serve spectators going to the Exposition.

Once in the center of the city we still had to make our way to the Bois de Boulogne which meant traveling by omnibusses all the way to the western edge where the lush park sprawled across almost 2000 acres.

As it was Bastille Day it didn't make it easy. The Bois de Boulogne was packed with many thousands celebrating the holiday and paying no attention to the events. We can't say the French didn't warn us.

Fears had been expressed that the day's military review might prove an occasion for political excitement for and against the Government and President Loubet. Nationalists and Socialists both announced their intention of marching and indulging in demonstrations and counter–demonstrations. Some conflict did arise between these groups not far enough from us—close enough anyway that we could hear it. Apparently several people were injured and a few were arrested.

I didn't notice any other problems, though. President Loubet was escorted by cavalry and was mostly cheered, except by one individual who shouted as the president was passing: "Death to Loubet!" He was immediately arrested. At least that's what the papers said.

So, with the Sunday/no-Sunday agreement in place, the games were about to get under way.

O O O O O

The first event was scheduled to go off at 9:30. It would be the 110 meter hurdles, which meant Kraenz would get things going for us. Who better to lead off for the team? Surely no one could touch him in this event. It was likely that if he had any competition at all it would come from others on our own team and he had already beaten all of them.

Expectations were high but if he was nervous, he didn't show it. He came across as a supremely confident (competitors say arrogant) athlete, which buoyed the confidence of the others.

The crowd was meager.

See, that's what we told you, said the French.

For some events, more athletes were on the field competing than spectators watching.

It's because of our national day, reiterated the French. But the reality was somewhat different because on the other days of the meet, the crowds were little better. The Exposition was bigger than the games tucked in here and there. Most Parisians in the hot summer of 1900 were there to experience the magnificence of the Exposition; few would also take in the games.

O O O O O

Those of us who didn't have to be warming up for another event were there to cheer our teammates on. At least those of us from Penn were. Some of the others were missing, perhaps expressing their pique at our school for not prohibiting Sunday competitors.

Jos and Trux were over warming up for the discus which would be the next event up, but Tewks and Bax, were there with me.

ALONZO STAGG   The track was not good. It was soft and uneven and I expected injuries to occur because of it—as was proven later to be the case.

ALVIN KRAENZLEIN   It took me a few practice runs to adapt to the French hurdles. They were 6 inches higher than those that I was used to and the grass takeoff was in places uneven.

And, of course, the distance was a little different from what I was used to. At home we ran 120 yards not 110 meters, meaning I would have to run about 10 yards farther. Mike thought this wouldn't present a problem. I agreed.

The French officials, however, did present a problem, especially the starter, who would not have been allowed to start schoolboy sports in America. Maybe this was not so much his fault as that of the traditional French style of starting. In France the starter says, *"Préparez-vous (Prepare),* and then three of four seconds later, *"Attention!"* and, in nine cases out of 10, he shoots the pistol immediately. I was told by a German competitor they have the same system. There the starter says, *"Sind Sie fertig, meine Herren?"* (Are you ready, gentlemen?), and a moment later, *"Achtung!"* and fires the gun. In both cases the runners start when they hear the first syllable of the word *"Attention!"* or *"Achtung!"* If the starter is not satisfied with the start, he shoots off the pistol twice, and the men come back and return to their same marks. So there is no penalty for stealing a head start by beating the pistol.

Figure 35 Sprint start

But here the starter was sloppy and inconsistent and no penalty was attached to any effort to "beat the pistol." The man who guessed the best moment when "Attention!" was about to be called, and was off, got the most yards. The starter came near to making a fiasco of the races.

Thank goodness, despite the sloppy starting, to no one's surprise, there are no surprises in the heats. Kraenz cruised to an easy win over the University of Chicago's Frederick Moloney and the University of Michigan's All-American football halfback, John McLean. The only other competitor in the first heat was a Frenchman, Choisel, who was so outclassed that he stepped off the track without clearing the last hurdle. In the second heat, the Indian runner, Norman Pritchard, beat out Remington. The third and final heat was a one-man affair in which the French ace, Jean Lécuyer, jogged to a walkover. Then in the repêchage heats, Maloney and McLean also advanced.

So the finals for the first event of these games was set to be contested between Kraenz, McLean, Moloney, Lécuyer and Pritchard.

O O O O O

As far as I could learn, there doesn't seem to be any reference to hurdle races in ancient Greek literature. But by the middle of the 19th century hurdle races were becoming common. Originally the standard distances in the USA were 120 yards, 220 yards and 440 yards, with 10 barriers at each distance. They were known as the "highs," the "lows" and the "intermediates."

The height of the hurdles for the lows was only 2'6" high meaning that sprinters often excelled in the lows. At 120 yards they were 3'6" high, placed at intervals of 10 yards from each other.

The earliest hurdles were often solid sheep fences, gates or sometimes taught ropes. Safe clearance was the goal so that while clearing the barrier the body was erect while the legs were raised and bent as they would be in a standing jump.

A British hurdler, Arthur Croome, may have been the first to attempt the straight-lead-leg style around 1886, but it never really caught on—until Kraenz perfected it and turned into a mainstream technique. By developing his sprinting, rather than sailing over the hurdles Kraenz became largely responsible for the eventual lowering of every high hurdle record then in existence.

CASPAR WHITNEY   America has always been strong in hurdlers. Somehow or other it seems natural for an American athlete to hurdle. This is only to be expected. Hurdling requires a strong pair of legs, plenty of nervous force, and best of all, a good sprint.

We are a nation of sprinters. Everything we do, we do in a hurry. We have always been strong in contests where nerve and sprints are concerned.

The hurdle event is the outcome of the old steeplechase, the distance being reduced to give the sprinters more of a chance to show their caliber. In the old days all the "pros" went in for the hurdles and the sprints.

No nation ever developed such a galaxy of hurdling stars as us. But the greatest hurdler of all undoubtedly was Al Kraenzlein. This elongated Dutchman was built ideally for a hurdler. He had it all over every other timber topper in this respect. A tall athlete with two of the longest legs the cinder path ever knew, he simply flew along in a race like a huge kangaroo. Where Kraenzlein is a better hurdler than the rest of the lot is simply in his wonderful sprinting powers.

Kraenzlein is always good for around 9 4/5 seconds for the century. Outside of possibly Tewksbury or maybe one or two others there is no hurdler in the world who can do better than 10 seconds on the flat for the century. He is that good.

It was none other than Kraenzlein who revolutionized the whole system of hurdling by running the hurdles as if he was running a flat race.

Figure 36 Kraenz hurdle style

MIKE MURPHY   The important thing in hurdling is to recognize that different sized men will do best with different styles. Al Kraenzlein could always sprint so when I first worked with him I let him go over the hurdles in his own way. I was looking at his natural gait. That would tell me if he had what it took to become a top hurdler. And did he ever! All he needed was to be shown the proper position in clearing the barriers.

I got him to make every motion of the body going forward with no hitch or backward movement going over the hurdles. When he went over the hurdle his head did not seem to rise at all.

He was a beautiful hurdler.

ALVIN KRAENZLEIN   Perhaps my ability as a hurdler and broad jumper is due to my height, combined with the unusual power with which nature has endowed me. Good hurdlers especially over the high obstacles, are generally tall men, so I usually advised the little fellows to stick to the low hurdles.

Some men easily acquire the knack of clearing the sticks fast and close, while it seems impossible for others to learn it. I myself experienced difficulty in learning the proper style. I had, however, unusual speed from the beginning and was never afraid of barking my shins.

Hurdling undoubtedly requires good eyesight and a little nerve. I fortunately possessed both.

Before I put myself under the tutelage of Murphy I used to clear the barriers any old way. I took a good while to rid myself of a very awkward style. A first-class hurdler is essentially an excellent sprinter and jumper. A man who cannot run the hundred in 10 1/5 seconds will seldom beat 16 seconds for the high hurdles.

Some athletes could hurdle with either leg, and this is a big advantage, especially when the path is wet, and you slip or trip. I could hurdle with either leg but I only practiced clearing the bars with the left leg. It is only when a man is thrown out of his stride that ability to hurdle with either leg is useful, and its use is confined to the low hurdles.

The start is even more important in hurdling than in sprinting. In both the high and low events the distance to the first obstacle is 15 yards and the number of steps taken is invariably nine. Hurdlers get off as fast as sprinters and clear the first obstacle at their greatest possible speed. It is only after the first two obstacles are cleared that style counts. A man who can just shave the top of the bars in a neat way will gain at least a foot on an awkward hurdler at each obstacle.

In the low hurdle event seven strides are taken between the obstacles and in the high hurdles three steps are taken.

Whether the hurdle be high or low, I always wanted to clear them close. All good performers on the cinder path run, to use an athletic expression, as close to the ground as possible. Time is always lost when a man bounds high in the air, instead of far forward. I understood this early and had always been given credit for having a good forward action.

Kraenz's style in topping the sticks proved as great a revelation to the Parisians as it had to the English athletes. They had never seen anyone clear the hurdles like he did, although several French athletes vowed to copy it.

O O O O O

While Kraenz was running away with the low hurdle heats, the discus throwers were warming up nearby for their qualification throws. The event drew a big group of big men. The top five throwers would go into the finals. Maybe. They are scheduled for the next day—Sunday.

The discus throw was the most classic of the throwing events and was richly illustrated in the art of ancient Greece, particularly in sculpture. Homer even mentions it as part of the Greeks' pentathlon event. They threw discs of bronze and iron from a rectangular platform known as a "balbis," but little is known about the rules they followed or the distances they threw. Their discs were apparently much heavier than the ones in use in Paris.

At the Athens Games, the Greeks assumed the event was theirs.

No one can throw the disc like a Greek. It is our heritage, our event.

But along came the brash 20-year-old Princeton student, Robert Garrett, who uncorked the longest throw they had ever seen. He had been practicing with a heavy steel discus and considered himself very much a novice at the event. But when he heard they would use a much lighter discus in Athens, he jumped at the chance to enter.

Garrett's story was rather amazing. Years ago discus just wasn't an event in which we participated. When he got to Princeton, Garrett had never even seen one, let alone touched one. He had read about the discus used in ancient Greece and became intrigued. So he asked his classics professor, William Milligan Sloane, if he knew anything about the event.

Well, professor Sloane knew of the ancient statues in museums with athletic young men in the coiled position ready to let loose with the implement. He gave Garrett pictures of the statues and suggested he take them to a local shop and see if he could find someone to make something akin to the discus they saw in the photos. He found a craftsman who made him one, except it weighed nearly 25 pounds. Throw it? He could barely lift it. He didn't know it at the time but a regulation discus weighed about 20 pounds less.

Figure 37 Robert Garrett

MIKE MURPHY   I'd trained quite a few good discus men and all had at least one quality in common—they had big hands with strong fingers. To hold the discus properly the hand had to cover as much of the outer surface of the discus as possible with the fingers firmly gripping the lower edge so that when it left the hand it skimmed along through the air with a twisting motion. Ability to get the correct elevation and to start the discus at the right angle from the hips was of prime importance.

Josiah McCracken was a good athlete and our best thrower at Penn. I had worked with him a lot on his technique although, truth be told, he was better with the shot and hammer.

He had to learn to pivot more quickly on his left foot. We worked on this. The instant the right foot touched the ground, the heave had to be made, the left foot swinging around and striking the ground to keep the body from going out of the ring.

It's the small points of discus that make the difference. I knew if he got these right he would have a chance in Paris.

McCracken was big, strong, fast and athletic. He was at the top of Penn's list of shot putters and hammer throwers and a member of the gymnastics team. But it was on the gridiron that he really stood out. He was named to the 1899 All-American football team as a guard.

As Murphy tells it, by mere strength with no science, he had made fair athletic records in the weight events before coming to Pennsylvania, but in the hammer throw in three years under Murphy's direction he gained 63 feet, and in the shot put nearly 6 feet.

He had his work cut out for him though. In addition to Garrett, the strong Hungarian, Rudolf Bauer, was there. So was our teammate, Richard Sheldon.

Like his older brother, Lewis, Richard was a standout performer for Yale and the New York Athletic Club. In '96 he won the intercollegiate shot title. The next year at the British Championships he placed second in the shot and third in the hammer. He was truly an all-around weight man who took the shot/discus double at the AAU Championships while setting a world record for the discus. He also starred on his football team. He must have been good, too, because the previous season Yale recorded eight shutouts and outscored its opponents by a combined score of 191 to 16.

Sheldon's figure attracted such attention that the Frenchmen christened him "The little baby."

Another of our football standouts, Truxtun Hare, would be competing, so would "the Irish Hercules," John Flanagan.

All the competitors were in shock as they looked down the bowered throwing lane. They had seen nothing like it before.

TRUXTUN HARE   What can I say about the conditions for the discus event other than they were ridiculous? We had to throw down a bowered lane between two rows of trees. Nice trees they were but they belonged in a garden not in a discus event. Now we had all trained to throw with some accuracy, but this was taking it to extremes. I remembered Mike hollering "Accuracy, accuracy," in so many practices back at Franklin Field. Maybe he knew something.

Warm up throws were going into the trees with such regularity that the Racing Club officials, who had refused to cut any down for the benefit of the athletes, must have been wondering how much damage a spinning disc could do to tree branches, several of which were snapped clean off.

Once the competition itself got started though, the big shock was the errant throws of the defending champion, Garrett. He was in the trees more often than a robin going to its nest. He was furious, but the angrier he became, the wilder went the discus.

Some spectators found this amusing. He didn't.

I overheard one of the competitors say, "Since when did this become target practice?"

The Hungarian, Rudolf Bauer, got off the longest throw of the day at 3 inches over 118 feet. Another Hungarian also qualified for the finals, as did a Greek, an athlete from Bohemia, and Dick Sheldon. That was it. Flanagan and Jos McCracken managed to get in legal throws but not long enough to make the finals, which since they would be held on Sunday, likely wouldn't have mattered anyway.

I have to say the discus event surprised us. We all thought that Sheldon or McCracken would win with some to spare. But this, as we came to learn, is a favorite sport in Hungary, where it is practiced assiduously. Bauer and Janda were their best and proved superior to all others. Sheldon managed several throws over 120 feet, but they were outside the boundary drawn according to the Continental practice which was different from the one we were used to.

Figure 38 Rudolf Bauer

Bauer deserves all credit for his victory, though, because as with his fellow countrymen, the discus left his hand and flew straight as an arrow without losing distance. Actually, the control of the discus was remarkable in all the European contestants. What was odd, however was the European style of stopping still at the front of the square and losing all their momentum. They might just as well have thrown from a stand.

The trees got the better of Garret and Trux and neither recorded a legal throw. It was another strange event in what would become a long list of them.

After the disappointing discus competition, I headed to the starting line to get a good view of the 110 hurdle finals.

O O O O O

The hurdlers all took their places at the starting line, but then again the ineptitude of the French starter (a man named Meiers) was on display. As soon as he said *Attention!* McLean caught a flyer, and not by a little either. He had to be a good 5 yards in front off the start.

Figure 39 John McLean

Assuming that his rival would be recalled, Kraenz remained on his mark. By the time he realized this was not to be, he took off after the Michigan man, who by that time was almost to the first hurdle. With each flight of the hurdles Kraenz closed the gap. He caught McLean at the eighth hurdle, flew past him and won by 3 yards in the phenomenal time of 15.4 seconds.

Figure 40 Kraenz in the lead

McLean held on to beat Moloney by inches. Pritchard, who hit a hurdle, failed to finish.

Had it been possible to have timed Kraenz from the moment he left his mark until he broke the tape, he would have established an amazing record. Add to this the fact that the race was on a soft dirt course, and some idea can be formed of what this superman could do when pressed or drawn out. Thanks though to the typical French incompetence, what would likely have been a lopsided race turned into an exciting one.

Naturally Kraenz was thrilled with the victory but angry at the starter.

That was crazy, he says.

Yeah, agrees Tewks.

Better be careful in your races.

You mean get a flyer?

Just pay attention.

I suspect that Moloney, who had beaten McLean easily in their heat, would have come second had it not been for McLean's flyer. While bent over catching his breath, Moloney stared intently at McLean. I don't know if the two ever had words but in reality McLean just took advantage of the inept French starting.

At any rate, we were off to a good start with a clean sweep in the first track event.

O O O O O

Now it was my turn—the 800 heats. We had every reason to believe we would get something out of this race. Of the 13 entrants, 10 were from the USA. So who would it be? Since Alex Grant was our 1900 national 800 champion, he was heavily favored. Actually, he was a Canadian but since he ran for us at Penn he was an honorary American and since the French weren't too keen on keeping things straight, they listed Alex, his brother Dick and George Orton—Canadians all—as competing for the USA. Maybe they thought Canada was a U.S. state. The band probably didn't even know *O Canada*.

Alex studied European History at Penn, and on the way over he had told us all a little about French history and while in Paris dug a little around in museums.

The Flaxen-haired Alex may have been a tad slow of speech but he sure was swift of foot.

He had also planned to run the 2500-meter steeplechase but as a devout Presbyterian he decided he wouldn't as it would now be on Sunday. Maybe he'd go in the 4000-meter steeplechase on Monday.

After Alex, John Cregan of the Princeton Tigers had to be considered a possible winner. He was perhaps our best miler, but since the 1500 was also to be run on Sunday he wouldn't be in that race. So if the 800 was to be his only race in Paris, I knew he'd be able to put a full effort into it. In London, he'd come second to the Englishman, Alfred Tysoe, but he said at the time that he wasn't in top shape. However, he insisted he would be by the time he arrived in Paris. Still, Johnny had been sick as a dog for days, and it wasn't certain he'd even line up to run.

Figure 41 John Cregan

That left Tysoe, a Lancashire farm hand, as the one to beat. In that race in London he not only won, but set a new world record.

Figure 42 Alfred Tysoe

Earlier in the year I had taken the intercollegiate mile title. That was my best distance but again, because it would be run Sunday, the 800 would be my only race in Paris. (Unless I entered a handicap event after the scratch events were over.) I was drawn to go in the second of three heats with the first two in each heat to go through to the finals on Monday.

The heats were scheduled to get going at 10:15, right on the heels of the hurdles which I had watched, so I warmed up during the first heat. Alex was in that. So was Tysoe. But what a double shocker it turned out to be. Howard Hayes of the University of Michigan got out of the gate like a shot and led most of the way, but in the stretch Tysoe and David Hall of Brown University made it a ding-dong finish as they both passed Hayes and ran stride for stride to the tape. Tysoe just nipped Hall in a fast time. Later we found out it was an Olympic record. That was the first shock because nobody expected records on a lumpy, grassy track. The second—and bigger—shock was that Alex Grant struggled home in sixth place. Sixth! He was out of the finals. Was he hurt? He didn't appear to be. I guess he just had one of those days. Maybe it was the travel, the French food, the track surface, too much Parisian night life? I don't know and he never said.

Anyway, I had other things to think about, like running my own race. It looked to be an easier heat. I knew nothing about the

Frenchman in the race—Henri Deloge. The Yale runner, Harrison Smith was also entered as was the University of Syracuse runner, Justus Scrafford. The other two runners were a Hungarian and an Italian.

We all got off to a good start and then settled into a slow-paced race. I hung back, but in hindsight, I would have been better served had I pushed the pace. When Deloge moved to the front, the French spectators who were otherwise seldom demonstrative cheered him on with great enthusiasm which may have motivated him. He won by 3 yards over the Hungarian. Scrafford was third, I came in fourth. Of course I was disappointed. Maybe deep down I never thought I could win but a second or third seemed possible. Alas, it was not to be. My Olympics were probably over.

The only upside to being eliminated was that I was now free to concentrate on keeping notes on the rest of the games. My plans were to be a journalist after graduation anyway. The practice couldn't hurt.

The final heat was a mostly American event, with only one foreigner, an Austrian.

Cregan was in this race, along with John Bray from Williams College, Harvey Lord running for the University of Chicago and Ed Mechling, my Penn teammate.

Cregan took his place on the line, looking no worse for wear from his recent sick spell. He spurted to an early lead and never relinquished it, winning by about 6 yards over Bray.

So the finals were set: Tysoe, Cregan, Hall, Deloge, Bray and the Hungarian, Spiedl.

Without Alex Grant, Tysoe and Cregan figured to duel it out on Monday.

I wish I could say I would also be a part of it, but such is the nature of sport. Everyone has to deal with losing sometimes. Well, maybe not Kraenz, but certainly the rest of us mortals.

It was time for the sprinters to shine. The 100 was next.

O O O O O

GEORGE ORTON   When it came to sprinting, we were pre-eminent. In the English championships, Tewksbury and Jarvis dominated.

The superiority of the American sprinters is due not only to our better physical condition, but to our methods. Simply put, we outclassed all the Continental runners in our style. Most Europeans ran awkwardly, not using the arms and shoulders to the best advantage. The legs and body do not work together as one piece of mechanism as with our sprinters. But even had the English, European, and Australian sprinters been able to run as fast, they would have been beaten because of their poor starting. Jarvis and Tewksbury opened the eyes of the Englishman through the quickness with which they left the mark and the celerity with which they got into their running. In England, the English champion, Wadsley, was beaten at 20 yards, simply run off his legs by Tewksbury.

The feeling among some of us in Paris was that the Europeans were practically beaten before they started.

Few English coaches had developed clear concepts about the mechanics of sprinting form, but much less about conditioning methods. However, one famous British coach, judge and co-founder of the British Amateur Athletics Association, put forth some ideas.

SIR MONTAGUE SHEARMAN   The best practice for a sprint race is to have continued bursts of 30 yards with another man, who is about as good or rather better than yourself. If practicing with a man who is inferior, you should give him a short start in the sprints and catch him as soon as you can. Such practice both helps a man to get into his running quickly and "pulls him out," to use a trainer's expression, i.e., leads him to do a little better than his previous best. After half a dozen of these sprints he should take a few minutes rest and then run the full distance, or at any rate a burst of 70 or 80 yards before he goes into have a rubdown and resume his clothes. For all practice it may be laid down that a man should rarely run a trial for over two-thirds of the distance for which he is training.

The first American sprint star, dubbed "America's Fastest Human," was the legendary Bernard Wefers. A big, powerful sprinter he originally enrolled at Boston College, but then transferred to Georgetown to study medicine. He is credited with having perfected the "shrug finish," throwing the body sideways across the finish line, with one arm high and the other back.

Figure 43 Wefers wins

In 1895 the first major confrontation between the sprint champs from both sides of the Atlantic took place in New York between Wefers and the British champion, Charles Bradley.

WILLIAM CURTIS   Some 8,500 spectators watched. It would have been several thousand more had it not been for the high prices, the cheapest admission being one dollar. On the 155th Street viaduct, which towered high above the roofs of the stands on the southern edge of the field, the sidewalk was thronged with spectators, who stood for four hours in the scorching sun. Probably 12,000 people inside and outside, saw the event. As the hundred yard runners thundered down the path, "Bradley wins" was heard more often and more loudly than "Wefers wins." But in the race the Englishmen lagged behind. He made a desperate attempt with 40 yards to go but Wefers answered so effectively that he finally won by about 4 feet and equaled the world's record.

MIKE MURPHY   One often hears it said that "sprinters, like poets, are born, not made." In a measure this is true, because it is just as natural for some men to outstrip their fellows in a foot race as it is for others to pass their mates in any mental or physical task. It would be a hopeless undertaking to develop a cart–horse into a trotter, because they are built for different purposes. So it is almost as hard to make sprinters out of some athletes. It requires a peculiar combination of strength, agility, and nervous energy to make one a successful sprinter, and if nature has not blessed the athlete with these attributes no amount of hard work or coaching can make him a world champion.

Tewksbury, Jarvis, Duffey, they were born to be sprinters. Kraenzlein, too.

At the same time, any man, no matter how slow he may be, can improve his speed eventually by constant practice and without harm to himself.

I want to correct a popular fallacy: that, to be a successful sprinter, some particular build is necessary. This is a big mistake, for I saw and trained champions of almost every conceivable build. Some were short of stature and inclined to be too heavy; some were very tall and thin, while others had an ideal physique. If there is any advantage to any type of man, I would say it lies with the one who is tall and strong like Kraenzlein.

Numerous trainers claim to have invented the "crouching start" for sprinters—Mike Murphy among them. He says it was while he was at Yale in 1887 and Charles Sherrill was the athlete. At the time all runners stood on the start line, crouched slightly, and pushed off with the rear foot. According to Murphy, when Sherrill dropped into a deep crouch, he was laughed at, and the starter, thinking that Sherrill did not understand how to start, held up the race to give him instructions. Sherrill informed him he knew exactly what he was doing, that he was simply using a new starting technique. When Sherrill consistently won his races, the crouching start caught on and eventually all sprinters used it.

Figure 44 Kraenz demonstrates crouching sprint start

O O O O O

These games had their own sprinting superstar—Arthur Duffey. In recent years he had dominated the 100 (either in meters or in yards) in the United States, Europe and Australia. "King of the English Sporting World" the Boston Globe called him. Other than Kraenzlein, there was probably not another competitor at these games considered more of a favorite to win his event. Duffey was also favored to win the 60 later in the afternoon.

While a student at Boston High School he tried pole vaulting but after skinning his knees and elbows so often his parents made him quit. He decided to try something less painful so he began sprinting. Within a year he entered the New England Intercollegiate Championships and became the first high school runner to post a time of 10 seconds flat for 100 yards. In a shocker, he beat Bernie Wefers. The press called him "the second Wefers." That fall he entered Georgetown University as Wefers' teammate but because he had previously run for a club team, he had to sit out the year. Wanting competition, he headed for London where he took the English 100-yard championship.

By the time he arrived in Paris he held the world record for the 120 yards and was the holder of all national records up to 135 yards. Naturally he inherited the "world's fastest man" label.

Figure 45 Arthur Duffey

Later he became embroiled in a major dust up with Sullivan when Sullivan claimed he had accepted money to run, was a professional, and therefor ineligible to compete as a track and field athlete in the Olympics.

JAMES SULLIVAN   Look, he brought the whole thing on himself. He wrote something suggesting he'd taken money … expense money he says while competing as an amateur. Well, that's simply against the rules. He knew it, we knew it, everybody connected with the sport knew it. He cheated and had to pay the price. It's as simple as that. When an athlete breaks an established law, a trial is unnecessary. He has disqualified himself.

ARTHUR DUFFEY   You want to know the truth about that? I'll tell you the God's honest gospel. The reason Sullivan had it in for me is that I didn't want to wear Spalding shoes, and I didn't wear

Spalding shoes. I had my own shoes and they had worked for me in the past so I wasn't about to change. Remember, Sullivan worked for Spalding. He was his errand boy and whatever Spalding said ... well, let's just say you didn't go up against Spalding without ... repercussions. My goal was to run fast enough to win races. Spalding's goal was to sell enough merchandise to make him rich ... if he wasn't already. That's it and I don't care what Sullivan or anybody else said about that or what was in the papers. This is the reason Sullivan had it out for me.

Spalding was out to corner the market in sporting goods and he damn near did. He had a big booth at the Exposition selling, or at least advertising, just about anything you could ever need as an athlete, shoes included.

I doubt if he really had an interest in any of us. Why was he even in Paris? As far as I could tell it had more to do with business than it did with sport. And I don't think I was the only one to think that.

Despite Sullivan's protestations, Duffey was in Paris. The question was would anybody else even come close to him? Jarvis, Tewks and the Australian, Stanley Rowley, would likely have to duke it out for second and third.

Tewks—John Walter Beardsley Tewksbury—was born in Ashley, Pennsylvania. After attending Wyoming Seminary, he enrolled in the University of Pennsylvania Dental School. He had never run a race in his life and did not know he could sprint until Murphy saw him running for fun and convinced him he could become a good sprinter if only he learned and practiced the proper techniques. So he worked with Mike and developed into not only a top sprinter but one good enough to win both the intercollegiate 100 and 220 yard championships.

Although not a good starter he usually came on strong in the last half of his races. He always looked slightly awkward but his staying power seemed to make up for that. Although he never trained especially for the quarter, Murphy felt that with his ability to come on late, if he trained for it he could be a very competitive quarter miler.

The 22-year-old Princeton flyer, Frank Jarvis, whose father had come from England, enjoyed the distinction of being a distant relation to George Washington. He was probably the second favorite after Duffey. His father had emigrated from England. He was both an outstanding student studying law at Princeton and was the first great Princeton sprinter.

Figure 46 Frank Jarvis

The other top sprinter was Stanley Rowley. As a schoolboy in New South Wales, Australia, he showed promise as a sprinter of the highest order. He won a lot of high school meets and then entered open competitions where he beat the then current Australasian champion. In 1897 and 1899 he won both sprints at the Australian Biannual Championships against the best athletes from Australia and New Zealand. And he set a whole bunch of records.

Figure 47 Stanley Rowley

STANLEY ROWLEY When the notice of the Paris Games came up, I was immediately interested. New South Wales is a bloody long way from Paris so I didn't exactly know how I would accomplish that. Then a boost came from the English Amateur Athletic Association. They had read about my sprinting times so they wrote to our amateur association asking for them to send me so I could run as a part of a Great Britain team. They knew that the Americans coming to England prior to Paris were strong in the sprints with men like Jarvis, Duffey, and Tewksbury and figured I could help bolster their British Empire team. And so I could.

The English Association wrote to the Australasian Association:

> In Australasian and British athletic circles it is felt that in view of the importance of our next championship festival, Stanley Rowley at least should be given a chance of measuring his speed against the crack sprinters who will be competing.

The AAU of Australasia is, unfortunately, poor, but our AAA has a very large sum of money in hand, and some of it could not be spent in a better cause than that suggested. The Australasian people are helping with men and money to maintain our supremacy in South Africa, and the AAA might therefore find some of the money, while Australasia finds the man to help our supremacy against the Americans on the athletic fields.

Our Amateur Athletic Association voted to send me to the English Championships. That was swell, but they didn't come up with enough money. I might have taken a train to Canberra on what they gave me, but that would have been about it. But I desperately wanted to go. I knew I was a bloody good sprinter at least by Australian standards. In the 15 open competition events I ran in, I won 13, dead-heated once, and came in second in the other. More than once I ran 9.9 for the 100 yards. Not many men can say that. I was in good shape—5 feet 9 1/2 inches, about 161 pounds. I was raring to go to test myself against the rest of the world. Hell, I really thought I could beat the rest of the world. All I needed was the chance. I kept asking the Athletic Association for more money, but they kept telling me they didn't have more, which is ridiculous when you think about it. I mean, how many other men would be representing Australia in front of the whole world? Actually, Freddie Lane was going, too, but he was a swimmer. I was the only track and field athlete, and those were the events that got most of the attention.

They put out a subscription and raised some of the money I needed, but not all. The only thing I knew to do was to dig up some money of my own, which wasn't easy. I wern't no millionaire. I worked for a living at a shipping company. Not only did I have to come up with the money but I also had to ask for a leaving from the shipping company where I worked. Eventually I barely scraped together the loot and to get a five months' leave. It would be a long and expensive trip for me but I figured it would be worth it to show I was the best sprinter in the world.

On April 24 I boarded a P & O Liner from Melbourne headed for Liverpool. The plan was to join up with some English and Scottish runners before hopefully heading to Paris.

It is a ridiculously long trip so I didn't get to London until June 3. I immediately took a train up to Glasgow and ran my first race a few days later. I wasn't in top shape after all that time traveling when I couldn't really train. It was a rainy day, the track was wet, and I was not in top form. I came in second. A few weeks later I beat Wadsley, the English champion by a good 2 yards.

Then it was time to meet the Americans. They were as good as advertised. They won all their heats except one. I won that one. Then in the final I came fourth.

All that did was give me more desire to beat them when we got to the Olympics. I knew I could. If I had their advantages, I could beat them.

Our athletic capacity was every bit as good as theirs. Maybe better, I don't know. We're a tough lot of people, we Aussies. But they have their strong club and university systems unlike anything we have. They have a lot of men to pick from, they have a lot of money, and they have top trainers like Murphy who I met and spent a little time with. They also had another big advantage: they run on cinder tracks whereas I had always run on grass.

Oh yes, give us what the American runners had and we'd beat the bejesus out of them. I really believe that.

After the English Championships, the English Association coughed up enough money to send me to Paris. I was ready to take on the Americans again.

The 100 had a packed field, no doubt about that. A decent crowd turned out for the heats set to begin at 10:30 in the leafy Bois be Boulogne with 20 athletes stripping to run. There would be five preliminary heats, four semifinals, and the finals with four runners.

Our runners were used to running on carefully manicured cinder or dirt tracks. How they would adapt to the slightly bumpy, slightly soggy, slightly slanting "track" on which they were to run here was wasn't clear. But no one, except perhaps the French officials, were happy with it.

Tewks jogged easily on the cloggy ground. A sprained ankle could spoil everything. His roommate, though, successfully navigated the course earlier in the morning. Try not to think about it, Kraenz advised. Just run your normal race.

The first rounds offered no surprises. Duffey, Jarvis, Tewks and the runner from India, Pritchard, all easily won their heats. Continued problems arose, however, with the uneven starting procedure used by the French starter, Meiers. Murphy and some of the other Americans complained yet again.

We simply cannot continue like this.

It's making a farce of these sprints.

Meiers was a terrible starter in the hurdles. He's worse here.

We need to do something. We need to change the starter.

George Sandford is here. He's very experienced. He's a well-known British starter and he's willing.

So after holding off the heats for a while, it was finally agreed to let Sandford start the remainder of the sprints and the races went off without further problems.

An official reminded them that the winner of each heat in the semis would advance to the final and that the second and third place runners would advance to the repéchargé heat.

With spectators crowding the lumpy straightaway, the first heat was won, as expected, by Duffey in a relatively slow time. Rowley took second, 5 feet behind.

Tewks would compete in the second heat along with the Americans, Clark Leiblee from the University of Michigan and Frederick Moloney from the University of Chicago. The other runner was a German.

Tewks moved to the starting line and dug his starting holes in the soft earth. Mike had trained him well, taught him to dig the holes so he would be as close to the starting line as possible and still have a proper angle to get away naturally and quickly. This he would do by getting down on one knee with the back leg even with the inner ankle of the forward foot. He had done this hundreds of times. The back knee would be on the ground when the starter gave the first of his three signals: "Get on your marks." With the next signal "Get set," he would rise on his hands and feet, leaning forward as far as possible without losing his balance. At the report of the pistol he would spring forward. At least those were the commands used back home.

Here on the soggy ground of Paris, Tewks easily dug his holes with his spiked shoes, one hole for each foot. He took the time to make sure they were deep and strong enough to give a firm grip. Using his spread hand, he measured the correct distances for the holes which had proved best for him as determined by Mike. The hands on the starting line were exactly 6 inches in front of the forward foot. This way he was well balanced and could get off without wobbling.

While waiting for the pistol, he let the weight of his body rest on his front leg, a little forward so the first drive of the leg would send his body forward and upward. His back leg was firmly in the hole he had dug. Although the German runner next to him was rocking back and forward a little, Tewks was still. Mike had drilled into him the idea that runners who aim to gradually move the body forward after getting set on the assumption they can perfectly time the pistol will be set back more than they gain.

At the gun he sprang forward with the impetus the crouch had given him. His first few strides were natural and easy. It was close to 20 yards before he was running erect, his arms helping the leg drive by swinging forward and upward with a hard cross motion. He ran naturally, making sure not to over stride.

Leiblee was running with him stride for stride with Moloney falling back. Out of the corner of his eye he saw the German runner pull up.

As they approached the finish line, Tewks leaned just enough to best Leiblee by inches. To his right he could see Mike offer a slight nod. That was a lean they had worked on a lot in practice.

The third four-man heat was made up of our Penn teammate Thaddeus McClain, Edmund "Cotton" Minahan, the Georgetown sprinter, the Brit/Indian Norman Pritchard and the overwhelming heat favorite, the "Princeton Flyer," Frank Jarvis.

The 18-year-old Cotton Minahan was one of the youngest competitors at the games and one of the biggest sprinters at 6' and 190 pounds.

Figure 48 Cotton Minahan

As expected, Jarvis cruised to victory, beating McClain by a yard with Pritchard third and Minahan fourth.

So with Duffey, Jarvis, and Tewks safely through to the finals it would be left to the repéchargé to settle on the fourth runner.

Rowley got off to a flying start and held off the fast charging Pritchard by a matter of a couple of inches and the final field was set.

O O O O O

After a brief interlude, the runners were asked to lineup for the finals.

Duffey remained the huge favorite to the onlookers.

He'll win, probably easily.

The best in the world ain't he.

By far.

Look how easily he won the preliminary and semifinal. Didn't even look like he was working hard.

Second and third are still up for grabs and none of the others were about to concede. Even the best can have off days, can't they?

Figure 49 Arthur Duffey in sprint start

The crowd went silent waiting for the pistol, the runners on their marks seemingly for a long time. When the gun finally went, Duffey was off like a shot, a good stride ahead of the tightly bunched trio behind him. Then at about the half way mark he wobbled a little. In a few more strides, while still in front, he tumbled to the lumpy ground. A groan of disappointment and sympathy arose from the American spectators. Jarvis was now in front—barely. At the tape he was 2 feet ahead of Tewks with Rowley a close third.

Where the focus of attention should have been on the winning Jarvis, most of it went to the prone Duffey.

ARTHUR DUFFEY I don't know why my leg gave way. I felt a peculiar twitching after going 20 yards. Then I seemed to lose control of my leg, and suddenly it gave out, throwing me on my face. But that is one of the fortunes of sport, and I can't complain. I didn't think I could compete again in Paris, but I am glad the event went to an American.

ALONZO STAGG   The track was not good. It was soft and uneven and doubtless led to Duffey's breakdown."

Mike Murphy looking on had seen this type of injury before. He suggested it was probably a tendon so it was not likely Duffey would be able to run again for at least several months. These things take time to heal.

STANLEY ROWLEY   Fourth against the Americans wasn't great, but it was better than any anybody else in the world could do.

Tewks who was barely beaten hung his head. "I should have had Jarvis," he said to Bax. "Maybe not Duffey, but Jarvis."
"For sure."
"Damn."

O O O O O

It was time for the big guys again. Everyone had expected the shot put heats to be a ding-dong battle between Dick Sheldon and yet another superb Irish weightman, the record holder, Denis Horgan. Shortly after setting the world's record in County Cork, Ireland, Horgan came to the U. S. and joined the Greater New York Irish Athletic Association. For a big man— 5' 10 1/2" and 210 pounds— he had remarkable agility as his performances in the running broad jump showed. As a shot putter, he dominated the event, but Sheldon wasn't far behind.

However, as much as this would likely have been an enticing match up, Horgan is a no show. Perhaps without belonging to a big club or being enrolled in a university, he couldn't come up with the funds for a trip to Paris. So that leaves it up to Sheldon to do battle with Garrett, McCracken, Hare, and whoever the Europeans can put up.

MIKE MURPHY   Very rarely does one become a champion at putting the shot and throwing the hammer. While both are obviously weight events, they call for different styles of training. Proficiency in one is obtained at the expense of proficiency in the other, and more often training for both prevents the athlete from excelling in either. In putting the shot, tone develops the "pushing" muscles, while throwing the hammer is a "pulling" exercise.

In training putters like McCracken and Hare, I often had to work with them to avoid the common fault of trying to "throw" the shot. Throwing the shot as opposed to putting it not only constitutes a foul, but also puts a severe strain on the arm.

They were big, strong athletes, both, but that alone wouldn't make them champions. Their putting techniques had to be maximized and they both worked long hours to get that right.

One paper observed that "The physique of these American giants compared favorably with the best of Europe's big men." Perhaps so, but we believed that in this event the Americans would easily outclass their European opponents.

The heats got started at about 11:00 with the top five competitors being advanced to the finals, which being on Sunday, meant that some competitors would be heat-only putters.

Figure 50 Richard Sheldon

The heats didn't offer up a whole lot of surprises. Sheldon got off the longest put with McCracken and Garrett not far behind. One little surprise though is that the best Trux Hare could do was eighth. He was capable of so much better, but on this day it just wasn't there. After the top three, a Hungarian and a Greek putted well enough to advance to the finals but their puts were considerably short of the three Americans.

Figure 51 McCracken in shot heats

So even though McCracken and Garrett easily qualified, there was next to no chance they would appear for the Sunday finals.

O O O O O

The 400-meter flat race saw 15 starters line up for the heats. Among them were seven Americans. Maxi Long running in the Columbia's blue and white stripe was the big favorite. He was usually our best 400 man, had won handily in London, and was a savvy tactical competitor, seeming able to sense where all the other runners were, even those behind him, and adjust his pace accordingly. He had won our AAU Championships in '98 and '99 but somehow lost the recent intercollegiate title when he was beaten by Yale's Dixon Boardman and Syracuse's Henry Lee. So it seems if anyone other than Maxie has a chance it would be Boardman or Lee, but in reality most of us figured Maxie must have just had an off day when he was beaten.

Figure 52 Maxie Long

That looked like a sage observation when in Saturday's first heat, he trotted home to an easy win over Lee. Boardman also won his heat, and so did the University of Chicago's Bill Moloney. Georgetown's William Holland came in second in Boardman's heat, and since the first two in each heat were to advance, everything looked to be set up for the finals: Long, Holland, Lee, Moloney and the Dane, Ernst Schulz all qualified.

But … since the finals are scheduled for the next day, Sunday, Boardman, Lee, and Moloney said they will be no shows.

The Sunday hiccup was certainly having an effect on these games. And it was about to have even more.

O O O O O

The most outlandish event in these strange games was about to begin.

It was widely anticipated that the long jump would be a remarkable competition between the three best long jumpers in the world—the Americans Kraenzlein and Meyer Prinstein and Ireland's Peter O'Connor. It turned out to be less than that.

Where is O'Connor?

He's a no show. Too bad. He would have given the two Americans a battle.

Still, the Kraenzlein-Prinstein feud should make for a great show.

O O O O O

Myer Prinstein was born in 1878 in Szczuczyn, a small city of some 3,000 inhabitants in Northeastern Poland which at the time was a part of Russia. His parents, Jacob and Julia Prinstein were Polish-Russian Jews. When Meyer, the third born of their nine children, was five the family emigrated to New York City. Jacob, a grocer, later moved the family to upstate New York and settled in Syracuse.

Prinstein first gained national notice when, in 1896 he won the New York Metropolitan long jump competition. He then enrolled at Syracuse where he established American and intercollegiate records and then snatched the world record at the New York Athletic Club Games. He was also the center on the Syracuse basketball team.

At the 1899 Penn Relays, Kraenzlein beat Prinstein and retook the long jump world record.

The fair-haired Prinstein, ever the strong competitor, fumed for a year and then when the Penn Relays came around again he reclaimed the world record. He also anchored the victorious Syracuse relay team by beating Maxie Long of Columbia on the anchor leg.

His duels, and resultant feud with Kraenzlein became one of the most storied in American track and field lore.

There was never any love lost between the two best long jumpers in the world.

Figure 53 Meyer Prinstein

Adding to the tension between the two men was the Sabbath issue.

MEYER PRINSTEIN   Look, I'm Jewish-American. Saturday is my Sabbath, not Sunday. Nevertheless, I was informed by my school that we would not be competing on Sunday, but naturally we would on Saturday. This was not fair. It was not fair to me and it wasn't fair to any other competitor at the games who might have been Jewish. They wanted us to compete on our Sabbath but not on the Sabbath of another religion. Of course, this kind of discrimination against Jews was nothing new.

So I suggested that the entire competition be postponed to Monday so everyone could compete. That seemed like a fair and reasonable thing to do. But I was told that no, the competition would go on as scheduled with the preliminary jumps on Saturday and the finals on Sunday.

Since Kraenzlein, who was a Gentile would be allowed to compete on Sunday if he chose to do so, this set up a ridiculous situation: the Jew couldn't jump on a day that wasn't his Sabbath while the Gentile could jump on a day that was his Sabbath! How absurd and how unfair!

ALVIN KRAENZLEIN   I didn't set the rules, I didn't set the schedule and I had no influence on those who did. That was all up to other people. I competed according to the schedule set by the organizers, period.

MEYER PRINSTEIN   We could hardly be classed as friends, but I assumed that Kraenzlein was a man of his word. When we met on the Friday before the competition he agreed either to wait until Monday if that could be arranged or at least not to jump on Sunday since I couldn't jump then.

So when they wouldn't change the schedule, the prelims got under way on Saturday with both of us jumping. In the long jump you can never be assured of the results because it's always possible to have a bad day or to get the takeoff all wrong and not make safe jumps, but let's face it, it would have taken extraordinary circumstances for me and Kraenzlein not to make the finals.

There were 12 jumpers in the prelims. Each of us would have

three jumps. All we had to do was to be one of the top five to make the finals.

So the agreement I had with Kraenzlein was that neither of us would jump on Sunday. Rather we would let our results from Saturday stand. According to the rules in play all marks made in qualifying would count toward the finals. There was no argument about this.

Near the end of the day the spectators gathered around the center of the grounds, where a space was reserved for the broad jump. It was one of the larger crowds for athletics at these Games. Such was the appeal of the potential Kraenzlein-Prinstein matchup.

Also as usual, a little nod from Prinstein to Kraenz was the only exchange between them.

MIKE MURPHY   The last 5 or 6 yards of the runway were inclined, a height of about 6 inches being reached at the takeoff board. I talked to Alvin about this. He needed to adjust his run up slightly. He spent a lot of time staring at the takeoff board. Clearly he was a little thrown by this and I think it showed.

Kraenz was one of the first to go. Many in the crowd knew who he was, knew he was a great jumper, expected he would be in a fierce battle with Prinstein. He was, though, maybe a little nonplussed by the runway situation. He stood motionless for a few moments staring down the grassy runway leading to the takeoff board. Then he moved forward, slowly picking up speed. He was gliding smoothly, running with apparent ease, no hint of strain. He reached the takeoff at full speed and soared into the air with his arms reaching overhead as if he were grasping for every last inch. The mostly American crowd broke into a cheer. They could sense, even before he landed that the jump was long—and so it was.

Prinstein followed with a jump almost as far. The battle was on.

Figure 54 Prinstein in long jump (broad jump)

From our Penn squad we also had Bill Remington and Thaddeus McClain competing and both were strong jumpers.

Thad was nothing if not a versatile athlete. Here he was in the long jump, had already run the 100 meters, and would later run the 200 meter-hurdles and the 4000-meter steeplechase.

Bill Remington had placed third in the 1900 Intercollegiate long jump so there was a reasonable expectation he would make the finals. But as one of our most devout athletes, he was preparing to enter the Episcopal ministry so there was no question that if he qualified for the Sunday finals he would not be there.

The other American competitor was John McLean the All-American halfback from the University of Michigan who already had a second place in the hurdles.

If for some strange reason Kraenzlein and Prinstein faltered, the Irishman, Patrick Leahy would have to be considered a possible winner.

There was also a German, a Frenchman, a couple of Hungarians and a couple of Swedes.

The styles of all these jumpers was ever so different.

ALVIN KRAENZLEIN   It is much easier to jump then to explain how to do it.

Unlike many branches of athletic sports, the broad jump does not call for any qualifications as regards height, weight or build. This is evidenced by the fact that the best broad jumpers were pretty well divided as to size. Newburn, the Irish champion, stood 6' 3" while Prinstein was comparatively speaking, a small man.

Figure 55 Kraenzlein practicing long jump

My style of jumping was rather different from the style of most of the Continental jumpers. I made my first mark about 35 to 40 feet from the takeoff. The second was about the same distance from the first mark, and the third 10 feet from the second, making the distance of the run from 80 to 90 feet. The first 10 feet of the run I used to lengthen my stride to keep me well within myself. As Mike Murphy drilled into me, I had to make sure the last part of the run was loose and easy and not push too hard because that would only lead to a shortening of the stride and a jerky run. All except the last two strides, that is. I wanted them to be shorter so they would pitch my body forward which would assist me in carrying my body high in the air. Just before landing I would shoot my legs out so that I was almost in a sitting position. This increased the distance covered.

My technique was usually pretty good but I was always eager to have Mike Murphy at the takeoff. I had the greatest confidence in him and his shouting to me to jump high seemed to encourage me.

MIKE MURPHY   Kraenzlein was a master technician. But so was Prinstein. What made Prinstein so successful was the rise which he got after leaving takeoff. He did not approach the takeoff with as much speed as Kraenzlein but he got higher in the air. He had an unusually pretty style. He knew what he was doing.

It has to be said that the Continental jumpers had not developed the jumping skills of the Americans and the Irishman who had their takeoffs down to a fine point. Several Continental jumpers marked off their takeoff distance, but had not practiced sufficiently, while others jumped, trusting only to their eye for making the proper striding distance. In general, also, the Continental jumpers failed to rise sufficiently.

The qualifications proceeded pretty much according to the book. The German, Hungarians and Swedes sat at the bottom of the table. The five jumpers who qualified were Kraenzlein, Prinstein,

Remington, Leahy and the Frenchman, Delannoy.

Prinstein took the lead with 7.185 meters to Kraenzlein's 6.93.

This was turning out to be the close competition everyone expected ... but not everybody liked. Kraenzlein's competitive juices were roiling.

That was it, Prinstein figured. He was the likely winner. With Kraenzlein agreeing not to compete on Sunday that left the finals field to Leahy and the Frenchman, neither of whom were likely to approach his mark. They could jump all day long on Sunday as far as he was concerned. At the end of the day's competition he went back to his hotel a very satisfied athlete.

But Kraenz was a champion and champions hate to lose. I could tell he was stewing, so I wasn't all that surprised at what came later.

O O O O O

Next up were the 400 hurdle heats. After watching Prinstein edge out Kraenz in the long jump qualifications, what was left of the crowd had to hustle over to the start line.

Here, unlike what the athletes were expecting—individual hurdles lined up in each lane—they found fences running across the width of the entire track. Most were made of 10 rows of wooden boards about 4 inches wide nailed to square upright posts and then cross-braced with diagonals. Others were telephone poles. They were as solid as any fence used to coral steers. Hit one and it would be like running into a wall. If that weren't enough, the final hurdle was a 15-foot water jump like they used in the steeplechase.

Tewks looked at it in some disbelief. "I've never seen anything like it before," he says. "And likely never will again. At least I hope not."

"Just think of them as regular hurdles," says Murphy.

Easier said than done. Telephone poles?

Unlike at some of the other events, this one was fairly crackling with excitement. The French were excited about their athlete—Henri Tauzin—a five-time French champion in the event and according to the stories going around, he had never been beaten.

Never?

What they say.

The 400 hurdles wasn't an event run much in the U.S. so Tewks had little experience to build on but he figured he'd give it his best shot. At the very least, coming in second to an unbeaten runner wouldn't be a disgrace.

But like so much else at these games, this turns into another bizarre event. Ten competitors were entered, but when Tewks reported to the starting area there were only five men ready to run.

What's going on? Tewks asks.

We're it, George Orton tells him.

Where are the other …?

Maybe they've conceded the race to the Frenchman.

So another absurd situation. They would run two heats with the first two finishers in each heat progressing to the Sunday finals. In other words, run two heats to reduce a five-man field to a four-man field.

To add to the ridiculousness, one entrant, Bill Lewis, will run for Syracuse University, and knowing their position on not letting their athletes compete on Sunday, and knowing that the finals would be on Sunday, he wouldn't run even if he made the finals. So it was highly probable that four would run to reduce the four-man field to a four-man field!

In the first heat Tewks took an early lead, stayed in front the whole way and beat out Lewis and an Austrian runner.

At least he didn't break his neck on a telephone pole.

In the second heat, accompanied by enthusiastic support from the home crowd, Tauzin edged out George Orton—but just barely. But it didn't matter one whit. With only two men in the race and with the first two to go through to the finals, it was a farce. Both men ran at a rather pedestrian pace little faster than a Sunday jog. Neither was about to show his hand to the other man.

The crowd was predictably disappointed with the race but encouraged that their champion was conserving his energy for what they anticipated would be sure victory in the finals.

At any rate, all they accomplished was to eliminate the Austrian.

Ah well, it was a good warmup for Sunday's final and gave Tewks the opportunity to practice going over telegraph poles and water jumps.

"The poles were tricky," he tells Murphy.

"They're not tricky, just big."

"I had to be extra careful to clear each fence with room to spare," Tewks insists. "This slowed me down some."

"But it also slowed down everyone else. You won easily, didn't you? Take confidence from that."

There wasn't much time to take it in, though, because the 60-meter sprint qualifications followed immediately with the finals to be run only 45 minutes after that.

O O O O O

Tewks figured to have a good chance to place in this one but he knew it wouldn't be easy. Kraenz was entered. So was the Indian, Pritchard, the Aussie, Rowley and the kid, Cotton Minahan.

Cotton is a likable Georgetown kid of 17. Despite being one of the biggest sprinters, he always got away fast and could get that big body down the track to put in good times in the shorter races. He was also a good right-handed baseball pitcher with aspirations—realistic as it turns out—to play in the Major Leagues.

The first of ..." to two heats went off at 2:00 with the first two finishers advancing to the finals. Cotton got off to his usual good start, but Kraenz came on strong and took him by about a half yard. Pritchard was third followed by a Frenchman and a Swede.

In the second heat Rowley and Tewks ran stride for stride the whole way. Tewks managed to best him by maybe a foot. Maybe. Bill Holland, the other Georgetown runner, came third. Two Hungarians trailed.

That was one tough race. Short but tough.

So there were no real surprises here. Tewks, Kraenz, Rowley, and Minahan would make up the foursome for the final to come in a few minutes.

O O O O O

What a day for Tewks! By the time the 60 finals rolled around he had to be fatigued. He had already run three heats of the 100, one of the 60, and two grueling 400 hurdle races.

WALTER TEWSKBURY Those 400s by themselves were enough to take something out of the legs but I was hoping snagging another gold would put a little spring back. This would be the seventh race in the last four hours. They weren't easy jogs either and it was hot. I must already have sweated out a bucket of water. OK, I wasn't the only one who must have been feeling the effects of a jam-packed day. Rowley had run in the same flat races as I had, and Minahan only missed the 100 final. Kraenz had run those 110 meter hurdles and had that intense long jump battle with Prinstein.

After a quick light lunch and a lot of water, I headed back out for the 60 finals. Three Americans and an Aussie lined up for the final race of the punishing day.

Kraenz and I couldn't have been closer together for the entire length of the run. At the end I leaned and thought I had him, but they said he won by a couple of inches. I had the silver and Rowley the bronze.

We all collapsed on the warm grass.

It had been a great day for me. I had two silvers. I was thrilled and exhausted at the same time.

Figure 56 60 meter finish Kraenz (left) beats Tewks (right)

The 60 finished the first day's competition. We had swept all three of the day's finals: Kraenz, the 110 hurdles and 60 meters flat; Jarvis, the 100 flat.

o o o o o

FREDERICK MUELLER   As an American businessman in Paris at the time of the Olympic Games and as a frequent and keen spectator of track and field meetings back home, I was eager to go out to the Bois de Boulogne and take in the big meet. I was there for all of that first day, right through the 60 finals.

What immediately surprised me was the relatively meager crowds. I was accustomed to see thousands at athletic contests of such international importance, but on this beautiful day, not over 1000 spectators were present, and the majority of these came from America. Maybe the slim attendance was because it was Bastille Day and there was an annual review of the troops of Paris by the president.

Only two small stands were provided for the spectators, and only one of these was fairly filled, chiefly with bright young American girls who wore the colors of the various American colleges competing and gave unstinted applause when our team secured victories. A portion of the best stand, gaily bedecked with the Stars and Stripes, was reserved for Americans.

The girls broke out into college cheers whenever one of their schoolmates appeared on the field. This was obviously a revelation to the Frenchman and other Europeans. At first yell they apparently imagined an invasion of wild Indians, but after hearing the cries about 100 times, they recognized that it was simply an outburst of American enthusiasm. The Frenchmen, however, could not become reconciled to this form of cheering, and they were heard to exclaim frequently, "what a band of savages!"

The odd techniques of the American jumpers and throwers were matters of considerable interest to the Europeans. So too, were the curious crouching postures of the American sprinters as they awaited the pistol, the elaborate to "preparations for fixing the run length for a jump, and the peculiar form of shot putting. Apparently they didn't have the equivalent of a Mike Murphy to train them.

The natty college costumes of the lads were a decided contrast to the homemade attire of some of the best European athletes, who instead of donning a sweater or a bathrobe after competing, walked about in straw hats and light overcoats.

A few contestants, and more than a few spectators complained about the disgusting odors drifting across the field from the agricultural show nearby. They were not nice.

Most athletes on the American team were of the tall, lanky variety, and this led a French official to remark that the Americans, with their long legs and thin bodies, were built perfectly for running. Most representatives of the Continental nations caused our boys to smile. Their style of running and jumping was clumsy and ludicrous.

Despite the sparse crowds, despite the odd conditions of the field, despite the intense heat, it was a very successful first day for us.

It was a long trip back to the hotel, but an oh, so satisfying one. Since it was Bastille Day, as we were walking through the city we could see the tricolor displayed everywhere. The central arteries of Paris were overhung with tastefully decorated arches which that evening were brilliantly lighted, forming a continuous, fairytale vault of colored electric lanterns.

The next day was the contentious Sunday. We were looking forward to the day's events but not the complications and conflict we knew would accompany them.

O O O O O

As we were leaving the athletic field that day we came upon an interesting temporary enclosure. Looking inside out of curiosity we found strange looking equipment and a French inventor.

Etienne-Jules Marey, as we were to learn, was an important French scientist, physiologist and chronophotographer who was obsessed with analyzing the laws that governed the movements of the human body. Toward that end he created what he called a "chronophotographic gun," an instrument that looked something like a sawed-off shotgun with a small magazine mounted on top of the barrel.

Figure 57 Marey's chronophotographic gun

To operate it, he placed the stock against his shoulder just as one would if firing a shotgun, aimed it directly at his subject and pulled the trigger. It must have been disconcerting when aimed directly at a human subject. Rather than firing ammunition it photographed 12 consecutive frames a second. Using this he famously studied the movement of many animals, including cats which he proved always landed on their feet.

He had for some years been interested in investigating the comparative muscular development of cyclists.

The bicycle had been used in France since the 1860s primarily as an expensive plaything of the elite, but by 1900 with the advent of replaceable pneumatic tires, cycling had become a popular sport with an estimated 3,000,000 cyclists in France. Marey, although not a rider himself, saw the healthful benefits of cycling. He analyzed and photographed cyclists on various models of bicycles to determine which ones caused the least fatigue.

From studying cyclists he moved on to study the movements of other athletes, so he could analyze how the most useful muscles could be trained.

Hence his interest in the athletes at the Paris Games. He wanted to chronophotograph elite athletes. Where better to find them than at the games? His interests were similar to those of Coubertin—sports as an agency of moral and social rearmament. Sports, he insisted, would advance "physical fitness, self-reliance, initiative, and adjustment to the modern world."

ETIENNE-JULES MAREY The prize-winners at athletic sports betray the secret of their success, perhaps unconsciously acquired, and which they would doubtless be incapable of defining themselves. My task was to investigate the precise methods and the effects of different sports on the organism and compare their values.

Figure 58 Marey at work

Marey set out to determine the relationship between an individual's physical attributes and his aptitude for a particular sport, or with track and field athletes, a particular event. He would have each competitor fill out a questionnaire answering questions on heredity, nutrition, and lifestyle and then analyze the athlete's motions, from the point of view of kinematics and dynamics.

In Paris it wasn't as easy a task as he had thought. The events were so spread out across the sprawling city that he found it difficult to move all the necessary equipment to each location. At the Racing Club, however, he could set up this temporary enclosure for his measuring equipment, dressing rooms, and a large canvas backdrop for the chronophotographic photographs. But after setting up everything he found that many athletes were less than enthusiastic about undergoing a battery of tests before competing.

We've got to get ready for our event.

OK, we'll give you photographs of yourself that you can take home. Mementos, souvenirs to show your families.

In that case …

One of the first and most eager volunteers was Jos McCracken. Standing in front of the canvas, McCracken, wearing only a pair of tight shorts, to permit the camera to capture the action of the muscles, stepped into an imaginary 7-foot circle. He held the discus nearly level, swung it a few times from left to right to gain momentum, then pivoted quickly on the left foot. The instant the right foot touched the ground, he launched the disc with the left foot swinging around and striking the ground to keep the body from going out of the circle. McCracken repeated this several times while Marey and his two assistants operated the equipment. They were able to get close to 50 images of the throwing action, each a split second apart.

Figure 59 Josiah McCracken

ETIENNE-JULES MAREY The films we made of the athletes showed the superiority of one champion over another. They were a precious guide for those who would have similar success.

His camera showed in minute details the variations in techniques that distinguished each athlete. He studied each movement split second by split second in slow motion long before slow motion photography was commonplace.

Later, after comparing the films, Marey came to a somewhat surprising conclusion. The films demonstrated that from a purely physiological aspect, the French athletes were on the whole in better shape than the Americans, yet the Americans won most of the events. What to make of the American prowess? Marey reached two conclusions: 1.) They were introduced to sports at an earlier age. 2.) Their techniques, as taught to them by trainers such as Mike Murphy, were more sophisticated than those of other competitors. For example, in the hurdles as exemplified by Kraenz, the Americans leaned forward as they cleared each obstacle, whereas the others were upright. For the shot put and discus they wound up their throws by spinning and whipping their arms around, whereas the others relied on their muscles alone. In the long jump Kraenzlein and Prinstein used their arms to increase their forward momentum. The high jump proved to be the biggest revelation. Instead of throwing the whole body over at once, Bax let one leg lead.

The Americans weren't better athletes; they were better coached. Maybe Mike Murphy was more responsible for the American's superb showing than anything else.

ETIENNE-JULES MAREY Chronography showed that the Americans had a real advantage over the others thanks to ingenious tricks that the rules did not prohibit.

EIGHT

S UNDAY MORNING and some athletes slept late, some found churches to their liking, some took in the sights of Paris.

Some American athletes competed; some didn't.

O O O O O

Events weren't scheduled to begin until midafternoon.

After all, people go to church on Sunday mornings but the afternoon should be free. What better way to spend a summer Sunday afternoon than a nice wine-accompanied lunch followed by a trip out to a lovely park to watch sportsman compete in a leafy glade?

The first event on what we knew would be a contentious day of competitions began with the shot finals.

No one was sure who would show up. Yes, most of the American universities had forbidden their athletes from competing Sunday, but the question remained: would any ignore the prohibitions? If they do what would be the repercussions? Probably some kind of sanctions from their schools. Might some risk that? Exactly who would show up is a topic of conversation around the grounds. The issue with the non-university athletes is simpler. If they wished to compete, they appeared free to do so, but some probably wouldn't.

At the announced starting time of 2:25, not surprisingly McCracken and Garrett did not strip to compete. They were there as spectators. Garrett's Princeton team had ordered him not to. Jos, of course, had been quite vocal about abstaining. So of the five qualifiers only three were there to compete in the finals—Sheldon, the American; Crettier, the Hungarian; and Paraskevopoulos, the Greek.

All three put the shot out farther than they had in the heats. Still, it was quite an anticlimax. Horgan wasn't even at the games, and two of the three American qualifiers were sitting in the stands as spectators.

Richard Sheldon of the New York Athletic Club, as expected, was the winner with what was touted as the world's record put. He was the youngest athlete to ever win the shot title. It would have been interesting to see how he would have fared against Horgan.

Based on their puts in the heats alone, McCracken was given second and Garrett third. The Hungarian was fourth, the Greek fifth.

Mike Murphy thinks that nearly every one of the European shot putters would have been disqualified in England or America. They did not put the shot out straight from the shoulder, as the rules require. Under these circumstances it was surprising they did no better, 36 feet being their best.

Now, would the Sabbath defection scene be repeated all day? If so it would cheapen the results whatever they turned out to be?

o o o o o

Next up: the 400 meter finals and another event compromised by the Sabbath issue. Five American runners had qualified for the final. Two American runners lined up for the start, Boardman, Moloney and Lee not among them.

Without Boardman and Lee, both of whom had beaten him in the past, Maxie Long was the clear favorite. Georgetown's William Holland and the Danish runner, Ernst Schulz, lined up next to Long.

So what had promised to be a sizzling final turned into a fizzling final from the point of view of who turned up. Every runner in the race was guaranteed a medal (assuming he made it to the finish, which given the bizarre events at these games, probably wasn't a certainty). Three runners would run for three medals.

At the crack of the pistol, Holland set a vicious pace and held it well into the stretch. Then Long, ever the careful tactician, caught him and the two ran stride for stride toward the tape.

Long's light blue and white Columbia jersey was similar to the jersey of the Racing Club, so many of the French spectators thought he was one of their own boys and cheered him heartily down the finishing straight. Actually the only Frenchman entered in the 400 was their champion, Charles-Robert Faidide, but he finished a disappointing third in his heat so wasn't even in the finals.

Long pulled ahead near the tape and took first, Holland hung on for second, Schulz third.

Figure 60 Maxie Long

So now Maxie Long had won both in England and in France.

Quite possibly we would have come 1-2-3 had Boardman, Moloney and Lee run.

Mike Murphy thought the Continental quarter-milers all lacked the speed necessary for such a short distance. OK, they may try to make up for it by sheer strength, he assured his runners, but it is not possible. The 400 meters is America's race.

O O O O O

Sunday abstinence was not an issue for the discus competition.

The five men who had qualified Saturday all turned up. The only American is Dick Sheldon who had qualified third. Jos McCracken wouldn't have been here Sunday, but he had failed to qualify anyway courtesy of the Bois de Boulogne trees.

Nothing ever seemed simple or straightforward in these games. Sheldon demonstrated the fine art of tree-dodging as he got off the longest throw of the day. However, consistent with the confusing rules, the French officials had put in place, the distances made Saturday were to stand in the finals. So the Hungarian, Bauer, is declared the winner since the best throw over both days was his from Saturday.

Will the rules ever be consistently applied?

Sheldon is clearly annoyed, as well he should have been. He made the longest throw in the finals didn't he?

But the gold went to Bauer anyway. The Bohemian athlete, Janda-Suk took second as a result of his Saturday heave. Sheldon had to settle for third despite the day's longest throw.

Figure 61 Bauer (center and in circle lower right) taking first place in the discus throw. Janda-Suk (circle upper left) and Richard Sheldon (circle upper right).

Then, just to but a bow on the absurd package, to honor Bauer the band played *The Star Spangled Banner*. Perhaps because of so many American victories, they had that anthem down pat. Bauer threw his arms up in frustration and complained loudly. The band leader looked sheepish and then indicated he understood. He said something to his players. Bauer struck a winners pose, and the band started again. This time it was the Austrian anthem. Perhaps they thought Hungary and Austria were close enough to each other geographically that it didn't matter.

Enough said.

We have a lot to learn. How did we lose that event?

Simple: Imperfect training.

The winner made the discus take flight like a bird on the wing.

Surely Mike Murphy took note and learned something he could take back home.

O O O O O

The 1500 meters and the Sabbath problem again.

Two of the best, Alex Grant and John Cregan both pulled out. Without doubt they would have affected this race. Perhaps they would even have come first and second. We will never know.

John Bray, a relative unknown from little Williams College showed up. So did David Hall from Brown. Hall was a very accomplished middle distance runner who set a national half-mile record. He claimed to have collected 107 trophies before he came to Paris, so maybe he would have given our absentees a run for their money had they competed.

Figure 62 David Hall

Seven other runners took their places on the line.

Right from the start, the race seemed a contest between Great Britain's Charles Bennett and France's Henri Deloge. They raced around the turns close together, albeit at a rather sluggish pace, but as they entered the stretch they turned it on and pulled away from the others. Then came a wild sprint finish. Bennett edged into the lead with Deloge right on his heels. Bennett held on to his lead all the way to the finish. Bray came third and Hall a somewhat disappointing fourth.

Figure 63 Bennett beating Deloge in the 1500

The time for the last lap was fast and Great Britain again proved to have very good middle distance runners.

GEORGE ORTON   The English distance runners were mostly plodders, running with dogged determination, with arms too far up and faulty stride. Bennett was the exception. He ran with good style. The work of Bennett showed that with equal strength the better style will usually win.

But another factor in athletic competition must be considered—possession of that grit, courage, or whatever it may be called, which so often wins races. The Continental athletes, especially the French, seemed to lack this quality. Perhaps it was for want of courage to struggle to the end which allows an athlete to urge himself along though his muscles are weary and exhausted. For example, at the end of the 1500 race Deloge walked away, while Bennett fell to the grass exhausted. Had the Frenchman the courage, he would have won the race.

On general results, however, we must grant England's superiority in distance running undoubtedly because there were more distance runners in England than in any other country.

It was clear we had work to do if we ever expected to beat them in the distance races.

O O O O O

Michael Sweeney had recently set the world high jump record. However, he had turned pro before Paris, so he wouldn't be competing in the Olympic high jump, but was in Paris to compete in a separate professional event. Without Sweeney then, it appeared as if Patrick Leahy, the jumper from Ireland representing Great Britain would be the most likely challenger to Bax. He was the British champ and one of seven jumping Leahy brothers from County Limerick.

IRVING BAXTER My first event was the high jump. I had every expectation of winning and didn't want to give that up because of the Sunday mess. I knew if I did, I would have regretted it the rest of my life.

PATRICK LEAHY   Things were definitely looking up for my chances of a medal in the high jump when two Americans—Remington and Carroll—were no shows because of the Sunday issue. I knew it wouldn't be a shoe-in, though, because Irv Baxter from the USA wasn't Sunday-averse and he was there. So were the Hungarian, Gónczy, a Norwegian, a German, a Frenchman and two Swedes.

For several months it looked as if we wouldn't even send a team from Great Britain. Why? Because of strained relations between England and France. Most politicians thought it would simply be wrong for any of us to head to Paris. What, do something to please the French? Ridiculous. They certainly wouldn't do anything to assist us. But those of us who were athletes, we weren't interested in politics. We were interested in competing and I was ... frustrated, angry even.

I was one of seven Leahy brothers who were all sportsmen. My brothers Con and Tim were also good jumpers and we had set our hearts on competing against the best in the world and the best were going to Paris. So we appealed to our Amateur Athletic Association. They were sympathetic but didn't want to ruffle the feathers of those politicians who stood to help us. Eventually, though, they sent a team selected from our championship winners.

So nine of us were chosen to go. I would enter the high jump, long jump, and triple jump and represent the leaping Leahys.

The event itself apparently goes back to the Celts, or at least to competitors in Scotland. The early jumpers used a prolonged straight-on approach where they ran directly at the bar and jumped something like a hurdler—feet first. Then what became real popular was the scissors technique in which the jumper approached the bar diagonally, then first threw the inside leg and then the other leg in a scissoring motion. But it was the relatively new Eastern cutoff technique that most jumpers were using in Paris. This was a variation of the scissors jump and produced higher clearances for just about everybody who mastered it. Mastering it, though wasn't that easy.

The athlete who came up with this was Michael Sweeney of the New York Athletic Club. He had set the world's record of 6-5 5/8 five years earlier in an international meet between the New York Athletic

Club and the London Athletic Club. He was widely recognized as the world's greatest high jumper, so let there be no doubt about this: If he had been in Paris he would have been highly favored and unless he landed on his head or something, he would probably have taken home the gold. Still his presence hung over us, not only in terms of the heights he had achieved, but also because earlier in the summer he had competed in professional competitions where not only did he win the high jump but he also won in the 100 meters and the long jump. As an athlete you always want to know you competed against the best when you won, but I can't honestly say I was unhappy that he wasn't jumping in the Olympics.

I knew I had a shot at a medal, maybe a gold, and I figured Irv Baxter of Penn would be my biggest challenger. I knew next to nothing about the other athletes, but I think I would have heard had they done anything noteworthy.

I had won the 1898 and 1899 AAA titles, but Baxter beat me in 1900.

In Paris, the circumstances were hardly ideal. It was hot, the field in the park was lumpy and slightly tilted. One good thing, though, was that because we didn't have a lot of jumpers, they decided we didn't need a qualifying round. That was one less chance to pull a muscle or have an off day.

The rules then were much the same as they still are: three misses and you're out.

It was clear that one bloke, the Swede, Tory Blom would go out early on, and so he did, not even managing 5 feet. The Frenchman, Monnier, was next out at 5' 4" and the Hungarian, Gónczy, the Norwegian, Andersen; the German, Steffen, and the other Swede, Lemming all went out at 5' 6." Then things got interesting. It was down to me and Baxter. We both rather easily cleared 5' 8," but then at 5' 10," I inexplicably missed at all three of my attempts. I had done that height before, done it numerous times, but on this day …

So Baxter, who cleanly cleared that to take first place, then had the bar moved up to equal the world record—6' 2." On his first try he almost made it, but his second and third attempts were rather poor.

IRVING BAXTER   I would have had the record were it not for the spectators all over the place distracting me. I mean they were being obstreperous. Rude really. I complained to the officials, but they did nothing. I wonder what they would have done if that had happened to a French athlete. I won, but that's about all I can say about the competition.

PATRICK LEAHY   I agree Baxter had a point. The French could be, and often were rather boorish and bad-mannered. However, we were glad to have any spectators, because on the whole, the games weren't at all well attended.

The high jump furnished a study in styles.

Bax was perhaps the most economical jumper in the world. His great natural spring allowed him to make a half turn while rising so he could throw his legs over sideways. This way he saved every inch. He wasn't far off on his 6' 6" attempt.

Figure 64 Baxter in the high jump

While we were in Paris we heard the most marvelous stories regarding a Hindoo who supposedly cleared a bar at 8 feet with no more difficulty than a bird has in flying over a stone fence. Report had it he began jumping in childhood and never missed a day's training because the climate where he lived was so moderate. It was said he jumped as a religious duty. I have my doubts about the veracity of the story but it was widely circulated at the games.

o o o o o

Sure enough, as expected, William Lewis did not show up for the 400-meter hurdle finals. That left it up to Tewks and Orton, to take on Tauzin, the popular and heavily favored Frenchman. He was the

"Great French Hope." The hosts hadn't won anything yet. Now it was their chance.

Warming up, Tauzin looked nervous. The more the French crowd encouraged him, the more the pressure built, the more nervous he appeared.

For some moments, Tewks stood watching how he warms up.

WALTER TEWKSBURY   The event was new for me and I didn't know for sure how I would run it. I could tuck in behind the Frenchman and assuming I could stay with him, adjust to his pace. I could go out slow, saving whatever I had left for a final kick. Finally, I thought yes, that should be my tactic. After all, there were only three timber toppers in the race. Just so long as I didn't embarrass myself by falling on my face after catching a trailing leg on one of those massive telegraph poles or by coming in so far behind that the spectators laugh at me, I was guaranteed a medal.

I thought it might be a good ploy to team up with Orton and try to outfox the Frenchman strategically. Maybe try to box him in near the line. I went over to Orton and asked him if he had any ideas.

"Not really," Orton said. "Let's just see how it goes. Where's Mike?"

"I think the high jump is just finishing. He's probably coming over now."

Both of us looked for the coach we knew we could trust. Right on cue Mike came striding into view.

"How'd the jumping go," I asked as he approached.

"Good. Bax. No problem."

"Great. What do you know about Tauzin?"

"Don't worry about him. You men run your race. That's all you think about. Your race. Hard the first hundred, find a comfortable rhythm the middle section, give it all you got the last hundred. Be conservative over the fences. Better to lose a second than to clip one. They won't give way. But you know that."

The three men were called to the line. Tewksbury lined up on Tauzin's right; Orton on his left.

At the gun Tewks's nervous energy got the better of him and the whippet thin runner went out like a shot. So much for his plans. His slight frame and loose-jointed gait helped him sail gracefully over the barriers. Mike Murphy taught him well.

Three quarters around and he was still well in front and showed no signs of fading. Tauzin, with the French spectators excitedly shouting encouragements, was about 4 yards behind; Orton 2 yards behind him.

The crowd was expecting Tauzin to make a big move as they cleared the water jump, but Tewks dug deep and held him off, throwing his arms up as he crossed the line. Tauzin followed in front of Orton.

The previously undefeated French champion slumped to the ground. First losses can be hard to take.

This was not a race our team was expected to win.

Murphy let loose his Irish smile and winked at his boys. With Penn leading the way, the meet was going even better than expected. America was showing off its power and confidence for the world to notice.

O O O O O

As absurd as the organization of the games had been to this point, they were about to become even more so. There were four separate pole vault contests.

Pole event #1.

Spalding reiterated that he had been assured by the French officials that because the event has been scheduled for Sunday, the results would not be considered final until the Americans vaulted in a special session Monday.

Some on the American team got the message, some didn't.

Charles Dvorak and Bascom Johnson, were the favorites to duel it out for the top pole vault honors. Dvorak, a big 22-year-old of Bohemian heritage competed in the colors of the University of Michigan. He had been working with his track coach, Keene Fitzpatrick, who taught him to jump with his hands closer together than most other vaulters. The results had been impressive.

Bascom Johnson, representing the New York Athletic Club, won the event in London. Surely they would take the top two places with Dvorak perhaps the slight favorite.

The event which the French program called *le championnat de saut à la perche* was another event with no preliminaries. So early Sunday afternoon, Johnson and Dvorak made their way out to the Racing Club in plenty of time to allow them to inspect the vaulting area and to warm up. They were lugging the long hickory poles they had brought with them from home.

Once they arrived, however, a French official told them that, because of the American objections to Sunday competitions, the pole vault had been rescheduled for Monday.

Nothing today?

Come back tomorrow.

So they left. No use wasting a nice Sunday afternoon.

A little later in the afternoon, Irving Baxter having just competed in the high jump, and Meredith Colket wandered over to the pole vault area expecting to see Bascom and Johnson getting ready to vault. Athletes were stripping down getting ready to compete. The poles were lined up, the officials were on hand, the spectators were assembling.

Where are Johnson and Dvorak?

They look around. Perhaps they're nearby. They aren't.

It takes questioning several French officials to determine they had left after being told that the event had been postponed.

Was it postponed?

No.

Why were they told it was?

Shrugs.

Are the French incompetent or duplicitous?

Shrugs.

So there will be a competition?

Starting in 10 minutes.

Bax had not figured to beat Johnson or Dvorak but if they weren't competing? Maybe he had a shot. The other American, Dan Horton wasn't there either as he had previously declared he would not compete Sunday.

Bax knew little about the other competitors, still he figured that at least now he had a chance. Meredith Colket would also vault, but Bax had gotten the better of him in most of their practices. Anyway, Meredith's best sport is tennis. He had organized Penn's first tennis team and played a good game of cricket. Still, he knew his way down a pole vault runway.

Seven other athletes stripped for the event and were stretching and running in place. Bax didn't need to. His high jump effort served as his preparation. Now, if his legs weren't too fatigued he would be OK. Like all good vaulters, despite his lean frame, his arms, shoulders and legs were well developed. While they didn't come into play much in the high jump, he would need them for the vault.

The Norwegian, Carl Anderson, is also vaulting. He had jumped against Bax in the high jump, placing fourth. Known as "Flisa," he was apparently an excellent gymnast and, as Bax knew, gymnasts, with their body control abilities could be dangerous in any pole vault competition. Three Swedish multisport athletes will compete. The 20-year-old Eric Lemming had also competed in the high jump, coming equal fourth with Anderson. A true all-rounder he had also already contested in the discus earlier in the afternoon, and in the qualifications for the long jump Saturday. As if that wasn't enough, he was set to enter the hammer throw and the triple jump on Monday. That would make seven competitions in three days. Surely that would take its toll. Karl Staaf would also compete in the hammer throw, the triple jump and the standing triple jump. Karl Nilsson had competed in the shot put. Émile Gontier, a Frenchman and the Hungarian, Jakab Kauser round out the field.

IRVING BAXTER   I rather fancied my chances … assuming I got everything right. No other event has so many technical parts to it—the run up, the plant, the takeoff, the slide, the push. It is an event which calls for lots of training and what Mike Murphy calls "scientific study." Without doubt it is one of the most fascinating of the field events and requires courage on the part of the vaulters.

Mike had spent many hours with me and Colket working on getting our form just so. We began by using 14-foot poles going over a bar at merely 6 feet. Initially I scoffed at such a low bar. I had already gone much higher when I was at Trinity University, before Mike began training me. To be honest, I could high jump higher than that without lugging a pole.

Mike had other ideas. He wanted me to make an easy run at the bar and then to strike the pole properly in the hole without actually launching myself. I thought this was ridiculous but I did this over and over while Mike watched and threw in comments occasionally. "Your hands are a little too far apart. Two feet apart is what I'm looking for. Thumbs hard on the pole." With a 6-foot bar, Murphy wanted the top hand on the pole 8 feet from the bottom. Exactly. He carried a tape measure to make sure. Mike left nothing to chance. He could be pedantic to be sure and he could frustrate us with so much repetition of techniques without us actually going through with our event. But we did it and we got better … a whole lot better.

"Take an easy run of 30 feet, keeping your eye on the hole where you are going to plant the pole, AND DON'T LOOK AT THE BAR." I must have heard those words a hundred times. I could hear them in my sleep. DON'T LOOK AT THE BAR."

Eventually Mike let me go over the 6-foot bar—about 20 times! It was ridiculously easy but as with all of Murphy's boys, I had come to appreciate the emphasis on technique which became second nature after so much repetition. Six foot became 7, then 8, then 9, then 11. Eleven was hard and produced more misses than clearances, but if I could do 11 in these games …

It was 4:30 by the time the event got under way, and as it had been every day since we arrived in Paris, it was hot and sticky with steel gray skies and a threat of rain that never comes.

Bax dug a little dirt from around the bottom of a bush and rubbed it briskly between his hands. Perspiration on such a hot day could easily allow his hands to slip on the slick ash pole. Mike had always insisted his vaulters use ash since it's the strongest pole you could get. When they did break, they gave the vaulter warning by signaling first with a series of cracks. Were all the other athletes using ash, too? Bax couldn't tell.

With the spectators circling the vault area, his normal inspection routine was a little cramped. They're too close again he thinks. They distracted him during the high jump. He finds a French official and, as he had done during the high jump, complained. The official either didn't understand English or didn't care. Either way, the spectators lurked. Bax would have to put them out of mind but it wouldn't be easy.

Bax was a jumper—long, high, triple or pole. He was born in Utica, New York, the second oldest of the seven children of John and Minnie Baxter. His father was a contractor. At Penn he was a member of the track team and the gymnastics team and secretary of the Chess Club. He was a favorite of Murphy's. Mike would sit for hours playing chess with him while rambling on about whatever training ideas were in his head.

Bax saw the uprights had the peg holes bored 1 inch apart except at the lower levels where they were closer together. The plank in the ground looked to be about six foot long which was what he is used to. The hole dug in front of the board he estimated to be about 6 inches deep. That, too, was what was expected. The landing pit was dirt. He would have preferred sawdust but dirt would work just so long as it was loose enough. It looked OK.

He took a short jog along the lumpy grass run up. He would have to be careful not to turn an ankle.

In the intercollegiate rules there was always a line known as the balk line drawn 15 feet in front of the bar and parallel to it. Stepping over it and not vaulting counted as a balk. Two balks constituted a try. There was no such line here. No matter, Bax thought. He seldom balked anyway.

Standing next to the plank, he walked back down the run up 11 precise strides and stuck a little twig in the ground at that point.

Then he walked back another 11 and placed a second twig. This is where he would start his easy run. If everything worked out as it should, his right foot would come down next to the first twig and he would be in position to strike the takeoff properly.

He waited his turn for a practice run. The run went perfectly. Now if only the spectators don't distract him further.

He chatted briefly with Colket while they waited to get under way.

Why can't the French do things right? At home the spectators would be in the stands, not milling around.

Ignore them … if you can.

Maybe some of them would like to vault. They're close enough.

The bar was set for the first try at 8' 5." Simple enough.

When it was his turn, Bax found his twig marks and took his place on the run up. He looked down at the bar and set his hands at what he thought to be the proper height on the pole. He checked the leaves on the nearby trees. They were still. Not a hint of wind.

Mike stood off to the side watching, looking composed. He said nothing to his vaulters. Everything he had to say had already been communicated.

As always Bax started his run slowly, then when he hit the second twig perfectly in stride, he increased his pace. Nearing the hole, he lowered his pole, and then inserted it. His arms were extended, making a triangle with the pole his body and the ground. Almost a perfect right angle. Taking off from his left foot, he swung his body smoothly upward and forward. Just as the pole was raised and the right foot struck the ground for the last time, he began his hand slide. His lower hand shifted quickly upward, gripped the pole hard. He knew, because Mike had drilled into him, that he could not move the top hand to a higher point after he left the ground, nor could he move the lower hand above the other hand. This was called climbing the pole. In England they used it, but elsewhere it was illegal. Sometimes the English athletes could get in three or even four shifts. It was a rather acrobatic move and it could be effective, but this was not a circus, Mike had reminded him.

When Bax's body and legs cleared the bar, he released his hands from the pole and gave it a little push backward. As he was taught, he landed on his feet. He had already seen athletes hurt by falling on their back or side.

One jump down.

All the competitors cleared this height.

The crowded-around spectators gave enthusiastic support to all the vaulters. They were daring gymnasts risking their necks by going over such a high bar. It was exciting, it was dangerous and it was compelling to watch. It was almost as if the athletes were held suspended high in the air over the bar before they came gently down to earth. Each successful clearance was greeted with collective cheers; each failure with groans.

The origins of pole vaulting, or pole jumping as it was often called, go back to early wartime activities like escaping from enemies or wild animals by using poles to get over obstacles—streams, fences, walls. When it became a competitive sport, results were initially measured in distance, rather than height. The pole was planted about 3 feet in front of the bar and the jumpers used a sitting position next to their pole as they swung up and, sometimes over the bar.

By the late 1880s the pole vault was being included in college meets. Using bamboo poles with sharp pointed ends, the athletes competed on grass, and because planting holes were not permitted, they jammed the point into the ground, launched themselves into the air and landed back on the grass.

Hugh Baxter was the sport's first real star. He dominated competitions for many years setting the world record of 11' 5." Despite sharing the same family name, Irving is not related to Hugh, a fact he has had to explain more than once. He also hadn't been jumping as high, a fact he also has to explain.

IRVING BAXTER From watching the French vaulters practice, we could see there was a potential problem ahead. Instead of planting their poles in the earth with an iron spike at the end, they planted them on a raised wooden platform. The rest of us had to plant ours in the earth, which immediately put us at a 6-inch disadvantage, that being the height of the wooden platform.

That would have been a much bigger problem but the only Frenchman of any merit at all didn't vault that high to begin with.

We complained, but the French officials simply ignored us.

Two Swedes were the first to go out with three misses. And both under 10 feet.

Bax hadn't missed yet, neither had Colket, nor Andersen.

The competition dragged on for some time. One by one, the Frenchman, the Hungarian and the last Swede went out, leaving the two Americans to duel it out with the Norwegian.

The bar was raised to 10' 4" and all three cleared the bar. At 10' 6" Andersen missed on his first attempt, but cleared it on his second. Colket and Bax both went clear. When the bar went up to 6' 8" Andersen missed on all three of his attempts. The Americans would finish first and second. Only the order was yet to be known.

Mike watched as both of his athletes readied themselves for the showdown.

They both eventually cleared 6' 8". At 6' 9" Colket went out, and Bax had secured his second gold medal of the day. He went on to clear 10' 10," and then set the bar at 11.' He barely missed on all three attempts.

Figure 65 Baxter pole vaulting

Things likely would have been different had Johnson and Dvorak not been sent away because of French ... inefficiency, but as it was, Bax was thrilled to be a double gold medal winner.

That ostensibly was the end of the pole vault competition, but given the French penchant for confusing issues, it wasn't. There would be three more.

Later in the day, Johnson and Dvorak responded angrily.

How can you be so incompetent!

You told us there would be no competition this afternoon, then you held it anyway! This is ridiculous.

We're sorry you misunderstood.

We didn't misunderstand anything. That's what we were told. You have to do … something.

For a while it looked as if they had taken a four-thousand-mile journey for nothing.

Some compromise had to be put in place.

So the officials put their heads together and arranged for a special vaulting event to take place Monday in which the missing Americans could compete. A consolation event.

IRVING BAXTER   To say the least I was annoyed. But what could I do? Johnson and Dvorak were teammates. I stewed, but kept my mouth shut.

O O O O O

In track and field history, steeplechase races were relatively new. According to legend, one afternoon in 1850 a group of Oxford students were talking about a horse race over fences which they had just completed. One, whose horse had fallen, is reported to have said: "I'd run across 2 miles of country on foot, rather than mount that camel again!" The idea of a steeplechase race was born. A few months later a two-mile run with 24 fences was held in a meadow near Oxford.

O O O O O

George Orton stood looking at the Bois de Boulogne steeplechase course. It was nothing like he had ever seen before. The circuit was the 500-meter oval used for the other races but now it looked more like the type of courses they laid out for horses to run in England. The barriers were an eclectic mix of stone fences, hedges, hurdles, water holes and various other barriers. Clipping any of these and you would quickly find yourself on the knobby ground. Add to that the uneven and sometimes slanting takeoff positions and this would present a considerable challenge.

The 27-year-old Orton was a sandy-haired, smallish athlete. Born in Strathroy, Ontario, he was seriously injured as a child, and took up strenuous exercise to overcome his injury. He found he liked running and that he could beat his mates, particularly at longer distances.

At the University of Toronto, he was a superb student earning double honors in modern languages.

He developed into Canada's dominant middle distance runner, winning 12 intercollegiate one-mile championships and then added American championships at 1-mile, 10 miles, cross- country and steeplechase.

Orton moved on to Penn to study romance languages. He remained there long enough to become fluent in nine languages while earning both M. A. and Ph.D. degrees.

Being Canadian, he couldn't get ice hockey out of his blood so he started the Penn hockey team and was its outstanding player. At Penn, he captained the track team in 1895 and 1896 and won two intercollegiate mile championships.

In Paris he was set to run in both the 2,500 meter and 4,000 meter steeplechases. He had already taken third place in the 400 meter hurdles and expected to figure in both steeplechases, particularly the 2,500 since the Sunday hiccup would eliminate some Americans who might otherwise be contenders.

The starting time was 4:00 and it was still blazingly hot. Surely that would slow everybody down on the five lap race.

The other American in the race was little Arthur Newton. Only 5' 2 1/2" and 112 pounds, he was running for the New York Athletic Club. At his height he might find some obstacles quite a challenge, but he was a plucky distance runner with good stamina.

Sidney Robinson figured to be Orton's stiffest competition. Robinson, who represented the Northampton Cycling & Athletics Club, was Britain's best. He had won the English steeplechase championship four times and the 10-mile championship twice. He was also the English National cross-country champion in 1897 and 1898.

The three other runners entered were a Frenchman, an Austrian and a German. Orton knew nothing about any of them.

At the gun, Orton, Newton, Robinson, and the Frenchman, Chastanié, took off quickly and before they were half way around the oval they had already dropped the German and the Austrian, who struggled with both the pace and the barriers. Everyone had to measure their steps carefully as they approached the sturdy barriers. They jumped up and over them with their legs folded under their torsos. Nothing like the sleek extended hurdling style of Kraenz. By the end of the first lap, Robinson and Chastanié, were sharing the lead with Orton. Newton was close on their heels. For the next three laps nothing changed other than the German and Austrian fell even farther behind. As they began the fifth and last lap, Orton lagged behind the first three and looked as if he had nothing left. Robinson and Chastanié were pressing each other for the lead which seemingly changed at each barrier. They rounded the final curve neck and neck and sprinted down the long straightaway. Orton, too, picked up the pace dropping Newton and slowly closed in on the two front runners. Then, finding an extra kick from someplace, he surged past both, neither of whom had anything left. Orton won going away by 10 yards over Robinson and 50 over Chastanié who had slowed to a shuffling walk. Newton came around in fourth easily outdistancing the German and Austrian stragglers.

Orton had added another victory to the American total which now stood at eight out of the nine finals contested so far, not counting the inconclusive pole vault. Never mind that Orton was Canadian. In Toronto the next day's headline in *The Toronto Daily Star* read "A FAMOUS VICTORY" and then went on to describe how Orton won for America.

O O O O O

It was time for the final Sunday event ... and the most contentious.

We all knew the friction between Kraenz and Prinstein had begun long before Paris but when Prinstein saw Kraenz on Sunday, their antagonism erupted into fury.

Since he was prohibited from jumping, Prinstein went out to the long jump pit to do the only thing he was allowed to do on a Sunday afternoon... watch. There, to his surprise he saw Kraenz warming up.

MEYER PRINSTEIN   I'd like to think that all the men on our team were gentlemen scholar/athletes and as such when they give you their word you can be sure that they will honor it. Apparently not. Kraenzlein had given me his word he would not compete Sunday, but when I went out to the field that afternoon, there he was warming up before the long jump finals.

ALVIN KRAENZLEIN   Meyer was dead wrong when he questioned my integrity. He said I promised him I wouldn't compete Sunday. I did not. I made no such promise. I told him I would consider it, and I did but then decided since I was eligible to compete I would compete.

MEYER PRINSTEIN   He's a liar. He went back on his word for one very obvious reason—he didn't think he could beat me. What kind of sportsmanship is that? I thought we were supposed to represent the best of America? I guess not.

WALTER TEWKSBURY   It wasn't a comfortable situation for Kraenz I know. There's a lot of pressure when you're the best and the press built him up like that. It becomes like a drug, and not everybody can manage that. Kraenz could, but it wasn't easy. Not when every time he competed he had to prove it.

So now on this Sunday Kraenz was getting six more shots at beating the mark Meyer had set Saturday. He would have nine jumps to outdo what Meyer did in three. That may sound unfair but those were the rules. He was entitled to those additional jumps regardless of what Meyer thought or said and he was saying plenty.

ALVIN KRAENZLEIN   Despite Prinstein's assertion that we had an agreement, we did not. I told him that if he could get the date changed to Monday then I would jump on Monday. If he couldn't, well then that's just the breaks. I was entitled to jump on Sunday, and jump I did.

WALTER TEWKSBURY   I have always known Kraenz to be a man of his word. If he said he didn't have an agreement with

Prinstein then I absolutely believed him. As far as I am concerned, either Meyer misunderstood any conversation they may have had or he was a liar.

The tension was apparent to everyone. Well, I don't know if the spectators could sense it or not but the competitors certainly could.

With Prinstein watching, Kraenz prepared to take his jumps. After Saturday's competition he was only a few centimeters behind his arch foe. He had it in him to make that up ... if he stayed calm. I could see Mike Murphy talking to him, most likely telling him to take his normal run up despite the odd incline to the runway, telling him to forget everything else and just do what he normally did.

Kraenz may have been nervous but Mike looked as unruffled and composed as always. He knew if he looked agitated it could rub off on his athletes so he was always a tranquil presence.

Prinstein was anything but calm. He watched every jump Kraenz made, every move, every gesture. He stared at him with all the intensity of a jeweler repairing a watch. Kraenz I'm sure could feel that glare. He couldn't blink an eye without Prinstein noticing.

WALTER TEWKSBURY   To say the least, the whole situation was bizarre. The Jew could jump on his Sabbath but couldn't jump on the Gentile's Sabbath while the Gentile could. It made no sense. But then a lot about these games didn't make sense.

The situation was strained as it was, but then when Kraenz put in a jump that measured one centimeter longer than Prinstein's best Saturday jump, well, Prinstein exploded. He charged across the grass like an enraged bull.

Truxtun Hare went after him immediately but Prinstein got by him before Trux could get a good grip on him. Prinstein grabbed

Kraenz by the arm.

"You lying S.O.B.," shouted the enraged Prinstein. "You said you wouldn't …"

Kraenz was an easygoing guy but he wasn't about to back down.

"I said I'd think about it which is exactly what I did."

"Monday. We'll have a jump off Monday. Tomorrow."

"Nobody's scheduled a jump off on Monday."

"You son-of-a-bitch."

"I jumped farther than you. That's how you win. I won."

"Are you afraid to meet me tomorrow?"

"It's over."

With his free arm, Prinstein swung wildly at Kraenzlein, hitting him square on the shoulder. That's when Hare's football instincts came into play. He was used to tackling runners. He flew at Prinstein, taking him to the ground with a perfectly executed flying tackle.

"That's enough," he said to the prone Syracuse man.

By now the confrontation had attracted enough onlookers that they were surrounded.

When Hare let him up Prinstein stormed off.

"That's what I'd call a sore loser," said Tewks.

"Yeah," was about all Kraenz said. He appeared to be shaken by the encounter but he put on a good face. No one wants to be seen to be weak in these types of situations.

WALTER TEWKSBURY   So much for the Olympic spirit of good sportsmanship. Kraenz put in a longer jump than any of Prinstein's and he did it within the rules. That's the bottom line.

This was the last event for the day so we all headed to our rides back to our hotels. Kraenz was upset by the incident. I know that, but we didn't talk about it on the way back. Rather we were enjoying the day's great successes.

O O O O O

The outcry over Sunday competition raged more bitterly among our athletes, supporters and press than it did between French and American Olympic officials. At issue was the perceived role of America's athletes as athletic missionaries and it boiled over into public recriminations.

If they don't set the standard for the world, who will?

It is their duty to impose their sporting culture on the rest of the world.

Caspar Whitney published a list back in America shaming all of those who competed on Sunday, portraying them as betraying America's sense of nationhood.

CASPAR WHITNEY   Those athletes who competed on Sunday were unscrupulous mug hunters—Alvin Kraenzlein, Richard Sheldon, Maxie Long, William Holland, Irving Baxter, Walter Tewksbury, Meredith Colket, George Orton, Arthur Newton. Simply put, they shrugged off the moral censure and went for glory.

What all this amounted to is this: Because we identified our athletic prowess with expressions of our culture, we tried—unsuccessfully as some saw it —to impose our sporting culture on the rest of the world. There was no doubt about it, we identified athletic practice with cultural, religious and political principles. Sport functioned as a tool for imposing a culture on the world as well as on our own nation.

The French weren't buying it.

But after all the negotiations were completed and the recriminations thrown about, after all the protestations were exhausted, the urge for nationalistic display, among some competitors trumped the desire for religious orthodoxy.

IRVING BAXTER   Look, we weren't stupid. Those of us from Penn who agreed to compete Sunday—me, Orton, Tewks, Kraenz, Colket—we understood, and accepted, the criticism we knew we were in for from the U.S. press. And boy, did we ever get it.

Back home, my mother cut out and saved one editorial.

> It is a pleasure to turn from the great and growing role that America is playing in the councils of the military world as a military, naval and commercial power to the frequent victories in the field of Olympic Games that our athletes have won in Paris. Judging from all accounts, nothing but a virtuous resolve not to profane the Sabbath day was the only thing that kept America from winning far more events than she has. It has long been known that strangers arriving in Rome presumably follow the same customs that obtain among the Romans, and it might have been expected that Americans, knowing the French propensity for making Sunday more of a holiday than anything else, would foresee that they would be required to play in events held Sunday afternoon. However, the Americans did not foresee it, and refused to play. Like the second

son in the parable, Kraenzlein afterward 'repented and went,' and on arriving found himself to be easily the best man in the game.

The other colleges, notably, Princeton, felt themselves much aggrieved by this action, for it was understood that all were to play or none. We cannot doubt that a large part of the national strength of England and America is due to the fact that there is behind both nations a strong religious spirit. By this we do not mean any weak or woman-ish sentimentality, but a belief that righteousness is essential, and that it consists largely in adhering to principle through thick and thin, and not changing one's views of right and wrong with a change of climate or sky. The nations and the men who have had principles and have held to them are the ones that have endured. And the men who refused to compete in Sunday games on principle have done something in itself more praiseworthy than winning any medal that could be offered at Paris or elsewhere.

Although I did not compete Sunday, I for one did not hold it against my teammates who did. They exercised their rights as Americans and behaved according to their conscience.

Kraenz, Tewks, and Bax were still rooming together and I know derogatory things were said to them by a couple of the other athletes. But they circled the wagons and defended their position.

ALVIN KRAENZLEIN   I got real sick of talking about it. I was permitted to compete. I did compete. I won. There was nothing else to say.

IRVING BAXTER   Those lads who criticized us had a right to do so. They were also dead wrong to do so. We didn't make the rules, we just followed them.

WALTER TEWKSBURY   I was not-so-politely informed I would go to hell for violating the Sabbath. Well, if I go to the hot hole it will be for offenses a lot worse than that.

To some of us, though, no matter what others thought, we believed with all our hearts that there was another principle in play, a principle separate from preserving the sanctity of the Sabbath. That principle—that our victory would confirm the special status of our nation as the strongest people in the world. That was worth something, wasn't it?

So we competed on Sunday for American glory, for patriotic glory and, yes, for personal glory, too.

ALONZO STAGG   Sabbath observance was a sign between ancient Israel and their God. Death was the decreed penalty for violations. And the matter of Sabbath observance remains to this day as one of the great tests which divides the righteous from the worldly and wicked.

I was ashamed of those who chose to compete on the Sabbath.

MEYER PRINSTEIN   We should have stood together. If some couldn't participate on Sunday, none should have participated on Sunday.

Were we angry at those who did? You bet we were. They showed a lack of character, a lack of morals, a lack of courage. None more so than Kraenzlein who ran from his biggest challenger by jumping on the Sabbath—particularly after he gave his word he wouldn't.

WILLIAM CURTIS   The athletes who participated on Sunday knew they would be soundly criticized in some circles. Still, I'm not sure how ready they were for the public recriminations that surfaced concerning the college and club teams not presenting a united front to the world. But the hypocritical American press which roundly applauded the ethical, religious stand and chastised the Sabbath violators, also lionized the victors.

The Sabbath issue aside, the American press was already gloating.

Let the Eagle scream and every true son of Uncle Sam cheer the Stars and Stripes and the grand specimens of American youth now in Paris defending the world–famed supremacy of our athletes!

Already our splendid fellows have asserted their supremacy in unmistakable fashion.

The Yankees were dominating everyone, to the amazement of their rivals from all parts of the world.

O O O O O

Even aside from the Sunday mess, I don't think it would be inaccurate to say that the management of the games was rather poor. Most events ran behind schedule and, some didn't finish until well after 7 p.m. although according to the program they were to have closed at least two hours earlier. In the management of games, the French had much to learn.

They used one set of officials for both the track and field events, and since the field events usually took much longer than they should have, the entire meet was delayed.

JAMES SULLIVAN   More than once we had to come to the rescue of the French officials, who, despite their good intentions, had no idea how to properly run a first-class track and field event. We did, and instructed them on organizational principles of games management.

The French eventually agreed to take American advice, and use two sets of officials. But since the second set were unprepared to take charge ... well, there were still problems.

O O O O O

The ever-chauvinistic Ferdinand Peck was never shy about reminding anyone who would listen, saying that in his flag-waving opinion, the United States deserved all the adulation—and more— that the French could muster.

FERDINAND PECK   The crowning event of the participation of the United States in the Universal Exposition was the erection and dedication of a memorial to Lafayette, the patriot and soldier important in the history of both the French and American republics. The monument was built by the pennies of the school children of the United States and placed in the heart of the Garden of the Louvre. When it was unveiled it took place in the presence of all nations. The great flag of the United States, dropped from the highest structure ever built by man, the Eiffel Tower, was the largest Stars and Stripes ever constructed. When the French mounted guard of honor moved from the unveiling of the monument in the heart of the Louvre, through the Garden of the Tuileries, along the grand avenue of the Champs Elysees, across the great Alexandrian Bridge to the United States Pavilion, followed by the United States Marine guards, amid the applause of all nations, it was the greatest peace event in all history.

As for the people of France and Paris they were almost one with the citizens of the United States on this remarkable occasion, being unable to do enough, apparently to show their fellow-republicans from across the sea honor and homage. The city of Paris was literally laid at the feet of visitors from the United States and the keys given over without provision. The American flag was draped along the boulevards and over the retail shops in elaborate profusion. It decorated public buildings and waved from private houses. The numerous boats that plied up and down the Seine carried the American colors at stem and stern all day and delivered the message of the American festival to the remotest ends of the city. Paris was absolutely *en fete* for the United States. "*Vive Amerique!*" rose from every square and thoroughfare, and it struck upon the ear with the same sincerity and vigor of sound and feeling as the familiar "*Vive la France.*" During the entire day Americans assembled and greeted each other with enthusiasm in the happy pride of their nationality.

Sousa's band took a prominent part in the celebration at the unveiling of the Lafayette Monument during the day, and at night when the band played in the open air in the Place de Opera, the heart of Paris.

The banquet given by the American Chamber of Commerce and the reception held later by the California commission, at which Sousa and his band assisted, also contributed to the general and hearty celebration of the day.

O O O O O

COL. R.G. LOWE   As I was a newspaper publisher I had the opportunity of observing Paris during the celebration on Bastille Day which was also the first day for the Olympic Games. Paris looked all gay and delightful with Chinese lanterns and frivolity. I compared it with the solidity and strength of London, and I was not favorably impressed with the French. They seemed to regard this as the last opportunity they would have of securing money. The hotel keepers and drivers were especially notorious in this regard.

The French have no use for anyone speaking the English language, and make no effort to conceal their hatred of it.

I have nothing good to say about the French. They were behind in their work, and did all they could to delay other nations. Strange as it may seem, this was particularly the case regarding the American exhibit, the French railroad companies being unable or unwilling to forward exhibits collected at Rouen.

NINE

CIVIL WAR BROKE OUT in the United States camp. Or perhaps un-Civil War would be a better description.

There was lingering anger from athletes who weren't allowed to compete Sunday.

There was anger directed at those who did compete Sunday—particularly those from the University of Pennsylvania.

There was anger aimed at the vacillating French officials.

Still, nine events were on the day's schedule and compete they would.

O O O O O

The 800 final figured to be a duel between Tysoe and Cregan and maybe Hall, and so it was. I had come in fourth in the heats so was relegated to observing.

To the delight of the French spectators, Henri Deloge took the early lead through a pedestrian first half. Except for a freak accident, Hall, Brown's first Olympian, might have been a gold medal winner.

Running a close second at the halfway mark, Hall suddenly had his right shoe torn off when Cregan accidentally stepped on his heel.

Then at the top of the final straight, both Tysoe and Cregan moved to the front. In the final few yards, Tysoe pulled away to a relatively comfortable victory. Cregan held on for second, but Deloge struggled down the stretch and was passed for third by Hall.

Figure 66 Tysoe winning 800 ahead of Cregan

You have to give it to the Brits. They are good in the middle distances. That may be it in terms of track and field prowess but it's better than most countries can boast. We ... well, we can claim more.

GEORGE ORTON   In the half-mile, Cregan's style and natural speed had to give way before the bulldog strength of the English man, Tysoe. And yet the standard of middle distance running is somewhat higher in America than in England. We had several runners who ran under two minutes.

The Continental half-milers ran in Paris in such poor form that they were not at all dangerous. They run, in general, with the arm drawn up in a cramped position, impeding rather than aiding them. Their stride is on natural and faulty. Either they run on their heels, with too short a stride, or use too long a one. The Hungarian and Danish and German runners were examples of the latter.

O O O O O

If ever there was a "sure thing" at these games it was Kraenz in the 200 hurdles. As far as the other runners were concerned, they were running for second and third.

There were two semifinals with the first two in each heat advancing to the finals.

In the first heat Kraenz cruised to a four-yard victory over the Frenchman, Eugène Choisel, who just edged out Frederick Moloney for the other place in the finals.

Kraenz was so good, he jogged the last half of the race—a virtual walkover.

Norman Pritchard took the second heat beating Tewks by 2 yards.

So the finals were set: Kraenzlein, Choisel, Pritchard, Tewks.

After a rather short break, the starter called the runners back to the line for the finals.

They were held for a long time, then Kraenz surprisingly false started.

What? Kraenz? Why in the world would he do that? Surely he wasn't worried about the competition. He looked as if he could stroll his way to victory.

He is penalized a yard by the starter.

No matter. On the restart he quickly took a five-yard lead on the field and easily maintained that all the way to the finish. Pritchard came second, Tewks third.

Figure 67 Kraenzlein (far left) easily wins

After the race, with what press there was crowded around him, Kraenz made an announcement:

ALVIN KRAENZLEIN   That was my last race. I am through with athletics and will devote myself to something more serious.

Really? You're at the height of your form.

I've accomplished all I set out to do.

But you'll change your mind. When the next big challenge comes, you'll get the itch.

I don't think so.

We'll see.

Kraenz had mentioned he might do this but I didn't think he was serious. Maybe the mess with Prinstein had something to do with it. Maybe the pressure to have to always prove you are the best caught up with him. He was constantly in the spotlight and that had to take its toll.

Mike Murphy didn't look surprised at the announcement. He may even have suggested it, but I doubt that.

So Kraenz stepped down, the owner of six world and four Olympic records.

WALTER TEWKSBURY   Me and Bax, we knew he would announce his retirement after his last race. After all, during our three days of competitions all he had done was win four titles establishing new Olympic records every time.

BARON de COUBERTIN   His performances in Paris where the stars of the world were competitors showed the marvel he was. In every event in which he contested he landed a winner, beating the champions of many countries with the greatest of ease. That alone placed him in a class by himself, and he was entitled honestly to the title of champion. He was an exponent of every sport of the field and track, with the possible exception of distance running.

His performances were truly remarkable, and the whole world was talking of him.

That Kraenz was the dominant track and field athlete at these games was obvious. I'd venture to say he was one of the greatest ever even if he was relatively forgotten in later years.

O O O O O

While Kraenz was still accepting congratulations for his accomplishments, the 4,000-meter steeplechase was about to begin. It would be run over the same bumpy obstacle course as the 2,500, water jumps and stone fences included. This time it would be for eight laps.

The Americans knew here the Brits would be difficult to beat. The steeplechase was one of their specialties. They entered three men. Sidney Robinson, Charles Bennett and John Rimmer.

Rimmer, a Lancashireman, was the British four-mile champion and figured to give Orton a run for his money. Bennett, a train driver from Dorset and a member of the Finchley Harriers was the British mile and cross-country champion.

Figure 68 John Rimmer

The Frenchman and the German who had competed in the 2500 Steeplechase were also entered as were Alex Grant and Thaddeus McClain, both teammates of mine at Penn. Grant, like Orton was Canadian. After graduating from the Toronto University, he matriculated at the University of Pennsylvania. He had been scheduled to run in the 2,500 Steeplechase, but as a devout Presbyterian, he was another athlete who skipped the Sunday event.

After winning Sunday's race Orton began feeling sick. Maybe it was something he had eaten, some French food with which he was not familiar. Or perhaps he was coming down with the flu. Or maybe he was just worn down from the effort in the 2,500 Steeplechase. Regardless, he said nothing to anyone and even though feeling somewhat weak, took his place on the starting line. When the gun sounded, he immediately dropped to the back of the six-man field. By the first obstacle, Rimmer had taken the lead, closely followed by Grant. Bennett, Robinson and the Frenchman, Chastanié lined out behind them. They remained in that order until the final lap when Rimmer pulled away from the quickly slowing Grant. Orton, was still lagging far behind the leaders.

Maybe it was a strategic decision.

Hadn't he run from behind yesterday in the shorter race?

He's just biding his time.

The last lap. That's when he'll come on.

But he never did. As Rimmer neared the finish line, Bennett, Robinson and Chastanié were coming on strong, but in an extremely close finish, Rimmer managed to hold them off. By then, both Grant and McClain had stopped completely.

What a tough race that was. Exciting but oh, so difficult. Four thousand meters over all those difficult and different barriers. The exhausted finishers sprawled on the grass. Bennett had come second, Robinson third, Chastanié fourth and Orton fifth, beating only the straggling German.

O O O O O

Since it was Monday, Meyer Prinstein was allowed to compete in the triple jump. He was still seething over the events around the long jump and would love to have faced Kraenzlein, but Kraenz didn't register for the event.

MEYER PRINSTEIN   Why didn't he compete? Is that a real question? The answer is obvious, isn't it?

ALVIN KRAENZLEIN   The triple jump wasn't my event. It's not something I competed in. I probably could have. I had the runway speed and the spring in my legs, but that event required a lot of practice to get the technique down and I had enough events to practice as it was.

It's a pity. It would have made for a dramatic confrontation— the angry Prinstein and the victorious (albeit recently retired) Kraenzlein.

The Irish and the Scots are the acknowledged fathers of the triple jump, or as it was often called, the hop, step and jump but they had no contestants in Paris.

The event, though, wasn't even on the original program as it was seldom contested. It was added at the request of the athletes.

Very few spectators had ever seen the event before and many thought the hop-step-and-jump sequence looked ridiculous. The leading French sports journal described it as "perfectly boring."

It had been contested, however, in the '96 Games where the first title awarded in the modern games went to James Connolly. In Athens he won the event by taking two hops with his right foot and one jump. It was then known as a jump-as-you-please event with each competitor free to decide how to make the trip down the jumping path.

Now in Paris a few spectators watched the odd contest in which Prinstein easily outdistanced Connolly and Lewis Sheldon. Prinstein had his gold medal but it did little to ease the anger over the long jump.

MEYER PRINSTEIN   I know I should have had two golds. I was beaten in the long jump by politics and deceit, not by skill.

O O O O O

Raymond Clarence Ewry, otherwise known as, Deac, otherwise known as "The Rubber Man," was a remarkable athlete with a remarkable story that reads like an inspirational film script. As a small boy growing up in rural Lafayette, Indiana, he was frail and sickly. Partially paralyzed by polio he was confined to a wheelchair. So when other boys his age were enjoying their boyhood, he was stuck in his chair or bed. His parents were naturally worried about him. Could he ever lead a normal life they wondered? Poor little Ray.

Then one day, the family doctor told him that rather than letting his legs atrophy he should do regular leg exercises. The doctor suggested a few simple calisthenics and Deac began ... tentatively at first. When he saw some early results, he increased the intensity, added new ones, and soon developed his own daily intensive workout program. After a while he added some easy jumps to his routine. All the while he was growing taller. He never put on much weight, though. At 6' 3," he was maybe 150 pounds on long, skinny legs that had become like taut springs. In time what had started as his therapy became his sport. He could jump high, he could jump long, but he didn't run well, so he practiced the standing jumps—the high jump, broad jump and triple jump. It took him a while, but eventually he developed the power techniques that allowed him to jump competitively.

His grandfather had been a Lafayette pioneer who lived next to John Purdue, founder of Purdue University so perhaps it was inevitable that Deac should go there. By the time he enrolled he was on the verge of becoming the greatest standing jumper of his day.

While at Purdue he studied mechanical engineering and earned a graduate degree. In his second year at the university the long-legged Deac participated in the first Purdue Field Day and set the state record for the standing long jump. By that time he had also developed his running well enough that he could play on the football team, but a shoulder injury put a rather quick end to any gridiron dreams he may have had. His jumping continued to improve, however. He was elected captain of the track team and became Purdue's most outstanding athlete.

Perhaps it is fair to say that he was a living example of Coubertin's philosophy that sport and health went hand in hand.

After graduation he took a job in New York as a city hydraulics engineer and joined the New York Athletic Club which sent him to Paris.

Figure 69 Ray Ewry

His technique was exceptional, without a run up, with his stationary feet firmly planted on the ground, everything depended on the spring of his coiled muscles. In some ways he was like Kraenz because he had springy legs, but that is about as far as the similarity went. He was a rather quiet, even shy, guy, who lacked the showmanship and charisma of Kraenz.

In Paris only three men were entered in the standing high jump—

Bax, Ewry and Dick Sheldon's older brother, Lewis, so obviously, all the medals would go to Americans. This was not Bax's best event. Not by a long shot but at least he was guaranteed a top-three placing.

To absolutely no one's surprise, Ewry easily beat Bax and Lewis. Then after winning, he announced he would go after his own world record. As was his wont, the tall lanky athlete in the winged foot emblem of the New York AC stood quietly by the bar for a few moments, then uncoiled those steel spring legs of his and went up and over at 5' 4." Knowing he had the new record, the crowd cheered wildly. So what did he do? He announced he would try to break his seconds old world record. Not being a cocky guy he just rather casually made the announcement and then took his place. This time he jumped even higher—5' 5." So within less than a minute, he had set the world record … twice!

Figure 70 Ray Ewry in standing high jump (1908)

He stopped there, having two more events in which to compete.

Indicative of how incredibly good he was, Bax came second with a jump of 5'—a full 5 inches lower than Ewry. Lewis was an inch behind Bax.

The standing long jump was next. It was the same three plus one Frenchman.

This time Ewry beat Bax by an even bigger margin. He jumped 10' 10." Again Bax was second. He did 10' 3 1/4." The Frenchman finished in third, Lewis came fourth, both jumping less than 10.'

Ray Ewry

Figure 71 Ewry in standing long jump

It was on to the triple jump. They were joined by Robert Garrett, Frank Jarvis, John McLean, Daniel Horton, a Swede, a German and a Hungarian.

Surprise, surprise! Ewry won that one, too and Bax was second. If there had been any doubt about who the best standing jumper in the world was, that was now over. Bax might claim to be the second best. Ewry's best jump was 34' 8 1/2." Bax managed 32' 7 1/4." American jumpers managed the first seven places.

Ray Ewry simply dominated the standing jumps like nobody else had ever done—clearly the star of the day. And he did everything on soggy grass instead of the firm takeoff platform he had been used to.

Later it was charged that he was actually a professional because he had participated in contests at circuses and at meetings not sanctioned by the Amateur Athletic Union. Whether true or not, it doesn't take away from his spectacular performances in Paris. The crippled youngster overcame his maladies to become one of the world's greatest athletes.

O O O O O

So Monday, although already packed with eight events, they managed to squeeze in another pole vault competition—Pole vault #2.

Dvorak never got the message.

In the anti-climactic added event Johnson, the only entrant, vaulted 11' 1/3" inches higher than the winning height for Bax on Sunday. So Johnson won and salvaged some pride.

Oh, but we have now decided this event will not be considered official.

You can't do that.

These vaults will not be part of the official record.

I vaulted higher than anyone else, insisted Johnson.

In an exhibition event.

That's not what you said.

It's what we're saying now, and it's official. Bax is the winner of the Olympic pole vault.

Johnson had to be content with knowing he out-jumped the Olympic champion, for whatever that was worth.

Two pole vault competitions down, two to go.

The Americans, headed by Spalding, continued their assault on the French officials about their Sunday vacillations.

If this nonsense continues, Spalding told the French, we will have to considering pulling out of the games altogether and going home.

The French didn't want that.

OK, we'll stage a another scratch pole vault competition for Dvorak and Horton—Pole vault #3.

Dvorak and Horton grumbled but they turned up. So did most of Sunday's competitors—as spectators. Dvorak, while warming up, snapped the hickory pole he had brought with him from Michigan. The bar was only at 9 feet when Dvorak launched himself up. There was a ripping, tearing noise and he hit the ground next to his pole broken and useless pole. Dvorak felt he had already received more than his share of misfortune and now his pole was gone. But one of the athletes from Sunday who had his pole with him, handed it to Dvorak. It was bamboo and he had never jumped with a bamboo pole but it seemed to be a better option than not competing.

Horton won by clearing 11' 3" and was declared the winner. Then the French Olympic Committee changed their minds yet again, decided Bax was to be the pole vault champion, and offered Horton an umbrella for his trouble.

Eventually the French invited the non-medal winning vaulters to participate in a pole vault handicap—Pole vault #4.

The Hungarian Jakob Kauser took first; the Swede, Lemming second; Colket, third.

Chaos reigned.

Bax had his gold medal.

Johnson jumped higher than Bax but had no medal.

Horton jumped higher than Bax and Johnson but he also had no medal.

Kauser had a handicap gold medal.

Colkett took a silver medal in one pole vault event and a third place in the handicap event.

O O O O O

Yes, there really was a tug-of-war event and it was actually a rather popular sport. As I understand it, it was once a royal sport practiced in ancient Egypt, Greece and China, where it was held in legend that the sun and moon played tug-of-war over the light and darkness. I don't know about that, but I know that the crowd loved it and showed unbridled enthusiasm the likes of which I did not see at many other events.

The rules were simple. The teams pulled on opposite ends of a large and long rope. The first team to pull the other 6 feet would be declared the winner. If after five minutes neither team had done so, the team that had pulled the other the farthest would be the winner.

At some point we decided to enter the Olympic tug-of-war event. Why not? Maybe we had no experienced tuggers, but we had some rather large and strong men—John "the Irish Hercules" Flanagan and our big football stars, Trux Hare and Jos McCracken.

To these very strong men we planned to add the Sheldon brothers, Lewis the jumper, and Dick the shot putter and discus thrower. Dick represented both Yale and the New York Athletic Club and had already demonstrated his skills as a weightman by taking the shot title. Before graduating from Yale, his brother Lewis won the IC4A long jump in 1895 and 1896, although why he wasn't entered in this event in Paris, I don't know. His only event in Paris was the standing high jump.

With these big, athletic men we figured we could easily take the tug-of-war. Heck, we thought we might dominate the event. We joked about that a lot.

If we don't fall down laughing first.

French soccer players against American football players?

However, with the ever-shifting schedule we didn't realize until just before the tug was scheduled that there was a big problem. It was scheduled right before the final of the hammer throw. Flanagan, Trux and Jos were all in it, up against two Swedes. Now there was no way on God's green earth they would strain their muscles right before the big event. That was obvious to everyone. I don't think anyone even tried to talk them into tugging away. So, at the last minute, we pulled out.

I went over to take a look nevertheless. Since the officials had expected the Americans, there was confusion when they realized we weren't going to turn out a team. What to do? Cancel the event?

If there was any thought that the American abdication would have brought on more competitors that was immediately dashed when the only full team that turned out was the French team. Since a one-team tug-of-war would be absurdly impossible (although the French officials were not above descending to the absurd), and since a large crown assembled to watch the groaning struggle, a Danish shooter/sprinter, Eugen Schmidt, came up with an idea. Why not cobble together a joint Danish/Swedish team to offer the French a little competition and the spectators a little amusement? Schmidt had been a competitor at the '96 Games where he placed twelfth in the military rifle event and fourth in a 100-meter heat but did not advance to the finals. He was strictly a spectator in Paris. At least he was a spectator until his joint team idea came about in which he would be one of the pullers. His motive was not so much to help the organizers stage the tug, but an expression of his longing to get Scandinavia a gold medal in one way or other. The Norwegians had only light runners and jumpers in Paris, so they weren't going to be any help.

It would be up to the Swedes and Danes to man a rope. The Swede, Söderström, was a big shot and discus man; his teammate Karl Staff, was a hammer thrower and vaulter. The other Swede,

August Nilsson, put the shot and vaulted. Schmidt recruited Charles Winckler, Denmark's best shot and discus man. They needed one more man, so Schmidt talked Edgar Aabye, a 35-year-old Danish journalist in Paris covering the games, into being the final man on the team. I guess he figured there was nothing like covering an event from the inside.

When the two teams lined up, it was quickly apparent that the Frenchmen were considerably lighter than the Swedes/Danes. I guess they figured technique would win out over bulk. Söderström and Winckler looked like hulks compared to the more athletic-looking French, who were mostly rugby football players. One man caught all of our attention. He was black. Constantin Henriquez de Zubiera was a Haitian-born rugby union footballer, playing as number eight, wing and center. As I later read, he was the first black man to appear in the Olympics. There may have been some strange looks from the spectators, but if there was any negative reaction from the competitors, I didn't see it.

Figure 72 Constantin Henriquez de Zubiera

On the shout of "go," both teams dug their heels in, leaned back and drove their legs into the ground with terrific force while the watching crowd shouted encouragement—of course, mostly to the French. The great effort by the pullers was evident in their strained faces, bulging muscles and grunts. I have to say, it really was captivating as these men put everything they had into it. For a minute or so, neither team seemed to be moving back, then ever so slowly, the Scandinavians began to move the Frenchmen forward. Already pulling with all the force they could muster, the French had no more to give and were soon pulled the required distance. All the competitors immediately sprawled on the ground looking absolutely drained. Most of the crowd, disappointed in the performance of their countrymen, urged them not to lose hope for the second pull, the contest being the best two out of three pulls.

Figure 73 Scandinavian tug-of-war team

After an interval deemed long enough for the men to regather their strength, they went to the rope again. This time the Scandinavians managed a quick jump on the French and steadily tugged to the win. The chapfallen spectators gave both teams robust applause.

The Scandinavians had their first, and it turned out, their only medal at these games. Nationalistic feelings ran high as both Denmark and Sweden subsequently claimed the honor of having entered the combined team.

The French did have some keen tuggers, it has to be said, and it was obvious that they had trained as a team whereas their opponents had not, but it quickly became apparent that aside from the raw muscle power needed for tug-of-war, it was also a technical sport. The cooperation or rhythm of team members was as important, if not more so, than their physical strength.

O O O O O

The final scheduled event of the day was the hammer throw. We had our three big men going for us: John Joseph Flanagan, and our two Penn football players, Trux Hare and Jos McCracken. Their only competition would come from two Swedes, so at the very least, we were guaranteed one medal, but expectations were higher than that. A lot higher. Since it was a Monday, there was no question as to who would show up, but even with all hands on deck "The Irish Hercules," Flanagan was the one to watch.

John Joseph Flanagan was the only member of the American team who wasn't a college man. He was one of New York City's finest—a city cop. Naturally he was an Irishman (born in the Kinkead home of his mother's family in County Limerick) as so many of New York's policemen were. There must have been some who weren't, but I never met any. John was a strong guy who threw the weights about as well as anybody ever. He'd throw anything heavy—the shot, the hammer, the discus. If it had heft, he'd pick it up and give it a fling.

As he tells it, Limerick and Tipperary had a tradition of weight throwing stretching back to the penal days. Their blend of Celtic and Norman blood produced a race of giants. Or at least, so he claims. Except that he wasn't the biggest of men himself—something under 6 foot. Apparently his father, Michael O'Flanagan, a champion weight thrower in the '60s and '70s was really big, but John was the shortest of the five Flanagan brothers. He made up in symmetry and power what he lacked in height. He was a handsome bloke with black curly hair, chest like a barrel, arms and legs like gate posts—a stocky, 5' 10" and all muscle. In Ireland, it was said he never lost a hammer event in his life and set several world records.

Figure 74 John Flanagan

JOHN FLANAGAN   The O'Flanagans and Kinkaids from the mountain foot of the Ballyhouras on the borders of Limerick, Cork and Tipperary were legendary throwers. We threw a hammer with a plain cane handle and straight grip and we threw it like no others.

He had an uncle in New York who was prominent in municipal affairs, so after John had crossed over to England and won the hammer championship there, he induced the 23-year old John to emigrate. John joined the New York Athletic Club and the New York Police and was put in the Bureau of Licenses where apparently, since there was a lot less to do than chasing bad guys, he had plenty of time to train.

Flanagan was one of scores of highly-successful Irish-American athletes. It's a wonder there were any top athletes left in Ireland, because so many had come over to compete in the U.S. Since almost all of them were non-university educated, they competed for the athletic clubs. Collectively, they were sometimes known as the "Irish Whales."

Of all the Emerald Isle immigrants who came to America, Flanagan was undoubtedly the most outstanding. In Ireland he had earned a reputation as a real all-rounder who, when not winning all the hammer contests he entered, got good results in the long and triple jumps and even the high jump. In the 1895 Irish Championships, he reportedly finished second in both the high and long jumps in the all-around event.

I think it is fair to say, in New York he opened an athletic career that put Irish athletics on the map. He worked hard to get himself in superb physical condition and established records with all manner of weights from 56 pounds down. Some of his records stayed on the books for many years.

But it was as a hammer thrower he made his name. He began in the 9-foot circle and then the 7-foot circle and then he began using a hammer with a wire handle in place of cane. Then he moved on to ball-bearing swivels and the double grip. John was responsible for the popularity of these evolutions. He also pioneered the three-turns-in-the-circle technique. According to stories I read, people would show up at meets just to see this powerful but graceful man pivoting in the circle. I remember one that called him "the greatest hammer-man, of his inches and poundage that ever lived."

John was a real sunny chap, modest about his achievements and you might say shy, generous and hospitable to a fault.

Mr. Spalding loved him because he helped advertise the Spalding Hammer. I still have one of those ads he did for a ball-bearing hammer complete with leather carrying case: "Gentlemen: I have tested the 16-pound hammer you made under my direction and found same to be perfect. I find it easier to stay in the circle when manipulating, and owing to its ball-bearing construction it gets less resistance from the air, leaves the hand smoother, and in fact fills the bill completely as to what a perfect hammer should be. I will use it in all competitions and will recommend same to those wishing to excel in hammer throwing. You have my permission to use my name."

We are indebted to the Irish and Scots for the hammer event. It was developed there and then transported to this country where it has been brought to its highest state of perfection.

At any rate, as the event was not included in the Athens Games, whoever won here would be the first Olympic hammer champ.

In the U.S., the rules for the hammer as established in 1887, called for an implement with a maximum length of 4 feet comprising an iron ball connected to a triangular handle with a steel chain. When thrown it had to be less than 16 pounds and was to be thrown from the 7-foot circle. Trux and Jos weren't sure if the same regulations would be in place when they got to Paris. As soon as they arrived at the throwing site, they found the circle was a little larger. Without measuring, they calculated it to be 9 feet but that didn't figure to pose a problem.

Flanagan's record suggested he was far and away the longest chain-chucker in the world. Trux and Jos knew that, but probably second and third would be up for grabs. Then, too, there was always the possibility that the trees of the Pré Catalan would take the big Irishman's throws as it did Garrett's and Trux's discus tosses. What the Swedes would do was anyone's guess.

Without doubt, Trux was one of Mike's absolute favorites, if for no other reason than he could give Mike a stiff challenge on the chess board ... and they played, I don't know how many games over the years, but a lot.

The irrepressible Thomas Truxtun Hare was born in Philadelphia to a carpenter father and dressmaker mother. Recognizing his outstanding attributes, his parents sent him to St. Marks School up in Southborough, Massachusetts. That was an Episcopal preparatory school stressing the classics. It was a school with high academic principles focusing on preparing the boys for the likes of Harvard, Yale, Princeton and Penn. Judging by Trux, they did a good job of it, too.

Figure 75 Truxtun Hare

As he tells it, his middle name—Truxtun—came from a relative, Commodore Thomas Truxtun, a naval officer in the years after the Revolutionary War. He was one of the first six commanders appointed to the new U.S. Navy by President Washington. He went on to a distinguished career as commander of several famous U.S. naval ships including the *USS Constellation* and *USS President.*

If there was something Trux couldn't do I sure don't know what it was. He was one of those people who exhibited the annoying habit of excelling at just about everything he did and he did a lot. Let's see if I can come up with at least a partial list. He was an excellent painter even as an undergraduate. He was always hesitant to show us his work, but when we saw any, well, they were impressive. And he could write about as well as he could paint (mostly poetry). He was a member of the Ancient and Honorable Order of the Sons of Rest which was a group of poets. He acted in our Mask and Wig productions, he served as toastmaster at class banquets, chaired scores of dance committees, was president of his class, manager of the musical clubs and the golf and tennis clubs, and he was active with the Delta Psi Fraternity. On the athletic fields he was an excellent archer, trap shooter and golfer. He was on the cricket team and naturally the track and field team where at various times he engaged in the hammer throw, shot put, discus, running broad jump, running high jump, the mile run, and the 120 and 220 yard hurdles.

To say he was an exceptional man is quite an understatement, and I haven't even mentioned his greatest college claim to fame. He was a regular on our football team for all four years while he was in school. His principle position was at guard but he also punted, kicked off, drop-kicked extra points, and ran with the ball out of the backfield. Not surprisingly, he captained the team and earned All-American honors ... every year. Oh yes, he played every minute of every game on both sides of the ball.

As if this wasn't enough, he had yet another skill that made him both popular and indispensable for us in Paris—he spoke fluent French. He was an officer of the *Cercle Francais* and to my ear, spoke French with hardly any accent. What a help that turned out to be!

Everybody looked up to Trux, and why not? When we came up against the stubborn French, he frequently came to our rescue.

GEORGE ORTON   Once in a while you come across a truly exceptional person. Trux was such a person. A true Renaissance man if ever there was one—athlete, scholar, artist. Leader.

TRUXTUN HARE   Throwing the hammer takes a lot of work on timing. When I first took up the implement, Mike Murphy showed me how to swing the missile around my head and get the proper elevation to it. He started by having me practice swinging the hammer around my head without actually making a throw, but getting the feel of the hammer reaching the highest elevation as it went over the left shoulder, and the lowest as it passed the right hip. For some days we practiced swinging the hammer three times around my head and then releasing it over my left shoulder without making any turn. I think we did this every day for two, or maybe even three weeks.

"Accuracy," he would shout every time I was about to release the hammer. "Accuracy Trux, accuracy."

Although the finished hammer thrower uses two turns before making the throw, he insisted that first I had to learn how to throw it with a single turn. The feet were to be 24 inches apart, the left foot thrown back 6 inches in a parallel line, with the right foot gripping the ground firmly, and the knees bent slightly. That's how detailed he was. That's why he was the greatest trainer in the world and that's why we were so good. We worked on the little things. Where he learned so much about so many events I don't know. When I asked him this once, he said "You watch the best." With the hammer, I guess that meant Flanagan.

Anyway, he showed me how to judge the speed of the turn— quickly enough that my body was ahead of the hammer. Make the turn too slow and the hammer makes its circuit too quickly and it's impossible to get full strength into the throw.

Eventually we got to where I was making the double turn resulting in increased body momentum. The tricky part here was to remain within the throwing circle. At first unconsciously I was finding myself taking more room for the turns than I needed. But after a while I got that straightened out and became a decent thrower— thanks to Mike.

There weren't many spectators on hand for the hammer, but those who were, were advised to move back to give the throwers a bigger target area. This proved not only to be a good idea, but maybe a lifesaving idea. The two Swedes, apparently had little experience with the deadly implement and sent it in all directions except toward the intended target area. The trees caught most, entangling the wire handles in branches and those that didn't sent those spectators who weren't running for their lives into fits of hilarity. Great amusement seemed to be the order of the day. Neither of the frustrated Swedes managed a legal throw. Even they found amusement in their ridiculous attempts.

Jos got off a throw measured at over 143 feet; Trux, one over 145. But big John, Flanagan, wearing the winged foot of the New York Athletic Club, was in a class by himself. He uncorked a throw of 151' 1" after which he jumped in the air and raised his fist. He was heartily cheered as it was thought he had set yet another record, but when the officials stretched out the measuring rope they found it 3 inches short. Still it was a magnificent throw. Even Trux and Jos applauded that one.

Interestingly enough, when talking with John it was clear that he always had an inkling he would be beaten. No matter how many records he put up, or how many titles he claimed, he always felt the day was coming when he would lose. So although he never was beaten, he put such pressure on himself that he was always nervous during competitions. When competing, he projected anything but the image of the typical happy-go-lucky Irishman.

Trux and Jos were happy with their second and third place finishes even if Jos thought he should have bested Trux.

So Day Three ended with us taking five more gold medals, three of which went to Deac Ewry. Prinstein had one although he was still fuming over the one he didn't have and Kraenz picked up one in what he said would be his final competition.

Actually, to be completely accurate, it wasn't exactly the end of the day's competitions.

O O O O O

The French-Scandinavian match should have been the end of tug-of-war matters. The crowd should have dispersed, the athletes should have returned to their hotels, the officials should have gone off to report the events. As it turned out that was just an intermission in the tug-of-war wars. Throughout the games, events going off at the announced scheduled times, were rare. At any rate, by this time, the hammer throw was over and onto the tug-of-war pitch strode Flanagan, Trux, and Jos beaming over their performances in the throw, claiming they were there to restore the tug-of-war honors to the Stars and Stripes.

But the event is over. You didn't show.

We'll challenge you anyway.

Too late.

It's never too late to have fun.

So after some discussion, with the crowd egging them on, the makeshift Scandinavian team agreed to pull against the U.S. in a friendly non-official match.

We assembled our team and were about to get into position to pull when one of the French pullers noticed our lads were all wearing the spiked shoes they used for their track and field events. The Frenchmen, who were wearing flat-soled shoes, protested loudly.

"That's what we always wear," countered Trux in his best French.

"But you don't always compete in the tug-of-war," said one of the Frenchmen. "Do the Americans want to be accused of cheating?"

When Trux translated this for his teammates, Jos took off his shoes and tossed them to the side. The others followed.

"Shod or unshod, it won't matter," said Trux.

"Vous allez voir," said the puller in the first position for the French.

"What'd he say?" asked Flanagan. "They quit?"

"He said all Americans are weaklings," Trux said with a wink.

As it turned out, competing barefoot was actually something of an advantage, as their un-shoed feet dug into the grass better than the slicker soles of the Scandinavians.

A spectator standing next to me, who apparently was an aficionado of friendly tugging said. "Neither team has the slightest science and no team of Irish policemen knows anything about the sport. The finest tug-of-war opponents in the world, would have beaten them."

As soon as the mighty tug got under way, he shouted "pull devil, pull baker." And pull they did.

I still have the article one of the papers wrote about the exhibition tug.

"With their shoes and socks off, the Americans dug their toes into the ground like Darwinian demons, the crowd gathered in close and yelled themselves hoarse, shouting, screaming, lashing the slaves tugging at the rope with their tongues, and sputtering "go arm," when the crack of their exhorting whip became exhausted. Then they changed sides and essayed again. It was the end of the day and the surrounding became a pandemonium. The men could scarcely breathe, the howling, crazy crowd almost treading on their feet. A sly pull of a bystander would have escaped attention, as dozens of willing hands itched to take five-card in the game. Dust! Heat! Five minutes tugging, surrounded by well-dressed people, who became for the moment barbarians, and again the weight and muscle of the United States pulled their opponents over the line. The tug-of-war was an object lesson in how not to do a thing."

What the writer of that didn't mention is that in the second pull, the Americans were struggling and dead tired. After all, half the team had already competed in a throwing event, and now there they were in a strenuous pull. So several spectators (me included) grabbed the rope and lent a hand. After exhausting ourselves for several minutes, both teams dropped to the ground.

Now the Scandinavians, led by Schmidt, didn't take too kindly to this and an unpleasant incident followed which almost ended in fisticuffs. Except, it was more in mock anger than real. Actually, the utmost good humor prevailed when all the literal dust settled.

Since the next track and field events wouldn't be contested until Thursday, we had a couple of days off to enjoy all that Paris had to offer.

O O O O O

Paris at the turn of the 20th century was an inspiration—
beautiful, romantic, a city of dreams. Even if there had not been
the Exposition, the city alone would have been more than enough
to take in.

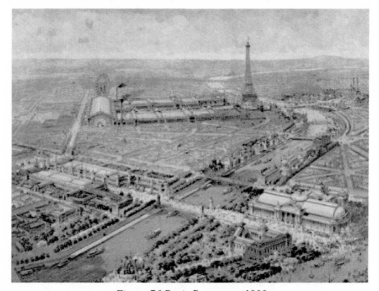

Figure 76 Paris Panorama 1900

When not practicing, competing or watching events, we found
time to explore much of this fascinating city.

We walked and we walked, strolling on the wide sidewalks of
grand boulevards under imperial chestnut trees and then veered off
into the endless little side streets.

I particularly remember walking down the rue de Richelieu
toward the Seine and then into the magnificent garden and arcade
of the Palais Royal. This huge garden with the fountain shooting

water was beautiful, not only on its own merits but also because it was enclosed by the Palais effectively shutting out the hubbub of the streets—the clattering wagons, shouting vendors, omnibuses and automobiles. Paris was a noisy city. The Palais Royal with the famous Louvre Museum and the Garden of the Tuileries were nearby. Up the street in the opposite direction was their stock exchange, the Bourse, sitting behind grandiose Doric columns making it look like a Greek temple.

Figure 77 Garden of the Tuilleries

The Garden of the Tuilleries covered over 60 acres surrounded by an iron fence. Inside were paths, statues, fountains, flower beds, lines of trees, all laid out in formal symmetry. The Seine ran along one side, the rue de Rivoli with its handsome townhouses ran along the other. From it you could see the beautiful Place Vendôme in the middle of which was the immense bronze column made of melted down cannons seized by Napoleon's army at the battle of Austerlitz.

Figure 78 Place Vendôme

I couldn't help thinking we might benefit from more beautiful public spaces like the Parisians do. We value land more by what could profitably be built on it. I've heard it said that Independence Square in Philadelphia was worth a thousand dollars a foot. How can you value a foot of the Tuilleries?

On a fine Sunday, three or four elegant carriages and countless promenading Parisians would travel two gently uphill miles of Grand Champs-Élysées from the immense Place de la Concorde to Napoleon's colossal Arc de Triumph—a parade of fancy horses and the latest high fashions.

Across the street from the Garden of the Tuilleries was Galignani's, the English language bookshop that carried American and English newspapers. We went there often to keep up with the news back home. Everyone except Trux, that is. He went to the French language book shops and bought a ton of books of French poetry. Show off!

Figure 79 Galignani's English Bookstore

Paris, with its twisty, winding streets was a complicated city to get around in. None of the streets ran parallel like the big cities I knew in the U.S. so *Galignani's New Paris Guide* was indispensable. You'd see people peering into the thick 800-page leather bound volume on street corners all over the city.

Galignani's Guide proclaimed the most fashionable promenade in Paris was between the Petit and Grand Palais. You could look down the long vista all the way across the Seine to the Invalides which held the body of Napoleon. On either sides were huge gold-topped statues. I have never seen anything like it. It was majestic.

Figure 80 Petit and Grand Palais

A magnificent view of the grand buildings of the Universal Exhibition could be had from the newly constructed Alexander III Bridge.

Figure 81 Alexander Bridge

The French took their time to savor things—a good meal, a glass of wine, a summer afternoon—probably more than we did. But then, they weren't accomplishing the things we were, either.

As far as I could tell, the French took most, if not all of their meals in public and took their time doing it. A leisurely meal, accompanied by wine and conversation could take hours. And, needless to say, the food could be great.

I loved the French breakfast. I loved the French coffee. I loved the *petit pain* which was a biscuit I can only describe as being halfway between bread and cake. It was usually served crisp and warm. Their bread was good and the butter exquisite.

One thing that stood out: the number and variety of cafés in the city. *Galignani's* guidebook said: "It is impossible to conceive either their number, variety or elegance, without having seen them. In no other city is there anything to resemble them; and they are not only unique, but in every way adapted for convenience and amusement."

I'll have to admit, though, that once you got out of the center a little, things changed. There were beggars, prostitutes, rag men. I saw a soap vendor with snakes wrapped around his neck.

Of course, I didn't visit them, but prostitutes of varying degrees of allure could easily be found, particularly around the Pigalle Nighborhood.

Paris was a city of real contrasts. Still, I didn't see many drunks reeling down the streets as I often did in Philadelphia. I didn't see men chewing tobacco, spitting or abusing public property. With so many marble statues in public gardens we might haves expected some to have been mistreated, but all I saw were statues as immaculate as any in the museums.

On the other side of the Seine, in what they called the Rive Gauche, was the Sorbonne. It was considered the finest educational institution in France—the equivalent of our great universities, our Ivy League schools. Over there, too was the École de Médecine one of the finest medical schools in the world. It was rather a crowded and compact area of the city but a very febrile one.

These were the long summer days of northern Europe. I had to remind myself that, although it didn't seem like it, we were as far north as Newfoundland.

Were the Parisians ever walkers. You could find people strolling up and down the wide boulevards all hours of the day and well into the evening—*flâneurs* they were called.

There were so many magnificently dressed women promenading along the Avenue Bois de Boulogne, some with little dogs on leashes. Dogs were everywhere. It seemed as if no lady of fashion would stroll the boulevards without her leashed little dog.

Figure 82 Fashionable ladies of Paris

They also had the famous Paris omnibuses, giant horse-drawn vehicles that went all over the city from eight in the morning until late at night. Sometimes when we were sitting on the top of one and it came to a roughly cobbled street it shook like crazy.

Figure 83 Paris omnibus

I have to say, the French people we met were always friendly, polite, and nearly always ready to help. Ask a Parisian for directions and he was likely to take you to the end of the street to show you.

Sunday in Paris always brought out great crowds. Did anyone keep the Sabbath? It didn't seem like it. This was not easy for us to get used to—or accept. Yeah, the church bells rang Sunday mornings, but they did on other days, too. The shops, cafes, restaurants were all jammed. Theaters had performances. So did the operas. The public gardens were more filled with people than on any other day and dancing went on in their rotundas. This, as much as anything, reminded us we were not in Philadelphia or any other American city for that matter.

Most of us tried to get by speaking a little school-learned French, although often with lousy accents, so the Tuilleries came out more like "Tullyrees" and garçons as "gassons," but the French appreciated our efforts anyway.

From the top of Montmartre hill you could look down at the

jumbled rooftops of Paris and the Cathedral of Notre Dame off in the distance towering above everything around it. You could see how big the city was. The population was something approaching 3 million people. Philadelphia was only about half that size.

If there ever was a marker of the immense difference between the Old World and the New, it had to be the Louvre. It was the world's greatest museum in what was at one time the royal palace built for Catherine de Medici in the 16th century. Its famous Grande Galerie they say was the longest room in the world. I can believe that.

Figure 84 Louvre Grande Galerie

More than anything, what I took away from Paris is that the glory of the arts of architecture and public spaces was indispensable to the enjoyment of life felt by the Parisians. In this respect, we had a lot we could learn from the French.

One great advantage the old countries had over us is that they have the treasures of great art and the love for it. We can't match that.

A favorite saying among the French was, "to be in Paris was to have the world at one's feet."

One image of Paris that I will never forget was the dazzling profusion of electric lighting. It was everywhere—in the pavilions, on the monuments, along the central boulevards, in the Palais de l'Électricité, and up the entire height of the Eiffel Tower.

Figure 85 Ornate electric lamps

Perhaps the most fascinating marvel of the entire Exposition though, was the moving sidewalk. Designed by two American engineers, it was a two-mile long, electric, three-tiered sidewalk. The outer track was stationary, the next moved at two-and-a-half miles per hour, the other at 5 miles per hour.

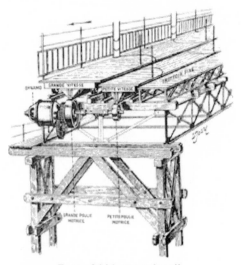

Figure 86 Moving sidewalk

I don't know how many trips I took on it, but it was a lot. All the lads rode it. From its moving tracks you could take in much of the Exposition. The arrangements of the three tracks, together with the balancing poles stationed conveniently along the margins of the platform enabled us to easily step from one to another and at the same time to regulate our progress to our wishes. The trip at night when all the buildings were gloriously lit with colored lights was particularly enjoyable.

Figure 87 Seeing the sights rom the moving sidewalk

I remember late one night Tewks decided to use the sidewalk to jog—in the opposite direction of the sidewalk's movement. He thought that was funny. The policeman who stopped him didn't.

We rode the giant Ferris wheel. I hated it when it stopped while we were at the very top. I guess it offered a great view of Paris way below us, but I'll admit to being so nervous at that point that I can't say I really enjoyed it.

Figure 88 Giant Ferris wheel

Here are a few other sights we took in:

Bastille Day confetti fights between top-hatted gentlemen erupting on the boulevards.

Dancers swirling on the Bastille Day ball along the Quai aux Fleurs.

The bird market, a meeting place for people of all ages and caged birds of all sizes.

Scores of horse-drawn carriages driven by well-attired men in top hats.

The grand apple market at the port du Mail, Quai de l'Hôtel-de-Ville.

Dockers working on the Quai du Louvre.

Bouquinists on Quai de Conti.

Women selling artichokes from Brittany on crowded streets.

Scores and scores of blue and white collar workers sitting on the terraces of cafes on Boulevard Garibaldi.

Sidewalk artists and organ grinders. Street peddlers raving about the benefits of a wonder product.

Goat's milk vendors with herds of goats wandering the streets.

Huge stacks of forage on the sidewalk for the city's 80,000 horses.

Little girls in white dresses, broad-brimmed sun hats and ankle-length boots on a carousel.

Nannies getting on with their knitting while watching over their protégés.

Engrossed kids watching a Guignol puppet show.

Children watching the guillotine being cleaned through the keyhole where it was kept at No. 60 Rue de la Folie-Regnault.

The Eiffel Tower being struck by lightning.

Stock brokers and agents rushing around the Paris Bourse stock exchange.

The Sacré-Couer being built on top of Montmartre.

The changing colors of the Seine depending on the time of day and the weather—brown, gray, silver, deep indigo.

Ragmen equipped with hooks for rummaging through dustbins to pick out things they could sell.

We watched as 11 people went up in the basket of a hot air balloon, and what an assortment of people it was. There were men in top hats, men in skimmers, men in turbans, and a daring finely dressed woman.

Inside the fruit and vegetable market of Les Halles, I saw strongmen unload trucks and carry the merchandise into the halls.

To do the job they had to carry 200 kilograms over 50 meters, so they used big hats made out of leather reinforced with lead for lugging the heavy loads on their heads.

On the Place de la Bastille, there was a huge telescope—maybe 20-feet long. You had to climb up on a ladder to see through the eyepiece.

Figure 89 The giant telescope

We were told by a manager of the telescope that a great contest was in progress over the eventual possession of it after the fair closed. The papal nuncio in Paris said that it ought to go to Rome and that he was raising a subscription among the Catholics of the world with the object of adding it to the great observatory at the Vatican. A wealthy New Yorker has been talking to several millionaire Americans with the idea of getting it to New York. Buffalo and St. Louis were also vying for it.

We looked down on a panorama of Avenue Kléber from the top of the Arc de Triomphe. I could see the Neo Moorish towers of the Palais du Trocadéro constructed for the 1878 Paris World's Fair. It absolutely dominated the cityscape.

We watched as waiters raced across the city carrying trays with a full bottle of wine and two glasses. The winner was the first to finish the race with the wine and glasses intact.

We were fortunate enough to see the incomparable Sarah Bernhardt playing the Duke of Reichstadt in Edmond Rostand's *L'Aiglon*—the tragic tale of the son and heir of Napoleon who died at 21. The "Divine Sarah," played the young man.

At the foot of the Montmartre hill, we stopped at the Moulin Rouge Cabaret's gardens for a glass of wine. Naturally we stayed to take in the fabulous dances at the Folies-Bergère and the Grand finale of the Cancan.

Figure 90 Moulin Rouge

We saw the grotesque mouth opening of the Cabaret de L'Enfer, on Boulevard de Clichy, and inside, the twisted subterranean decor where devilish waiters served 'a sinner's cocktail with a pinch of sulpher,' in the form of a coffee laced with cognac.

Oh yes, I feel fortunate to have taken all this in. They claim there is no other place in the world like it. I can easily believe that.

EDMUND MINAHAN   I know it sounds silly to say it, but I was struck by how completely French Paris was. All the signs and posted notices were in French. Nobody in the cafes spoke anything but French ... and that included the waiters. That may have been good for someone like Truxtun Hare who spoke the lingo pretty good, but some of us, me included, had to work hard to deal with getting around and eating in restaurants when none of our French speakers was around. I got so I could use a few words, like *gauche, droite, garcon* and *boulanger*. Pronouncing them was another story altogether. Some words were the same, though. Like "rat."

And the French money, that was hard to figure out—not like dollars and cents.

O O O O O

While we were in Paris at least two serious accidents occurred. One I witnessed, the other I heard and read about.

Sometimes it takes a little luck to get through the day. I got up one morning and could feel the sticky heat of the day already building so I went for an early morning walk. I was just about to step on the footbridge over the Boulevard de la Tour. The wooden bridge was already packed with people on their way ... to wherever a hot July day's activity would take them. Within a few feet of the bridge I heard a loud cracking sound as if the bridge was about to collapse. The crowd already on the bridge rushed to the opposite side causing enormous pressure on the outside railing, which when it became too great, gave way. Screaming accompanied scores of people who poured onto the roadway which I judged to be a full 20 feet below.

What a tangled mess of wood and injured—some apparently seriously. I rushed over to see what help I could offer. An older woman was struggling to get to her feet. I gave her a hand up and led her away from the accident. She was continually mumbling something in French I couldn't understand. When we came to a bench she sat, still mumbling. I went back to see if I could help anyone else but by that time there were so many people, both the injured and those helping, that I stayed off to the side.

I saw several people being carried off, presumably to hospitals. Later I read that two people had died as a result of their injuries.

Naturally, this put a real damper on the day.

The other serious accident occurred at a ballooning exhibition.

Ballooning was becoming hugely popular in France. Ever since the days of the Montgolfier brothers in latter part of the 18th century, the French had been fascinated with the thoughts of flying and had created numerous aeronautical societies. They were rather fanatical about it, too.

Several balloon ascensions were arranged as part of the Exposition. For one, 6000 people were jammed into the Place Barault to watch Capt. Mouton take his balloon up. Every space between the buildings on the four sides of the square was occupied and thousands more tried to push in from outside the square. The police just stood around and watched while what they should have been doing was controlling the mob. Maybe they felt overwhelmed by the size of the crowd and thought there was little constraint they could offer.

The wind kicked up enough that Capt. Mouton delayed starting at the announced time. The crowd not understanding the cause for the delay began to hoot and jeer, until the aeronaut, unduly influenced by these cries, sprang into the car where his assistant, a man who apparently had only made one ascension before, was already seated. Mouton gave the order to let go.

The balloon had hardly risen above the housetops when a sharp gust of wind blew it to the left causing it to bump against the telegraph wires. A little ballast was thrown out and the balloon swayed up and rose again a little, but two more puffs of wind blew it against the roofs of the houses on the right-hand side of the square, where it knocked a chimney over, and tore away several window shutters. Then the car became caught in the network of telegraph wires behind it.

Suddenly the dragging of the car across the wires established an electrical short circuit. A spark and a small tongue of flame which licked the base and sides of the balloon were seen by all the onlookers in the square below.

Shrieking with terror, the immense crowd surged this way and that, throwing down women, old men and children and trampling them underfoot. The crowd fought madly to get into the passages and halls of the houses on the square, breaking the windows of the apartments on the ground floor and clambering in for safety, and altogether behaving more like a stampeded herd of wild cattle fleeing from a blazing forest than a crowd of frightened human beings.

Capt. Mouton quickly opened the safety valve of the balloon, but he was too late to prevent the explosion of the gas. There was a report like that of a huge cannon, and the immense pear-shaped vessel flared up, hissing and smoking with a blaze which was perceptible all over Paris. In an instant the upper floors of one of the houses on the square caught fire, while the howls and cries came from those within.

The assistant miraculously escaped serious injury by falling from the balloon's car on to two crossed wires and climbing to the ground down the pole. He was badly burned by the flames which had enveloped him. Capt. Mouton, in trying to cut the car away from the body of the balloon, became entangled in the cords, and although half suffocated by the smoke, and badly bruised, was not more seriously hurt.

Twenty people were taken to hospitals, some badly injured.

It was two hours before the firemen who had been summoned could get the flames under control.

TEN

A S STRANGE AS SOME OF THE TRACK AND FIELD
EVENTS HAD BEEN, they were about to get even stranger.

The marathon was the only event held Thursday, and it was …
extraordinary and not necessarily in a good way. The Paris marathon
was anything but efficiently organized. If we were wont to criticize
the French for their lack of organizational acumen, the marathon
gave us ample cause.

Interest in marathon running was greatly enhanced by athletes
returning from the Athens Games. Subsequently marathons were
established in several countries in Europe, Canada and the United
States. Distances varied, but most were between 15 and 25 miles.
In September 1896, the Knickerbocker Athletic Club organized the
first marathon race in the United States. It was run from Stamford,
Connecticut to New York City, a distance of 25 miles. Thirty runners
took the train from New York City to Stamford, and then ran back
in the rain. John McDermott was the winner, covering the distance
in 3:26.

The first Boston marathon was run a few months later. The
conceit was to run the course ridden by Paul Revere, but myth
outdistanced reality as the course mostly ran parallel to the railroad
line from Metcalf's Mill in Ashland, Massachusetts to the Oval
on Irvington Street in downtown Boston. McDermott also ran this
race which included a long steady uphill climb through the city
of Newton followed by a 6-mile-long downhill to the finish. The
course was about 24 1/2 miles long and became the focal point for
distance running in the United States. McDermott took the lead from

Harvard's Dick Grant over the Newton hill. Although forced to walk often in the finishing miles, he still won by a considerable margin.

Now in Paris, Grant and Arthur Newton, would carry America's hopes—even if Grant was Canadian.

Newton, the diminutive runner from Vermont, while working for the Wood Motor Vehicle Company in Manhattan, competed for the New York Athletic Club in races throughout the Northeast and won regularly. He had beaten most of the best distance runners we had to offer in middle and long-distance runs, in cross-country races and in the marathon. He had even entered a few hurdle races. *The New York Journal* referred to him as "that little wonder from Vermont." A whole lot was expected from him in Paris.

Long-distance running was popular in France. A few months before the Paris Olympic marathon, 191 runners entered a 25-mile race from Paris to Conflans. The race was won by a British runner, Len Hurst. Since he was considered a professional, he wasn't eligible to run at the Olympics. However, the second place runner, the Frenchman Georges Touquet-Daunis, was an amateur and so was entered.

Figure 91 Georges Touquet-Daunis

CASPAR WHITNEY The French organizers, as was their wont, were late in sending out the announcement of the marathon course and as originally described it was to go from Versailles to Paris.

But then, after the runners had already studied the route, the French officials switched to a course of four laps around the Racing Club oval at Pré Catalan in the Bois de Boulogne and then a big circle around Paris.

MIKE MURPHY   We had two good lads entered in the marathon—Arthur Newton representing the New York Athletic Club, and Dick Grant running in the Harvard colors.

Now I can't rightly say we excelled in the really long runs but we were coming on and Newton and Grant figured to do well in Paris.

In the early days of our history, professionals indulged in long runs, frequently competing in distances greater than what became the standard marathon length. But the amateurs took it up only after it was made such a feature of the revival of the Olympic Games in 1896.

When I saw to what extent the marathon craze was being pursued by boys and immature young men not properly trained, I sounded a warning against it, and tried to persuade our lads not fitted for a race which requires so much endurance to leave it alone. No one under 18 should run this distance. Twenty years is young enough for so great an effort.

By the way, Grant was 22 but Newton, only 17. Young for this event, but as I wasn't his college coach I had no say in his training.

I had preached for years that before an athlete takes up marathon running he needed to make sure he had the endurance for a long run, the marathon distance being approximately 25 miles. The fact that a man could run 5 miles is not good evidence he could run 25. I have always gone on this theory, that if one can run 5 miles comfortably, he can also run 10 miles without injury. And if one finds that 10 or 12 miles can be covered without great distress the chances are that with the proper training he can go the marathon distance.

The number of men fitted by nature to run the marathon distance is very few. Unless a man can get all the sleep and rest he needs he should not take up the marathon.

To get in marathon condition a man should be able to run frequently for more than an hour. Often he needs to run two hours or more and such long periods of hard work call for a corresponding period of rest.

The best kind of training is a combination of cross-country running, walking and jogging. A cross-country walk combined with a slow jog which will take a man a mile in about 7 or eight minutes is the best way to get the legs and wind in condition. This can be done two or three times a week, gradually increasing the distance from 5 to 10 or 15 miles according to the athlete's condition.

A man should not expect to get in condition for the marathon with less than eight or 10 weeks of training.

More than anything, though, the marathon runner needs to acquire the art of running easily.

The essentials are plenty of work, though not an excess of it, a good diet, plenty of sleep and rest, and no alcohol or tobacco.

A great many marathon races are lost because of a runner's desire to keep up with too fast a pace at the start. So I talked with both Newton and Grant on the morning of the marathon and reminded them to go off easy and to make sure they drank enough because it looked as if the day would be another scorcher.

DICK GRANT It had been hot the entire time we were in Paris, but on the day of the marathon, it was unbelievably hot—well over 100 degrees in the shade and there was scant little of that. Perspiration dripped from me from the moment I awoke. It was a day I'll never forget—Thursday, July 19. Boiling Thursday. Running 25 miles is difficult enough as it is; running in that heat was crazy.

E. ION POOL   The whole conduct of the race on the part of the responsible organizers, beginning with the tardy date of the announcement sent abroad, down to the smallest details of providing, or rather failing to provide, for the convenience of contestants on the appointed day, and the entire absence of precautions to ensure fair play, can only be characterized by a single word: Preposterous, with a capital "P." Add to this the nonsporting demeanor of the French populace and it becomes easy to explain the extent of the troubles that variously beset the foreign runners.

ARTHUR NEWTON   Even though it was the hottest summer anyone in Paris could ever remember, they didn't get the marathon going until 2:30 in the afternoon. It was 102 degrees—the hottest July day on record. Only the French! Had we gotten going early in the morning it would have been much, much better for us, but as it was, that wasn't the biggest problem we would face on that blistering hot July day without a cloud in sight. And to top it off, I wasn't feeling particularly well. I don't know if it was all the travel or maybe eating food I wasn't acquainted with, but I wasn't feeling right. I hoped that the feeling would pass after a few miles of running. Sometimes you can run through these types of things.

Since it was Thursday and nothing else was on the track and field schedule that day, Mike Murphy and some of the team were there for the start. Dick Grant, the Canadian runner from Harvard, lined up next to me on the starting line in the Bois de Boulogne. So did his countryman, Ronald MacDonald, a Canadian running as a Canadian.

Figure 92 Ronald MaDonald

Michel Théato, a Luxembourger, was running for France. E. Ion Pool was a Brit actually running for Great Britain. Four other Frenchmen also started—Emile Champion, Eugène Besse, Auguste Marchais and George Touquet-Daunis. All together I counted 16 of us crazy enough to set off for a 25-mile run around Paris in that scorching heat. Interestingly enough, though, there were no Greeks and this was supposed to be their race since the idea came from a runner who ran from the plain of Marathon on the Greek coast to Athens to warn the Greeks that an attack force was on the way. That may have been more myth than reality, but the story says the runner then dropped dead from the exertion. Maybe he didn't like the heat either. Anyway, for the '96 Games, the Greeks trained on their home course. Fourteen Greeks entered the race to run against four foreigners. What a surprise, a Greek won.

DICK GRANT   What a motley group of runners we were in as many different outfits as there were competitors. Some wore hats to fend off the blazing sun. A few wore straw skimmers, a few wore those French style berets, at least one looked like a floppy beach hat. One runner wore what must have been a military officer's cap. A few others I wouldn't know what to call them, other than odd. I wore no hat because that was the way I was used to running and I didn't think the Olympic marathon was a good time to experiment. We all wore long shorts that came down to our knees and leather shoes with leather soles.

ARTHUR NEWTON   A Frenchman named Fernand Meiers introduced himself as the starter. He was supposed to be their champion 1500-meter runner from a few years earlier, but I guess he was smart enough to not want to run in that heat. Anyway, he fired the pistol and we all set off to run four laps around the same lumpy 500-meter oval they used for all the other running events. We started off slowly enough but we had barely come around the first lap when one of the two Swedish runners called it quits. He must have been sick or something ... or maybe already overheated. Given what transpired over the rest of the race, he may have been the smart one.

Figure 93 The marathon runners get under way

I knew enough to hang back and run at my own pace. So did Grant. The race would not be won on that oval but it sure as hell could have been lost … as the Swede found out.

We were all still bunched up for the track laps with Marchais in the lead group with a couple of his compatriots and the Swedish runner, Ernst Fast, right on their heels. Grant and I were close behind. I still wasn't feeling great, but as the pace was easy I wasn't in any real trouble. The "track" was pretty much tree covered, so it wasn't nearly as hot as it would become once we hit the Paris streets.

Figure 94 Ernst Fast

After the four laps we headed down a trail leading out of the park and into the city proper. This was really cross-country running. Paths were crisscrossing in front of us seemingly every few yards, and of course, no guidance came from the organizers. So by necessity the French runners were out in front. The rest of us followed like good little running sheep.

Then came the first of what would be many confusions. As we went through the Porte de Passy we had to make a turn to head along Paris streets. Now you would have thought there would be a course marshal or a big sign pointing out the turn. But, of course, this being a race organized by the French, no such help existed. The Frenchmen in the lead turned left but the young Fast didn't see them and turned right. After a while he noticed he was all by his lonesome, so he had to turn around and play catch up. Just what he needed—to run even farther in the heat.

This was only the first of several confusing turns on the course. Maybe they were expecting us to carry maps!

The Porte de Passy was supposed to be the first of seven control points along the way and as far as I could see, there wasn't the slightest hint of controlling anything going on. What, I wondered did that presage for the remainder of the race?

I figure we were about 5 miles into the race when we got to the Porte Maillot, which as I understand was one of the ancient city gate entry points in the old wall around the city. I had by then moved up to a close fourth behind two Frenchmen and the Swede who had run really hard to catch up after his sightseeing detour.

Indicative of how damn brutal the conditions were, somewhere around this point, the three British runners called it a day and dropped out. We hadn't even run the first quarter of the course. If I didn't know how difficult this would be before, I sure did then. The three Brits who retired had taken the first three places in the London to Brighton ultradistance race the year before. So these were anything but novices at long running. They were excellent, experienced runners—and if they couldn't make a go of it, I wasn't at all sure I could. But I pushed on anyway.

E. ION POOL   At best the marathon proved a steeplechase, with bicycles and cars for obstacles. Twenty-five miles is really too far for a steeplechase, but that was a mere incidental to the heat that got to me.

Figure 95 The marathoners dodging traffic

I was at the Porte de Passy as the competitors came out of the Bois de Boulogne, and was able to see them at two other points as they circled the city. I have nothing but admiration for these men, running in such abominable conditions and running for so long. It had to be dangerous. I understand there were a few doctors stationed somewhere around the course in case anyone ran into serious medical difficulty. What I didn't see a lot of, however, were race officials keeping onlookers and pedestrians clear of the runners. It looked as if the marathoners were running through crowds.

ARTHUR NEWTON   Since the course was not closed, we were constantly dodging pedestrians, horses, carriages, automobiles, motorcycles, dogs and various other animals, bicycles and I don't know all what else. At times, bicyclists pedaled alongside us as if they were racing us.

I don't think there was ever an announcement in the papers that the marathon race would be coming through and around Paris, so the Parisians seeing men running down their streets treated us merely as annoyances to their getting to … wherever they were going.

In other long races I'd run there was always lots of support from the race officials. But here, they were basically nonexistent. Oh, there were a couple of control points along the way, but other than that, I didn't see anything set up to help us—like water stations.

DICK GRANT   At several points along the course, I saw other runners running with us who weren't there at the start. I don't know who the hell they were. Someone said they were professionals. Where they came from and where they went I can't say. The marathon is a unique event in that for much of the race you rarely saw all or even any of the other competitors. This was strange, though—runners coming and going.

ARTHUR NEWTON   Close to the Paris slaughterhouse, we picked our way through sheep and cattle ... and a few goats. The spectators? Hell, most didn't even know a race was being run. They either ignored us or shouted what sure sounded like French profanities when they thought we got in their way. Apparently goats in the road didn't bother them but runners did.

Somewhere around 10 miles—near the Porte d'Ornano—the Frenchman who had led the race most of the way up to that point, Touquet-Daunis, decided he was thirsty. Real thirsty, since he had also run an additional quarter mile when he made a wrong turn. So to slake his thirst, he dropped into a café for a beer. Actually two beers. He was still there when I passed. He waved and returned to his brew. As far as I know, he was still there when the race ended.

If the heat accounted for nothing else, at least the competition was getting thinner all the time. My chances were getting better, but there was still a long way to go and I was feeling even less chippy than I was at the start. Amazingly, I was still very much in contention only yards behind the leaders. I'm not sure how far behind me Dick Grant was, or for that matter if he was still behind me at all.

A few miles on, at the Porte Villette, we ran past the Paris abattoir, which was a big, smelly slaughterhouse. Sheep and cows were all over the place in the road. We had to zig and zag like we were running a bizarre moving obstacle course. I didn't see anyone run over by a cow but it could have happened.

Then, as if the already difficult race wasn't torturous enough, the paved road turned into rough cobblestone. That was simply hell to run on with tender feet, tired muscles and slippery leather-soled shoes. You had to really concentrate so as not to turn an ankle … or worse.

Several times somebody sprayed us with water from big hoses. I can't say the cooling was unwelcome, but it sure could take your breath away when you weren't expecting it.

Figure 96 Cooling the marathon runners

It was at the Porte de Vincennes, which was about half way (there were no course markers to tell us for sure) that the Swede who had earlier taken the wrong direction, stopped running and walked. Apparently he had a leg cramp. Given the conditions, I'm surprised more of us didn't. Eventually, though, he got back to running.

I slogged on, the heat slowing me considerably.

After this, things got … even more confusing.

Figure 97 Théato crossing marathon finish line

I made my way to the finish line to see the French going positively wild when Théato was the first to cross the line. French spectators poured onto the track that used only light rope as a barrier and carried Michel around on their shoulders, while enthusiastic cheers resounded across the grounds. It was the last scratch race on the schedule and so it was the only win for a Frenchman at these games.

I had to wait for quite some time for our boys—Newton and Grant—which was surprising. They were both excellent long-distance men and that they were beaten so soundly seemed … peculiar. Art Newton more than an hour behind Théato? And Dick Grant was behind him. That is hard to explain. I understand other runners might be faster, but more than an hour on a 25-mile course seemed like a lot.

By the time they arrived, most spectators imagined that all save those who had arrived had abandoned the race and most onlookers had gone home. So Newton's arrival passed almost unnoticed except by us few remaining Americans who gave him an encouraging cheer as he entered the track for his final three laps. This he did walking. Grant and MacDonald arrived a little later. Grant quite done in, dropped on the grass after passing the finish line and seem to be in a fainting condition. He received attention from Murphy and a few Frenchmen, who stood over him fanning him. Finally, he recovered and walked to a dressing room, leaning on Murphy's arm.

All sorts of accusations were put forward, mostly claiming that Théato and Champion took short cuts. But how does that explain Fast, the Swede? Was he just close enough to the two Frenchmen that he could follow them? Fast, true to his name, was an amazing runner. First he went the wrong way, then he had to slow to a walk, and he still managed to come third.

Maybe these three were just really good and deserved their places. Maybe. Théato's time was just 40 seconds longer than the winner of the Athens Olympic marathon four years earlier. The distances for both races were marked at 25 miles although the course profiles were quite different, so it is not inconceivable that Théato's performance at Paris was on the up and up.

Still, the question lingers: Did everyone run the same course? We'll never know as there is no proof of exactly which course every competitor ran.

ARTHUR NEWTON   Théato was credited with a time of 2:59:45, Champion more than three minutes behind him, Fast 23 minutes behind Champion. Besse came fourth more than an hour later, and then me at 4:05:12. The only other two finishers were the Canadian, Ronald MacDonald and Grant at 4:24. Everyone else had dropped out along the way.

Those are the official results. What the true results were ... well, that may be another story altogether.

DICK GRANT   OK, here's the big question: Who won the marathon? I know the official results. That's not what I'm asking. I'm asking who actually won.

Well, I can state this as a fact: Just as I was about to pass Théato, a bicycle came whizzing up the street, smashed into me from behind, and sent me flying to the pavement. I was startled, slightly bloodied and furious. It was no accident I can tell you that. There was no way he didn't see me. We were in an open street and there was plenty of room to pass on either side of me. I think the cyclist had been following us for some time and when it looked like I was about to go into the lead, he took me down. Probably a pre-arranged strategy set up by Théato or maybe his trainer ... if he had one. And the cyclist didn't stop either, he just took off like a thief in the night. Absolutely it was no accident but just another lousy example of the French lack of fair play sensibility.

As soon as I crossed the finish line I dropped to the ground for a few moments to recover and had to be fanned. Then when I could I corralled a French official and complained vociferously about being knocked down by that cyclist. I even showed him some blood on my arm. He shrugged and walked away, either not understanding or nor caring—probably the latter.

That night, Mr. Spalding helped me prepare an official protest which we delivered the next day. Naturally, I wasn't surprised when nobody paid any attention to it.

After the games were over, I filed a lawsuit stating that the collision was intentional—and it sure as hell was. I know it. But, surprise, surprise, that was turned down, too.

The words "fair play," and "French" just don't go together.

Maybe I wouldn't have won that race but I would have liked an honest shot at it.

In all fairness one thing has to be said about that confusing race. Théato later set a French record for 10,000 meters. So he was no slouch as a runner. Art Newton's time was far off Théato's, but perhaps was the result of his getting lost on the course and therefore running farther than the prescribed distance.

E. ION POOL   The marathon turned out a dismal fiasco. Suffice it to say that when the first three finishers in the London to Brighton race the year before found it necessary to retire within 4 miles, and Arthur Newton, that well-known long-distance runner record breaker in the United States, who was unwise enough to finish, took almost longer than walking time to complete the distance, it shows that everything was very, very wrong. I could a further tale unfold … but "no mattah."

ARTHUR NEWTON   Did Théato and Champion cheat? Maybe. I know this much for sure: They were both behind me at least until Porte de Chatillon and neither of them ever passed me. It may have been so hot, I may have been struggling and I'll grant I might not have been as sharp as normal, but I didn't miss either of them going ahead of me. Théato was hard to miss under any circumstances. He was tall and dressed in the colors of his club, the Club Athletique de Sainte Mandé, which was mostly black. Fact: nobody in black passed me. I would have noticed.

I heard later that he was a Paris baker and that he knew the streets so well that he used several shortcuts to get in front. That would explain how he got ahead of me without my seeing him. Also as a baker, he would have been more used to the extreme heat than the rest of us.

For a long time after the games stories went around that Théato was a baker's assistant who was able to cheat because he knew the confusing Paris streets so well as the result of delivering croissants and baguettes every morning to customers all around the city.

Well, after that story received so much attention, someone looked into it further and found out that he was actually a woodworker. Anyway, bakers didn't even deliver breads, customers came to local boulangeries to pick up their daily baguettes and croissants. That was a long-standing French tradition.

DICK GRANT   I can't say for sure that Théato was a cheat, but I'll mention just for the record, that on the very day of the marathon, July 19, 1900, Paris opened its first underground railway—the Paris Metro. It ran from Porte Maillot to Porte Vincennes, both places we ran through. The Porte de Vincennes we reached at just about the half way mark. Could he and Champion have jumped on a train there for some distance? That's a question, not an accusation. But something was fishy.

Here's another thing to consider: The night before the marathon it rained fairly heavily and not all of the marathon course was run on paved roads. So how do you account for the fact that Théato finished with the cleanest legs you ever saw? Mine were mud-splattered. Odd. What did he do, stop and wash up after the dirt roads? Or maybe he didn't run the same course the rest of us did.

I suspect, and I'm sure as hell not the only one, that the course had been specifically designed with short cuts that the hometown contestants knew about and used.

And, too, there are other serious questions about the fairness of the event. I know for a fact that Ernst Fast, the little Swede became so lost at one point that he stopped and asked a policeman for directions. The gendarme pointed him in the wrong direction. On purpose? Who knows? One story though that floated around later was that the police officer became so distraught over "his mistake" that he shot himself. That, too may well be another one of those legends about the games perpetuated by the French.

CASPAR WHITNEY   After the Paris Games, a story came out that Théato accepted participation money but we never saw any real proof of that. With Grant's lawsuit that dragged on for months, Théato's victory remained questionable and somewhat hollow. The French still insist Théato won fair and square, and he is still officially considered the winner. But the controversy lingers ... as well it should.

O O O O O

It was hot all that summer. Very hot, very often. A few storms blew through which freshened the air for short periods, but the stifling heat always returned with a vengeance.

The *New York Times* began publishing a Paris edition and in it they reported that the heat in the city had sent the death rate soaring, especially among children. The hospitals were so overcrowded that 1,200 cots were added. Horses suffered terribly, the streetcar companies alone reported losing more than a thousand animals.

Due to the shortage in the water supply, service was cut off between 11 o'clock at night and 6 o'clock in the morning. Even during the day there were local shut-offs and numerous reports of restaurants being unable to draw enough water to meet their needs.

We were staying outside the city and so had no such inconveniences, but we were competing in the sweltering heat and that didn't make for ideal running conditions. During the marathon the temperature reached 102 in the shade, making it the hottest day ever recorded in Paris.

The efforts to keep cool assumed some amusing forms. Many men and women carried a little Japanese fan, known in Paris under the picturesque name of "The Little North Wind." Horses wore big straw sunbonnets, and men and women everywhere were attired in the most airy clothing. Boulevard cafés were crowded late at night with iced drinks being the drinks of choice.

Naturally when it got this hot, attendance at the Exposition and the Games dropped off considerably. This brought about a big slump in the price of tickets to many of the Exposition venues. Tickets which sold at 75 centimes when the show opened dropped gradually to 45 centimes and then to 20 which was equal to about 4 cents in American money.

Sales of electric fans, however, soared.

Figure 98 Voucher for ticket reduction

O O O O O

Robert Roosevelt, the congressman and Minister to The Hague, upon visiting the American Pavilion claimed that the structure was not safe. He said that he was there on the opening day and the building was less than half-full, adding that if all the people who had been turned back had got in at once he believed that the buildings would have fallen.

Henri Dumay, the Paris correspondent of the *New York World* picked up the story and wrote extensively about it. According to him the American Pavilion was a mere shell of light timbers covered over with plaster, and because the huge interior included four galleries it was unstable. He wrote that testing architects told the United States Commission that if the lower floor and galleries were allowed to be filled the whole structure would inevitably collapse toward the center, and the great dome would fall on top of the heap.

According to Dumay, great efforts were made it to keep the

information within the United States Commission, and strict orders were issued not to let newspaper correspondents learn it. It was only because Mr. Roosevelt made his assertion that the issue had become known.

Dumay promptly was challenged to a duel by Morin Gustiaux, the assistant architect of the American Pavilion.

Pistols were demanded by Dumay who was, according to reports, a crack shot. He refused to apologize, asserting that he was only doing his duty as a correspondent when he wrote that the pavilion was unsafe.

Because of the bad publicity, Commissioner Peck had to assure the public that the story was wrong. He had an engineer put out a statement that the building was, in fact built of steel and stone and not of timber and plaster. His explanation of the reason only a limited number of people had been admitted inside the pavilion on the opening day was that two weeks before that event the Russian Commissioners had opened wide the doors of the Russian building and invited all to come in. All visitors were treated to plenty of Champagne, and all got riotously drunk. So the United States Commissioners decided they would go their Russian colleagues one better, and if the Russians had served Champagne in buckets the Americans would bring it in barrels. They were then flooded with so many applications for admission that they had to limit the tickets to friends and "important people."

In the end, the American Pavilion did not collapse and Mr. Gustiaux was not shot in a duel with Mr. Dumay.

ELEVEN

SUNDAY AGAIN. There were 30 entries for the 200 but only eight men turned up for the start. Perhaps it was because the race was run more than a week after the track events had begun and some men had decided it was hot enough that they headed home. Maybe it was because the USA competitors had proved to be so dominant that they saw little chance for victory. Or, more likely it was the Sunday affair again. At any rate Tewks and William Holland, the Georgetown runner, were there. So were Norman Pritchard and Stan Rowley.

Norman Pritchard was listed as an Indian representing that country. The fact is, however, like many other confusing issues of these games, Pritchard was neither an Indian nor did he represent India. OK, he was born in Calcutta, but both his parents were English and members of the large British community that had lived and prospered in the sub-continent for generations.

Figure 99 Norman Pritchard

Pritchard worked for a large jute trading house in Calcutta where he was an excellent soccer player and a competitive sprinter, winning the Bengal 100 yards for 7 consecutive years. He also won titles there in the 440 and 120 yard hurdles. From about 1893 on, he was considered the best athlete in India.

It was on business that Pritchard visited England in 1900, knowing nothing of the scheduled Olympic Games. This did not make him unique since the games were not widely publicized in any part of Europe.

On arriving in London in June he joined the London Athletic Club and quickly won the club's Challenge Cup in the 120 and 440 yard hurdles, the 100 yard flat.

Then when we were in London, he came runner-up to Kraenz in the 120 hurdles, after which his club elected to send him to Paris for the Olympics.

The first heat saw Holland easily beat Pritchard with a Frenchman a poor third and a Hungarian trailing. But since the first two advanced to the finals, it looked as if by the halfway point Pritchard knew he would easily qualify so he backed off leaving first to Holland.

The second, and last heat, played out in a similar fashion. Rowley and Tewks took first and second, badly outdistancing a Norwegian and a German.

So, as expected, the Americans Holland and Tewks were pitted against Rowley and Pritchard in what turned out to be a magnificent tussle and one of the best track events of the Games. Tewks, Pritchard, and Rowley got off the mark together and sprinted up the track with Holland close behind. At first Pritchard had a very slight lead, but Tewks pulled even and the two ran neck and neck to the finish. At the line Tewks bested Pritchard by 6 inches. Rowley was a good third but he was clearly agitated.

STANLEY ROWLEY Plain and simple: I was interfered with. I had the extreme outside, and after making up the distance lost there, I was blocked at about 150 yards, and had to round the field and was only beaten to third place by the Indian, Pritchard—and then only by a yard.

Despite his complaints, the results stood. Other than the ridiculous 5000-meter team race, the track and field competitions had come to a formal conclusion. Tewks had finished them off in style.

O O O O O

STANLEY ROWLEY At some point they added an event they called The Course De Nations. I don't know where they scraped up that, but it was a 5000-meter run. Not a relay, but a race where everybody would run the whole damn way. That's 3 1/4 miles. Just fancy me running that distance. The race was really a team race with five men on each team. As far as I know, they asked all the countries to turn out a team, but only France came up with a complete one. Great Britain was close. They found four runners who were willing to run that number of times around in a circle. I certainly wasn't about to do that. But then they ganged up on me—the Brits.

Charley Bennett and John Rimmer corralled me soon after completing the 200-meter sprint. I was resting under a nice shady tree minding my own business.

Bennett flashed his big grin. "We need another runner for the 5000. We've got four. We're short one."

I smiled right back at him. "That so?"

"We were thinking maybe you could be the fifth."

"Think again."

"Seeing that Australia is a part of the British Empire and all."

"I hadn't heard."

"Trust me on this one."

"I couldn't run 500 meters if a rabid roo was chasing me."

Bennett brought the smile back. "Don't really matter."

"Does to me."

"Because the way we got it figured," chimed in Rimmer, "is that no matter what you do we can win the thing."

"In that case what I'll do is sit right here and you go and win the thing."

"We've got to enter five. You can start, run as far as you like. A 100-meter sprint. I don't care. Then slow down. Walk if you want to."

"In case you haven't noticed, there are no walking races."

"Yet," said Bennett.

"The crowd will roast me alive."

"No, they'll love it. Great entertainment."

"I'm a runner, not an entertainer."

"I'd say we're all entertainers, and you, I know you love the attention of the crowd."

I'd have to say he was right about that. I'll have to admit to being something of a showman.

"For the sake of the British Empire then?"

"I'll probably regret this, but OK just so long as you guarantee me I won't have to run all 5000 meters. It ain't healthy."

So that's how I became part of the one and only race of the mighty Great Britain 5000-meter team.

Sunday turned out to be yet another scorcher, making the idea of walking even more appealing than it did when initially presented to me. I waxed and trimmed my big (am I allowed to say "impressive"?)

moustache even more carefully than I might have otherwise. Us showman, we've got to make the proper impression, especially if there are young ladies to impress. And there most definitely were some very comely French demoiselles about just waiting to be impressed.

When I got to the track, the others were already there. I suppose they got there early to warm up or something. I had no idea how to warm up for a long race, and besides, I didn't see the point. I wasn't going to run very far anyway and I knew damn well none of them could beat me in the first hundred yards so that would be my race.

I lined up at the start, just like the others, set off in a sprint, easily leaving the others in my wake, then slowed like I was pulling a wagon load of stones.

Well, the spectators were mighty amused. They cheered me in fun every time I crossed by the grandstand, where I would stop and bow politely, raise my cap, have some refreshment, in the form of soda water, take half a lemon in my hand, and resume my march amid the laughter of the French spectators. But when the race was over I still had four more laps to do so I called Pritchard out to accompany me round the track, which we did arm-and-arm until an official allowed me to stop, seeing I could only get last place. It caused great amusement all around.

DICK GRANT The 5000 team run was on Sunday which meant that we weren't going to be able to put together a team of men who could make it that far. Too bad, too, because me and my brother and maybe Orton and Thad McClain would have made a pretty fair team. This, however, didn't seem to stop the Brits who put the sprinter, Rowley on their team. Well, he made a joke of it, hamming it up for the crowd. He was a brawny lad with a big handlebar mustache that curled up on the ends in true style. He looked a little bit like a dandy, but seeing as how he was Australian, that didn't seem so odd.

The race itself was really nothing more than a club contest with a team from the Racing Club de France and the makeshift team from the Amateur Athletic Association of Great Britain with Rowley as the comic relief. He ran a little way then walked … or maybe more accurately, strutted. Other than Rowley the jester, it was a close race most of the way. Rimmer led for the first 1500 meters with Bennett in second and, save for the clown, the rest of the field bunched. On the last lap, Bennett closed in on Rimmer easily in the sprint to the finish, beating his countryman by 25 yards. Two Frenchmen came in third and fourth. When the last runner, a Frenchman, crossed the finish line, Rowley was still on his seventh lap. An official stepped onto the track, stopped him by the elbow and announced he was being awarded 10 points "for finishing in 10th place," except he never actually finished. Maybe they were sympathy points. I don't know how they figured the score, but they said France scored 29 points, and Great Britain/Australia 26. Good old French arithmetic. One of many mysteries of those games.

JOSIAH McCRACKEN Rowley turned what might have been a good race into a charade. It was an unbecoming display of buffoonery and frankly, something of a disgrace to the Olympic ideals. Ironically Rowley received a metal for a race he never finished.

O O O O O

Although not considered an official part of the Olympic Games, the organizers scheduled a few competitions for professionals only. Races were held at 100, 400, 1,500 and 5,000 meters, 110 meter hurdles, 2500-meter steeplechase and a six-hour race with 1,500 French francs going to the winner—a Frenchman. No Americans were entered in any of these. However, America's Michael Sweeney and Otto Schoenfield took first and second respectively in the high jump and long jump events. Schoenfeld also took first in the professional shot put.

Then, too, there were the track and field handicap events.

The idea behind them was to equalize the competition. The times and distances of each contestant in the championship races and field events were taken as yardsticks for the assignment of handicaps, but after the showing made by our men, potential entrants knew that they would have to face heavy handicaps. The handicaps were so severe that they would have little chance to win, so very few even entered, proving that either the Frenchmen were so determined to prevent us from winning any of the handicaps or that they were ignorant of the true system of handicapping. The purpose of handicaps was not to let inferior athletes win, but to put to them on an equal footing, as nearly as possible, with men of acknowledged superiority. In other words, to place everyone in the same class. In all athletic contests the best man ought to have a chance to win, but in the Paris handicaps, that was not the case. To arrange handicaps so that inferior competitors would carry off the prizes seems to me to do injustice to the concept of fair competition.

Handicap competitions were held for the 100, 400, 800 and 1500 meters; 100 and 400 meter hurdles, 2500-meter steeplechase, high jump, long jump, pole vault, shot put and discus.

A few Americans did compete and maybe a few others might have had not some events been held on a Sunday.

Cotton Minahan won the 100 meters (after beating Prinstein in a first round heat) despite a 6-meter handicap, Holland came second with a 4-meter handicap and Pritchard with a 3-meter handicap. David Hall came in fifth in the 400 meters.

I had no intention of running in any handicap race, but at the last moment I gave in and entered the 800-meter. In my heat I lost out to Brown's David Hall. My Olympic running career was over, but there was still a lot in Paris to experience, not the least of which were the non-track and field events.

TWELVE

NUMEROUS SPORTING EVENTS were staged throughout the summer, some of which were or would come to be considered Olympic events, some weren't.

O O O O O

The problem with cricket? It's not widely played outside the United Kingdom and its former colonies. The Brits, though, wanted "their game" at these games.

To the French the seemingly endless boring game was incomprehensible. Baseball was bad enough, but cricket! The English are madmen!

WILLIAM DONNE The French were just too excitable to enjoy the game. No Frenchman could be persuaded to play more than once. A Cricketer in France is a stranger in a strange land looked upon with mingled awe and contempt by the average Frenchman.

Cricket had been originally scheduled for the '96 Games but they couldn't find two teams to compete. So plans for what would have been the only team sport at the first modern Olympics were scuttled.

But blimey, the Brits were determined this time a true cricket match would be played.

After all, we play hard but we always play fair. That's what cricket is and isn't that exactly what Coubertin want? Wasn't that his Olympic ideal?

On Sunday, August 19 and Monday, August 20 a cricket match, which remains unique in Olympic history, took place. It was played at the Municipal Velodrome de Vincennes with its banked cycle track forming an unusual boundary for a cricket pitch. The Velodrome was located out past the western side of the city, far from the Bois de Boulogne where the track and field events were contested.

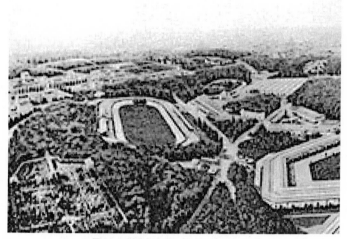

Figure 100 Velodrome de Vincennes

The match was between a British team and a "French team," which was actually a team of English expatriates representing a club formed by English workmen imported to construct the Eiffel Tower.

The British, designated as the visiting side, were represented by the Devon & Somerset Wanderers Cricket Club, a noted touring side. They had been formed six years earlier by William Donne who was on the team in Paris. Players were selected solely based on who was available and who had the funds to travel to Paris.

Both teams comprised distinctly average English club cricketers.

The match had been originally arranged with the usual 11 players on each team, but, by agreement, an additional player was brought into each team at the last minute. Although the game was essentially between two club sides, posters and handbills gave the occasion a fuller international flavor by announcing that it was a match between France and England.

Figure 101 Announcing the cricket match

Play began Sunday at 11 o'clock. The Velodrome, which could seat 20,000 spectators, had maybe 20 bemused gendarmes as the entire audience for this strange sport.

An hour's break for lunch was taken at noon. When play resumed in the afternoon the visitors were all out for 117 runs. The host "French" team replied with a score of 78 and play finished for the day at 5 p.m. With an overnight lead of 39 the Wanderers gave a vastly improved batting display in the second innings and declared their innings closed at 145 runs for five wickets. Needing 185 runs to win, the "French" batting fell apart in the second innings. After losing 10 wickets for only 11 runs the French attempted to play out time but the Wanderers finally won by 158 runs with five minutes to spare.

After the convivial post-match dinner, it was claimed that "England had retained the Olympic title!" No note was made of there being no title to be retained as it was the first and, to date, the only cricket match played during the Olympics.

The victorious team's trip back to the hotel was perhaps more interesting than the match they had just played. They traveled in two coaches. One crashed, causing minor injuries to some passengers; the other was driven by a coachman who had imbibed liberally during the match and had to be replaced.

O O O O O

Plans had been laid for rowing to be part of the 1896 Athens Games. The rowers assembled, but rough water in the Piraeus Harbor forced the cancellation of the regatta. So Paris saw rowing as an Olympic event for the first time.

Figure 102 The rowing competition on the Seine

Rather large crowds lined the banks of the Seine between Courbevoie and Asnières to watch their teams, most of which were French. The official announcement of the regatta said the races would be contested over a course of 1 1/2 miles. In reality, the course was only about one-mile long. The only U.S. representation was by the

Vesper Boat Club from Philadelphia.

As was commonplace in these games, controversy reigned. Throughout the regatta there was wrangling, protests, crew changes and the farce of two finals in the coxed fours, both of which counted in official medal tables.

In the single sculls 12 scullers entered, nine from France and one each from Great Britain, Italy and Spain.

In the first heat the only British sculler in Paris, Saint-George Ashe, rowed far out of his lane and interfered with the Frenchman, Raymond Benoit. Clearly this was grounds for disqualification. Nevertheless, his victory was allowed to stand. Two Frenchmen, Barrelet (actually a Swiss.) and Gaudin, protested and refused to race if Ashe was in the final. After considerable arguing with officials, they reluctantly gave in and agreed to compete.

During the race, another French rower fell in the river and was unable to finish. After climbing out of the water he vehemently protested that he had been interfered with. The officials were unmoved by his protestations. Barrelet won easily. Ashe finished third, 40 seconds behind the winner.

Ten crews entered the coxed fours—five from France, three from Germany and one each from the Netherlands and Spain. What resulted was perhaps the most controversial Olympic rowing event ever. Following protests that crews eliminated in heats two and three had posted better times than the winner of heat one, the regatta jury ignored their own rules and for some reason known only to them, announced a further qualifying round.

Except they didn't announce it to everybody. Some crews never got the word.

So, what to do?

They decided to let the heat winners and the three fastest losers compete in the finals—six boats in all.

Except the course only had four lanes.

So what to do?

Hold two finals.

The heat winners protested and refused to compete.

So the final was held among the runner-up in heat two, and the second and third place finishers in heat three.

Complaints came from competitors and spectators: this isn't a valid championship.

So what to do?

The heat winners then agreed to race each other.

Except the team which had won the "first" final refused to have to compete again.

So the "first" and "second" finals were both officially considered the final finals.

Only three countries entered for the coxed pairs event; France had five crews; Belgium and the Netherlands had one each.

In the heats, the favored Dutch pair of Francois Brandt and Roelof Klein with Dr. Hermanus Gerardus Brockmann as the coxswain, were beaten by a French team but still qualified for the finals by coming second.

FRANCOIS BRANDT   We rowed the best we could, we were stronger than our opponents, we both had many years of rowing experience, we were never beaten in Holland. Therefore, we should have the possibility to win, if only the circumstances were equal! But these were not equal. All those French teams rowed with children in the coxes-chair. As soon as they grew to 25 kilograms they were replaced by lighter ones. And we had to pull 60 kilograms which was the weight of Dr. Brockmann.

When we heard we were in the finals as the fastest losers, our coach, Dr. Meurer, in consultation with our board members who were present decided we should search for a young boy. We found one, a boy who had formerly coxed some French teams. He weighed 33 kilograms. When he sat in the boat the rudder came above the water surface so we had to use an extra lead weight of 5 kilograms attached to the rudder. That brought the fin under the water surface.

Before the final race started we had received information that the French teams, against whom we had to compete and who apparently were scared about our performance, had decided that one of their boats would initially give everything to try to cut across our front and give us 'foul' water, while in the meantime their other boat would keep up with us and then after half the distance row past us. And that is exactly what they did.

We came fourth.

DR. MEURER   It was clear to me that the French should never again compete in rowing races in France. Their conception of sport and the organization of races was more than 25 years outdated!

Figure 103 Brandt, Klein and?

Who was the young boy who coxed that day? His name has been lost, but almost certainly he was the youngest Olympic competitor ever. Most likely he was about 12 years old.

In the coxed eights the Vesper Club of Philadelphia were the American champions, an outstanding club and the odds-on favorites to win the race.

Founded in 1865 they raced on Philadelphia's Schuylkill River and quickly became one of the most celebrated rowing clubs in the world.

In their first heat they were up against a French boat representing the Société de la Marne. It was another warm day and the boats rowed downstream making for fast times. The two-team race quickly turned into a one-team race as the Vesper boat got off to a flying start. The French boat struggled to keep pace and failed to finish the course.

For the finals held the next day, the weather had turned cool and they raced against a headwind and heavy tide. The lineup saw the Vesper Club lined up against a Belgian club, a Dutch club and a combined German/Belgian club.

As soon as they got under way, a fierce headwind raged at them, but they dug grimly in and after a dozen strokes opened a lead they would never yield beating the Belgians by a full six seconds.

Figure 104 The victorious Vesper crew

O O O O O

Coubertin was particularly eager to see rugby played at these games.

BARON DE COUBERTIN   What is admirable in rugby is the perpetual mix of individualism and discipline, the necessity for each man to think, anticipate, take a decision and subordinate one's reasoning, thoughts and decisions to those of the captain. And even the referee's whistle stopping a player for a 'fault' one teammate has made and he hasn't seen, tests his character and patience. For all that, rugby is truly the reflection of life, a lesson experimenting in the real world, a first-rate educational tool.

Rugby was not included in the inaugural games in '96 perhaps because Greece did not play the game, but for Paris, Coubertin gathered three teams: A Parisian team, the Union des Sociétés de Sports Athletiques captained by the legendary Frantz Reichel who was not coincidentally a friend of de Coubertin, the Frankfurt Football Club representing Germany, and the Moseley Wanderers from the United Kingdom.

Figure 105 Franz Reichel

Reichel had competed at the '96 Games as a track and field athlete running the 400 meters and the 110 meter hurdles. He was also considered the best rugby player in France and captained their team.

Also on that team playing wing and center was the Hatian-born Zubiera who had tugged on the French tug-of-war team.

The schedule for the matches had the teams playing on Sundays three weeks apart.

Figure 106 French rugby team

Three things were of particular interest in the rugby competitions:

1.) They drew the biggest crowds of any sport at these games—6,000 for one match.

2.) The first and only black athlete competed.

3.) Two of the three competing teams were awarded medals although they never won a match.

The first Sunday saw the French team play the German team in the Velodrome Municipal at Vincennes. They played using a unique scoring system proposed by de Coubertin. A try or a penalty goal were worth 3 points; a conversion, 2 points, a dropped goal, 4 points.

France came out on top 27–17.

Figure 107 France/Germany rugby match

Figure 108 Scoreboard showing rugby result

The following Sunday Germany was scheduled to play Great Britain but the Germans were nowhere to be found. They were back in Germany. When contacted they said they couldn't remain in Paris for the entire 15 days it would have taken to complete the tournament.

The next week the Mosely Wanderers took on the French side.

The 15-man Mosely Wanderers, captained by J. Henry Birtles, their 26-year-old star, comprised players from nine English clubs. They were a strong team but a tired team, as several of their key players had played Saturday afternoon matches in the Midlands, boarded a train to London immediately after the match and then transferred to another train to the coast. Early Sunday morning they took the cross-channel steamer to France, then a train from the coast to Paris, and another train from central Paris out to Vincennes. They were exhausted before ever setting foot onto the field and France cruised to a 27–8 victory.

So despite not having completed the round-robin tournament as planned, France was given first place. Although neither Germany nor Great Britain had won a match, Germany was awarded second place on the basis that they scored more points than Great Britain. That left third place for the Mosely Wanderers.

O O O O O

Fencing was the most popular sport among French spectators and they turned out in large numbers for the events held all over the city, stretching from the middle of May to the end of June. French fencing fanaticism was on display and the French press covered fencing like no other events.

It is our sport! Nowhere in the world can people handle the blades like we do in France.

The French fencing master is supreme in the world.

French fencing masters were paid to give lessons. Some made their living by arranging duels for aggrieved combatants.

They were professional swordsmen.

Initially Coubertin balked at the fencing professionals but he came to realize that the sport was so popular in France and the top fencing masters so well-known, there would be no denying them entrance. Of the 258 competitors, 211 were French, two were from the USA—Messrs. Weill and Orleans. Neither advanced out of their pools.

Figure 109 Fencing poster

Events were held for the épée (the dueling sword), the sabre (the ancient scimitar like combat weapon) and the foil (the artistic instrument).

The French dominated … with one major exception.

Ramon Fonst was a sensational young Cuban épée swordsman.

He was a 17-year-old slim, tall fencer. With his épée seemingly always perfectly aligned he showed a sharp riposte and an accurate advancing attack. His patience and tenacity in the face of adversity were exceptional.

What a genuinely skilled fencer he was.

He may have been Cuban but he lived and trained in France. The French would have to be content with that.

After his victory he told the French press he owed it all to his French instructor, master Ayat.

Figure 110 Albert Ayat

He is also a genuinely skilled politician.

The amateur part of the tournament with 154 swordsmen, opened the proceedings with 17 qualifying rounds. The top two from each round progressed to the semifinals and after 36 bouts, the top three from each of the three semifinals competed.

In the final barrage in épée, Fonst touched Perrée and was declared the first Olympic champion from Latin America.

RAMON FONST   I was only 17, and despite the frank and powerful hostility of the judges, who not only saw me as a foreigner, a Latin American, an intruder, but a boy who should be studying in high school and not defeating consecrated idols, I won the Olympic championship.

In the masters épée event for the professionals, the nine-man final was an all-French affair bringing together the famous names in French fencing. The champion was the celebrated Albert Ayat. Emile Bougno came in second. Both were exciting to watch with very strong attacks and confident parries.

Then it was time for the amateurs and professionals to compete in the same event. This is not exactly what Coubertin had in mind, but it was what the French officials had in mind.

The top four amateurs and the top four professionals competed. Much to the delight of their supporters, Ayat and Fonst, were the top professional and amateur, respectively. Ayat walked away with 3000 francs for winning without sustaining a single touch.

Figure 111 Fonst (left) parries Ayat

Since the foil event was considered the most artful, in the early rounds the fencers were judged by a panel of judges on their level of "skill and artistry." Those with the highest score advanced to the next round.

Who cares who wins each contest? The best looking fencers move on.

So if you win your round you may not get to the next round?

That's right.

But if you lose you might?

That's right.

The French love their fencing despite—or maybe because—it has its peculiarities.

O O O O O

The shooting competition was nothing if not confusing.

Six thousand, three hundred and 51 marksmen competed. Of those 6,098 were French.

Of the 38 events contested, some were considered Olympic events, some were not depending on who was doing the considering.

Some events were limited to competitors from sanctioned shooting societies. Some were handicapped events; some were restricted to certain classes of shooters such as army officers.

Virtually all marksmen were competing for prize money— sometimes lots of prize money.

The official Olympic report shows that 518,602 shots were fired.

Competitions were held for military rifles, free rifles, military pistols, free pistols, small-bore rifles and shotguns.

Figure 112 The shooting stand

There were competitions for "youth" military rifle shooting, shooting at silhouettes of a human form, and various competitions for military personnel in separate categories for active army soldiers, territory army soldiers, and officers only.

The event attracting the most competitors (201) was the popular running wild boar shooting event. Competitors aimed at a moving model of a wild boar from a distance of 40 meters.

In the only competition in Olympic history when animals were purposely killed, almost 300 pigeons were shot from the sky. The live pigeon shooting event saw 52 marksmen shoot from a distance of 27 meters from where the birds were released. The day consisted of two rounds of shooting with each shooter getting a shot at one bird. On the second day, shooters continued to shoot until they missed two birds. The prize on offer was 20,000 French francs. However, before the final birds were brought down, the four remaining shooters decided they would split the prize equally. A Belgian shooter, Léon de Lunden, who killed 21 birds, took top honors and the 7,340 franc prize share.

Figure 113 Léon de Lunden looks for pigeons

Among the four Americans in the day's pigeon massacre was Albert Spalding, who missed all but four birds. The best American shot was Hannibal Crittenden Robinson, a 43-year-old Oklahoman sharpshooter. He came in third by bringing down 18 pigeons and so was one of the four who split the top prize.

By the end of the third day the field at the Bois de Boulogne was littered with pigeon blood and feathers. Presumably more than a few Paris restaurants that night offered roast pigeon on the menu of the day.

O O O O O

Not all the pigeons of Paris were killed in the pigeon slaughtering event, however.

Pigeon racing was an event in which trained birds were released into the air and then assuming they avoided the skies above the pigeon shooting competitions, they returned to a designated location. The fastest pigeon was the winner.

Seven pigeon racing events were contested. The names of the medal winners were not recorded.

O O O O O

If this sounds confusing, it is because it is. In polo there were multiple tournaments with teams that kept changing representing various nations with no apparent rhyme or reason. A team called Compiègne represented France and another represented Mexico whose riders were identified as Spanish. The best French player, Maurice Raoul-Duval, played for both the French team and the Bagatelle Polo Club de Paris with all French players except their captain, Agnew Gill, who was British. Perhaps his position as their manager somehow qualified him as French. Another team, BLO Polo Club Rugby, combined players from Great Britain and the United States. A team called the Foxhunters had players from Great Britain, Ireland, and two players from the United States—John Mackay and the irrepressible Foxhall Parker Keene, one of the more interesting characters of these games.

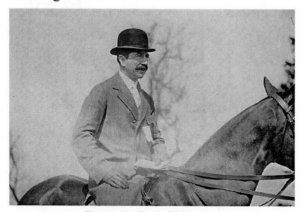

Figure 114 Foxhall Keene

Thanks to his father, who had accumulated millions by investing in mining stock, Foxy Keene had enough money to play at anything he chose and he chose many things, work not being one of them. He was the epitome of the gentleman sportsman. He rode in fox hunts, rode in steeplechases, bred racehorses. As a golfer he competed in the U. S. Open. As a tennis player he competed in the U. S. Championships. As a race car driver he competed in the prestigious Gordon Bennett Cup in Ireland. As a boxer he won numerous tournaments. As a polo player he was rated the best all-around player in the United States for eight consecutive years.

Above all, though, he was a horse person through and through. He says his first memory is running after a horse. When he was seven his father said they were moving to a place he called "the East." Foxy was upset and asked his father if they could take his horse in their private car with his fighting cocks.

FOXHALL KEENE We moved to a fashionable community out on Long Island. It was a very sporting community. Everyone rode, hunted, played polo, fairly lived out of doors. Sunday mornings you could see 40 or 50 men riding over the countryside, larking over the fences and having a wonderful carefree time. I was just 14 when I was invited to join the prestigious Rockaway Hunting Club.

I began fox hunting mounted on a pony and scrambled over fences like a dog. Soon I was riding horses against adults in steeplechase races.

In my first steeplechase race my hands and forearms were so tired that that I could scarcely hold the reins. Half a mile from the finish, the reins dropped from my fingers altogether and I held on by matting my hands in the mane. I won by 150 yards. I have to admit I was more dead than alive at the end. I told myself you can't do anything well in this world unless you work at it, so I set out to develop my own system of training as a boy in a man's game. My secret goal was to become the best amateur jockey in the U.S. My training was rigorous. Before breakfast I would go on 30-yard sprints, increasing to 80 yards as my muscles tuned up. Often I ran a mile on the beach at dawn or jogged for hours on the roads, holding the tail gate of a wagon and wearing a rubber shirt.

I decided a steeplechaser should hunt seriously. I learned to follow hounds straight across country like an express train and never to turn my head while hunting. I wasn't the only bold rider around, however. I was mightily impressed when Mr. Theodore Roosevelt came a crumpler and broke his arm, yet remounted and finished the hunt. That's the kind of dedication I was after.

Before my 17th birthday I became the nation's champion jockey, amateur or professional over the sticks. In one season I won 79 of the 101 races I entered while thousands of bettors blessed my name.

The professional jockeys with whom I competed were no altarboys, so I had to be ready and willing to fight both on the course and after the race in the paddock. That's when I took on a professional trainer to teach me to box. The game is for blood, with everything to the fit man.

Somehow I found time to take up polo in an organized way.

Foxy was a great partner for adult golfers and tennis players and entered several 10-mile walking races. It wasn't long before he discovered he was very good at shooting. His father even offered to bet $100,000 on his son at $10,000 each in any 10 sports, but his reputation as an all-around sportsman was so great that there were no takers.

FOXHALL KEENE One day a great pigeon shoot was announced. A man named Colonel Wagstaff bought me in a pool for $2, lent me a shotgun and told me to fire away. I bet $5 on myself, killed 13 pigeons in a row and won $565.

Figure 115 Polo in the Bois de Boulogne

All the polo matches took place at the Bagatelle Polo Club in the Bois de Boulogne. It was a straight elimination contest. In the preliminary round the Foxhunters rode roughshod over Compiegne winning 10 goals to none. Then they beat Bagatelle 6-4. In the second semifinal, Rugby defeated Mexico 8-0. Then in a tightly fought final match, the Foxhunters defeated Rugby 3-1 and the other teams were jointly awarded third place.

Foxy Keene was the obvious ringleader of his side. Whereas most players in the match concentrated on short passes to move the ball toward the opposition's goal Foxy had other ideas, sending long passes downfield to teammates who had broken away from the pack at a full gallop. They played a high speed game that none of the others could keep up with. And did Foxy ever enjoy himself. His exuberance and daring play was on glorious display for the appreciative crowd.

O O O O O

By the turn of the century athletic options for women were ... limited. Maybe a little golf on a shortened course, a gentle game of tennis or croquet. Ladies would not appear in public without a full-length dress and hat, so why in the world would they ever be seen in anything resembling athletic uniforms. Nothing sweaty to be sure. Nothing that required too much muscle. Nothing that would get a lady dirty or overly tired. In any sport in which they competed, the focus was on correct posture, a feminine body and always ladylike behavior. Not many women entered competitive events, and the few who did were looked on with disfavor. And no lady would ever compete against a man. Good heavens, whatever would happen if a woman won!

A woman's body was just not up to the rigors of athletic competition. Their reproductive systems were too fragile, so refraining from competing was a matter of protecting their health.

Baron de Coubertin could see no role for women in the Olympics. It was not a woman's place to compete. A woman's place was to encourage her sons to compete and excel.

In the ancient Greek Games not only were women not allowed to participate, they weren't even permitted to watch. In the '96 Games they could watch but not participate.

Except one did ... sort of.

A Greek woman, Stamata Revithi showed up to run the marathon.

Don't be ridiculous, said the officials. Women can't run a marathon. You'll get hurt.

I know I can finish.

Not allowed.

So either because she had been told that to run the marathon and win was to get rich, or because she wanted to prove a point about women's athletic abilities, she ran the marathon course ... the day after the men. Starting at 8:00 in the morning, she had various people sign a testament as to her starting time and then began her long solo run. When she arrived at the finishing stadium 5 1/2 hours later she was denied entry and had to run around the outside of the stadium. The officials called her Melpomene, after the Greek muse of tragedy.

By 1900 things had changed. Much to Coubertin's chagrin, women made their first Olympic appearance.

Because the International Olympic Committee, which was against women competitors, was less influential than the Exposition authorities, 23 women from five countries (Great Britain, Switzerland, France, USA and Bohemia) were allowed to compete in ballooning, croquet, golf, equestrianism and tennis.

The one thing the women competitors in 1900 had in common was that they were socialites all.

Margaret Abbott was a Chicago socialite. She played golf well and she was in Paris. Born in Calcutta, India to wealthy parents, her father, Charles Abbott, was a successful merchant. After they moved to Chicago, her mother, Mary, became a novelist and respected newspaper editor.

In Chicago the family was very much a part of the active social scene and members of the Chicago Golf Club, the oldest 18-hole course in North America and one of the five clubs which formed the United States Golf Association in 1894. Its founder, Charles MacDonald, learned the game while a student in Scotland. He returned to Chicago with a set of clubs in 1892, and after passing the hat among friends, collected enough to create the course.

Women's golf was one of the few sports open to women. Why not? It was a non-contact sport, did not require exertion beyond a woman's capabilities, did not injure the female organs, and did not require women to wear unsightly uniforms or special dress. Fashionable golf attire became quite the thing.

To participate, a woman had to have the means to finance clubs and club membership, so only the well-heeled played. The idea of public golf courses was still some time off.

Encouraged by her mother, Mary took up the game and soon became recognized as a fierce competitor—at least insofar as women could be considered fierce. *The Chicago Tribune* said that she had "acquired the same fierce driving ability and accuracy of putting that characterizes the play of her instructor, Edward Frost."

Representing the Chicago Golf Club with a handicap of two, she won the prestigious Deering Cup shooting a 61 for nine holes. She was awarded a gold belt.

Throughout the 1898 season she entered five ladies and mixed foursome matches, usually partnered with her brother who was then a student at Harvard.

At nearly 6 feet, she was tall for her generation and could generate considerable club speed allowing her to win at least one ladies long driving contest.

Margaret played in a long dress, flat leather shoes, a smart blouse and tie. Her long hair was put up under a hat.

MARGARET ABBOTT   My mother was a good player and encouraged me in my playing but golf wasn't in our plans when we sailed to France. We were set for an extended stay in Paris where I would study art and use the city as a base to tour other parts of Europe. Paris had long been a favorite of Chicago's "steamship set."

The trip was planned so that while in Paris we could enjoy the great Paris World's Fair.

Once settled in Paris, however, we learned that as part of the Fair, there would be a ladies international golf tournament. Why not enter, suggested Mother. I felt I was good enough to compete with the best women golfers, and Mother, while not as strong a player as I was, could hold her own.

So we both entered the match held at the course in Compiegne, a town on the edge of a forest about 60 miles north of Paris. The course itself, nestled in the beautiful forest, was laid out within the horse racing track. A mostly flat course, its fairways were lined with dense rough. The greens, as was the typical of the times, were postage-stamp size.

Ten women were entered. Five were French. Besides Mother and I, there were three other Americans—Pauline Whittier, Daria Pratt and Ellen Ridgeway.

Daria Pratt was vacationing in France. She was a member of the Dinard Club in Brittany and traveled in the highest of social circles. She and her husband spent much of their time in Europe socializing with royalty. After her husband died, she would marry a Serbian prince and become Princess Alexis Karageorgevitch of Serbia. Polly Whittier was from a wealthy Boston family and was studying at St. Moritz in Switzerland. She was a descendant of the famous poet, John Greenleaf Whittier.

The men played 36 holes stroke play, we played nine. Our tees set a course of 1,336 yards, or 139 yards shorter than theirs. The longest hole was the sixth at 213 yards; the shortest, the second at 64 yards.

Golf was catching on among the higher class French women so there were quite a few spectators who turned out for our event. So many if fact that we had difficulty getting off some shots because they crowded so close.

Right from the start the French ladies showed they were not the American's equal. They were eager but did not have the skills either in driving the fairways or reading the greens.

The match was a good contest between me, Polly Wittier and Daria Pratt. At the end I shot a 47 to take a two shot victory over Polly and six over Daria. Mother finished seventh with a 65. The last place French woman shot 80.

Figure 116 Ladies golf

DARIA PRATT So we won Olympic titles ... but we didn't know it. Not then. We all understood it was an international tournament, something we would never have found back in the U.S., but it was years before I realized we were part of the Olympics. I'm not sure Margaret ever knew.

Twelve gentlemen contested their event, also on the Compiegne course. Charles Sands, of the St. Andrews Golf Club in Yonkers, won by a single shot over Walter Rutherford of Jedburgh, Scotland. Sands was a well-known athlete. Primarily a tennis player, he was the United States champion in court tennis.

Figure 117 Charles Sands on the course

The event was well attended by the Paris society elite including a prince, a princess, several Comptes and Comtesses.

O O O O O

The English woman, Charlotte Cooper, was a three time Wimbledon champion. The youngest daughter of a successful miller, she learned to play tennis at the Ealing Lawn Tennis Club in England. It wasn't long after taking up the game that she began to win regularly.

Known for an attacking style of tennis seldom seen in ladies' tennis, she was one of the few women anywhere who served overhead. It was said she could volley like a man and match anyone tactically.

Perhaps her aggressive play was compensation for her deafness.

Not very ladylike, though, is it?

The times, they are a' changing.

Figure 118 Charlotte Cooper

The tennis events were held at the L'île de Puteaux club set beautifully on a small island in the middle of the River Seine. It was where the fashionable set met to socialize, dine and play tennis.

The L'ïlle de Puteaux sports club began in 1886 when the racquet sport was still unknown by the majority of France, but it was at the vanguard of spreading the popularity of lawn tennis throughout France.

CHARLOTTE COOPER   The surroundings were enchanting and the shade of the island provided a welcome respite from the extreme heat of the city. The Olympic event was wonderful, the competition was wonderful, the weather ideal, and the organization perfect. It was quite an elegant affair.

The turnout was rather small, but everyone there seemed to enjoy the magnificent setting, the engaging atmosphere, and the quality of the competition.

Several other top players were entered in the women's event. Probably the strongest group of women tennis players ever to meet in one event.

Marion Jones, the reigning U.S. champion, was the daughter of Nevada Senator John Percival Jones, founder of the town of Santa Monica in California.

Hélène Prévost was the winner of the French Open Women's Singles Championship and said to be the best player in Europe.

Figure 119 Hélène Prévost

Hedwiga Rosenbaumová was from Bohemia and thought to be at least the second best lady player in Europe.

All the matches were to be decided in straight sets.

Cooper went up against Jones in the first match and came out on top. In the second match Prévost beat Rosenbaumová in a close game.

The title went Cooper's way when she beat Prévost rather easily.

CHARLOTTE COOPER Then later in the mixed doubles I teamed up with Reggie Doherty, known to all simply as "R.F." I have to say we were a rather formidable pair as he was simply a magnificent and very stylish player. In the semis we played Marion Jones and R.F.'s younger brother Laurence, at least the equal of R.F. I think everyone was expecting it to be a tight contest, but it wasn't. We took it in straight sets and then easily won again against Hélène and her partner, Harold Mahony, the Scottish born Irish player, to take the title.

Charlotte Cooper demonstrated that she was the strongest lady player in the world who competed like a man, but with the grace and elegance of a true woman.

Although not many people witnessed the ladies' tennis, those who did came away impressed. Those ladies could play.

On the men's side, all suspense was lost when the Doherty brothers announced they would play as teammates in the doubles events. They were so dominant it looked as if had they needed to, they could have won every point. As it was, they won easily. Hugh took the singles over Harold Mahony, with his brother Reginald coming third.

Figure 120 The Doherty brothers face Mahony and Norris

O O O O O

An expensive sand court in a field of the Bois de Boulogne was built for croquet, but only one paying viewer turned up to watch the all-French event.

Figure 121 Croquet competition

Since croquet was regarded as an appropriate activity for women, three female athletes competed—Mme. Filleaul Brophy, Mlle, Marie Ohnier and Mme. Després. All three competed in the singles competition, an elimination contest with several rounds. They competed on an equal basis with men.

French men won all four events—singles for one ball, singles for two balls, doubles and a handicap singles event.

O O O O O

Of the 135 contestants in gymnastics, 108 were French. None were from the United States.

Events at the Velodrome at Vincennes consisted of horizontal bar, parallel bar, rings, pommel horse, floor exercises, long horse vault, high jump, long jump, pole vault and rope climbing. However, only the "combined exercises," counted as an Olympic event. The athletes were scored for "style" points as they met certain pre-set standards. In the long jump they were expected to jump 5 meters; in the pole vault 2.20 meters. In a combined high and long jumps they had to jump over a rope held at 1.25 meters while taking off from a point 1 meter from the rope. In rope climbing they climbed hand over hand up a 6-meter-long rope. In weightlifting they scored 2 points for each overhead lift of a 50 kg. However, the scoring topped out at 10 repetitions for 20 points.

Three Frenchmen, Sandras, Bas and Démanet took the honors.

O O O O O

Four football games loosely connected to the Olympics were scheduled, all involving the French team. The matches were to be against Switzerland, Belgium, Germany and Great Britain. However, neither the Swiss nor German teams made it to Paris. So the two football games they could play were in reality, exhibition matches between France and Great Britain and then France and Belgium. In the first game, Great Britain, represented by the Upton Park Football Club easily defeated France 4-0. J. Nicholas scored two goals and then retired injured. In the second game France topped Belgium, 6-2.

So much for the world's most popular game.

Figure 122 Belgian football team

O O O O O

The swimming events were, if nothing else, unusual, even by the standards of these Games. Held quite some distance from Paris at Asnières, a muddy section of the Seine, the swimmers had to contend with boats and garbage.

Figure 123 Swimming competitors ready to enter the Seine

Events included the 200-meter obstacle course in which the competitors had to first climb a tall pole, then scramble over a row of boats, then dive back in the river and swim under a second row of boats. Frederick Lane, the celebrated Australian swimmer climbed, scrambled, dove and swam faster than anyone else and took gold.

Lane also won the 200-meter freestyle event. The swimmers were propelled downstream so fast that he beat the world's record by 13 seconds.

In the underwater swimming competition, swimmers were awarded two points for each meter swum and one point for each second they stayed underwater. The best swimmer was the Dane, Peder Lykkeberg, who covered over 60 meters, but he swam in circles. The officials, though measured the distance in a straight line from the starting point so Lykkeberg was given third place even though he swam the farthest. Charles de Vendeville, a Frenchman was awarded first.

Figure 124 Beginning of swimming race

In the 200-meter team swimming event the British team was favored but they showed up late and missed the start.

In the 200-meter backstroke event the swimmers first dove from a high perch and then turned on their backs. Ernst Hoppenberg won the event by a wide margin.

John Jarvis of Great Britain won the downstream 4000-meter freestyle event by over two minutes.

A French swimmer named Verbecke won his heat in the 1000-meter freestyle by almost seven minutes and then came in eighth in the finals. John Jarvis took that event also.

The only two American swimmers in these competitions swam in the fourth heat of the 200-meter freestyle event. Neither advanced to the finals.

O O O O O

By 1900 cycling had become hugely popular in the United States. Millions of men, women and children were a-wheel. In the larger cities cycle racing was popular, attracting both amateurs and professionals.

Although at a directors meeting of the American Bicycle Company it had been decided to send an American cycle racing team to Paris made up of at least three riders and maybe as many as seven, only one amateur cyclist from New York City arrived in Paris. John Lake, a member of the big Harlem Wheelman cycle club, had set national records at eight, nine and 10 miles.

Figure 125 Racing on the Vincennes track

Events were held for amateurs and professionals and included handicap and tandem races. Cycling was the leading sport in France, and some of the greatest racers of the day competed, including French standouts Ferdinand Vasserot, Georges Taillander and Ferdinand Sanz.

In the premier event, the 200-meter match sprint, 21 heats preceded the finals. Lake won his three rounds of heats but was soundly beaten by Taillander and Sanz, settling for third in the finals.

Figure 126 Taillander, Sanz and Lake line up for 200-meter final

O O O O O

The equestrian events included the horse high jump won by an Italian rider at a height of 1.85 meters. The horse long jump event required rider and horse to clear a barrier 4.50 meters wide and then barriers of increasing lengths. A Belgian rider won that on a horse called Extra-Dry. In the horse combined jumping event, horse and riders had to clear one double jump, one triple jump and one 4-meter-wide river jump. A Belgian rider on Benton II took those top honors.

There was also a mail coach event in which competitors drove carriages drawn by four horses. They had to demonstrate control of their horses in precise prancing, cross-country driving and obstacle course navigation. Another Belgian won that.

A Frenchman named Napoleon won the Hacks and Hunter Combined event on a horse named The General owned by a princess. During the event hunter hacks were scored on their manners, gait, arc and stride over fences.

Figure 127 Louis de Champsavin on Terpsichore

O O O O O

Eight sailing classes made up the yachting competitions. The six smaller classes competed in the Seine near Meulan. Most sailors were from France but there were some from Great Britain, Germany, The Netherlands, Switzerland and the United States.

The conditions along the east-west river were hardly ideal. Buildings and trees along the banks partly blocked what little north-easterly breeze there was.

Figure 128 Yachts racing on the Seine

In the opening event—the Open Class— due largely to the still conditions, of the 49 yachts that started, only seven finished within the time limit. Of the seven finishers, two were disqualified for using "other means of propulsion than the sail."

The next three days of racing found the river so blocked with vessels of all sizes that it was virtually impossible for the yachts to steer clear of each other.

One yachting competitor was already famous; one would soon be. Édouard Alphonse James de Rothschild was an aristocrat, financier and member of the prominent Rothschild Banking family of France. Hélène de Pourtalès was an American born yachtswoman competing in the Swiss boat *Lérina*, which won the gold medal in the 2-3-ton class and thus became the first woman to win an Olympic gold medal.

OOOOO

The water polo tournament featured teams from Belgium, France, Germany and Great Britain. The Osborne Swimming Club from Manchester, England, dominated the three-round tournament and easily defeated the swimmers from Belgium for the gold medal.

Figure 129 Water polo match

O O O O O

Open to anyone with a bow and arrow, some 5,200 archers competed in events ranging from target shooting at 20 meters to 50 meters.

The archers assembled on the Place de Nation to beating drums and flying colors. They then marched in columns of four to the Velodrome at Vincennes with the strung bows carried in their right hands. The French archery champions of 1898 and 1899 attired in distinctive scarves, had the honor of leading the parade with the drums beating and the colors flying all the way.

Eighteen events were won by Frenchmen; one by a Belgian.

Shooting at a stuffed popinjay at the top of a tall pole was unquestionably the crowd favorite.

Figure 130 Archery competitors shooting at popinjay

O O O O O

Three events had been organized for Pelota Basque competitors—two for amateurs; one for professionals. However, only two events were contested as there were no entrants for the open palm event. Spanish teams won both contested events.

Figure 131 Pelota Basque

O O O O O

A few events were from the outset, always considered demonstration sports.

Baseball may have been a big deal back home, but it was ignored by the Europeans, who, when it came to team games, much preferred their football. At Mr. Spalding's urging, however, a game was organized. After all baseball was his sport.

A single game was played by two American teams. One team was formed from the guard corps of the United States Commission and the other from men in the publishers building in the Exposition. The guard corps won 19 to 9.

O O O O O

It wasn't long after the invention of the combustion engine that France became the country where motorsport flourished. As early as 1894 auto races were run from Paris to Rouen, a distance of about 82 miles. The first winner was Emile Levassor, driving a Panhard-Levassor car. The Paris-Bordeaux-Paris race saw Andre Michelin drive a car equipped with the new pneumatic tires. France was in love with auto racing so it was perhaps inevitable that motorsport races should be part of their Exposition, if not officially part of the games.

Sixteen events for automobiles and motorcycles were contested. The organizers had trouble getting permission to close off the route and could only do so a few days before it began. Almost all drivers were French.

The 835 mile Paris-Toulouse-Paris race was 835 miles long and got started at 3:07 in the morning with the contestants departing at two minute intervals. The cars had to pass each of the 82 control points. Fifty-five large cars started the race; 21 finished. First place medals went to the two drivers who averaged over 35 miles an hour and other medals to five others who averaged over 25 mph. Eight smaller cars also entered. Three finished.

Other events were held on a 30-mile loop near Vincennes. The cars drove one lap in the morning and two in the afternoon. They were not to exceed 18 mph in open areas, and 12 mph in inhabited areas. Several cars were excluded from receiving the prizes for belonging to jury members, exceeding the speed limits, or failing to meet the weight requirements. In the race with smaller cars, Armand

Peugeot took the first place prize. Louis Renault was among the other winners.

Figure 132 Louis Renault

Motorcycles had to complete 70 laps of the track; 30 in the morning, 40 in the afternoon.

Other events included races between taxis, delivery cars and trucks.

O O O O O

The invention of kites is said to have occurred in China, some 2,800 years ago.

Who doesn't love the exhilarating feel of a soaring, darting kite silhouetted against the summer sky on the end of a taut piece of rope?

It's a natural for the Olympics, isn't it?

Kites?

Sure, why not?

So three competitions were held with (athletes?) attempting to fly their kites in the most stylish, imaginative, artistic manner possible. The trickier the moves the better. The more elaborate the maneuvers, the more points were awarded.

The wind, however, was not a cooperative Olympic supporter. Kites were continuously getting tangled with other kites. After a strong gust of the French summer wind blew most competitors kites into nearby trees, the judges huddled.

Maybe we need to rethink this event.

Maybe it's not … right for the Olympics.

O O O O O

In an attempt to appeal to audiences who wanted to see lives put on the line (there's a reason gladiatorial games were once so popular), the Olympic Committee instated lifesaving as an exhibition sport.

Competitions included those between fire departments in the woods of Vincennes and lifeguards in the Seine.

ALBERT SPALDING   Kansas City sent its famous engine and hook and ladder company No. 1, $15,000 having been raised due to the personal efforts of the patriotic mayor of that city. The rapid and perfect manner in which the company, under the command of its captain, George C. Hale, performed its maneuvers and thrilling life–saving drills excited the admiration and the repeated and long applause of the great crowds assembled to witness this, one of the most interesting features of the exhibition sports.

Figure 133 Kansas City Hook & Ladder Company

Besides the obvious superiority of the professional personnel of the Kansas City brigade, the American engine was also superior, throwing two streams of water at the same time of greater volume and 50 feet farther and higher than its nearest competitor, which only threw one. The horses were 'war circus' horses, especially trained for the occasion. Kansas City was awarded the Grand Prix de l'Exposition and excluded from further competitions because … they were too good.

In the amateur ranks, teams from Portugal and Hungary took top honors.

O O O O O

The French, being keen balloonists, insisted on including ballooning competitions for the Games—just so long as they were held away from the shooting and archery events. Weather conditions had to be just right, air currents needed to be optimal and cloud cover had to be minimal. Large crowds turned up for the contests which took place in the Air Station at Vincennes. The competitions were for races of free balloons (including reproductions of famous balloons), and montgolfiers. Prizes were awarded for the longest distance traveled, greatest height achieved, longest time traveled, the shortest distance traveled to a fixed point and targeted stopping competitions which involved flying over a target and dropping a weighted marker to see who could get closest. And some people think soccer is a dull sport.

The overall winner was the Frenchman, Comte Henry de la Vaulx.

Figure 134 The ballooning competition getting under way

Vaulx set a distance record of 1,193 miles and didn't come down until he reached Korosticheff, Russia.

Competitions were held for the different systems of inflating with suitable prizes awarded to those judged to be the most rapid, and in contests of photography taken from balloons, prizes were awarded according to the perceived excellence of the pictures.

Figure 135 Judging the fishing competitors

A contest for fishing for live fish in the Seine seemed to stir the enthusiasm of the Parisians. Some 600 fishermen from six countries cast their lines in the Seine.

The fish won.

O O O O O

Motor boats from 6.5 to 15 meters long competed in eight races at distances from 12 to 60 kilometers. All the competitors were French. They were also the only competitors in both bowls events and the longue-paume tournament, an ancestor of modern tennis still popular in parts of France.

THIRTEEN

AFTER THE TRACK AND FIELD EVENTS CONCLUDED, the American athletes were invited to a splashy reception at the American Pavilion with Commissioner Peck playing majordomo.

A table laid out in the form of a horseshoe occupied the entire first floor of the United States Pavilion. The galleries were filled, mostly with American women who, as *The Clipper* reported, "greatly enjoyed the scene and the many good things said, even if they did not partake of the choice edibles and bibbles so relished by the participating athletes and guests."

Toasts were offered up by Peck, Ambassador Porter and Director Spalding, each receiving a rousing cheer.

Good feelings ran rife throughout the pavilion. Why not? The team performed splendidly at the games, didn't it? We expected to do well, but we did even better than we might have expected before setting sail for Europe. Who knew how stiff the competition would be from the rest of the world? OK, we received a hint when we whipped the English athletes so soundly before Paris, but we knew other challenges were ahead. Now the challenges were behind us and we had a right to celebrate, and celebrate we did.

Our college teams serenaded the guests with lively renditions of our college songs and cheers as might have been heard at football games.

Toast: To Mike Murphy, the greatest trainer in the world.

Toast: To the entire American track and field team. The greatest track and field team in the world.

After the toasts, Ambassador Porter stood, looked around the impressive athletic assemblage and offered up comments.

HORACE PORTER   You are the men who in the future will be our leaders. As you led the field these days in athletics, so will you lead in the future our businesses and our industries and in the affairs of state. I regret that when I was a youth I had not the opportunity to become an athlete that is afforded to you young men of today, which would have enabled me to build up a body and constitution that would be with me through my entire career.

Athletics, as it is understood, benefits the American race as it has the English race. England is a great country and the home of outdoor recreation, yet we Americans who have only been 20 or 25 years in the athletic field now excel England in many respects.

If you travel the world over and see the young men entering upon the 20th century, men who will be the fathers of the future, and you place them side-by-side in athletic competition, you will be convinced that the leaders of the 20th century will be giants in every respect, physically, mentally and morally.

George Orton responded for us with a rousing speech. He had studied up on a few words in half a dozen foreign languages and tossed them all in for good luck and with the best intentions in the world.

After the party ended, led by Kraenz we headed jubilantly out into the streets of Paris where we scrambled up the steps leading to the facade of the Opéra Garnier. There, standing in front of the giant classical columns and the busts of Beethoven, Mozart, Rossini and other famous composers we celebrated in high style.

O O O O O

On the final day of the Exposition it rained in the afternoon, but by night it was clear and crisp. All the pavilions were flooded with light. The entrance gate, the arcades, the illuminated fountains drew all the power Paris could muster. At ten o'clock a cannon cracked from the Eiffel Tower and colored filters were changed all over the Exposition. As the fog moved in the Exposition ended in a surreal glow. An appropriate ending to the surreal games.

O O O O O

Back in Philadelphia, Kraenz, Tewks and Bax sit on a rock under the red and gold autumn colors of a sprawling maple tree. The late October setting sun casts long shadows on the Schuylkill River unwinding like a thin, black ribbon in front of them.

Together they had won 14 track and field medals in Paris—more than any single country other than the United States. Still, when they had arrived back in Philadelphia a week earlier, they were publicly denounced in some reports for having competed on Sunday.

Gentleman, it's about that time, Kraenz says.

Tewks and Bax nod in agreement.

They take their shoes that had carried them to so many victories and without saying another word, they heave them far out into the river.

Their athletic careers are over.

In the years to come, the Olympic movement will flourish and become the world's biggest, most celebrated sporting spectacle. The transcendent athletic accomplishments of Kraenz, Tewks and Bax will largely be forgotten.

FOURTEEN

WITHOUT DOUBT many more athletes competed in Paris than in Athens four years earlier. But how many more? It is impossible to say with any accuracy. How many sports were included? It is impossible to say with any accuracy. How many events were contested? Also impossible to say with any accuracy.

The figures for the number of athletes competing is generally given as around 1,300 but the question remains: which events were Olympic and which were not? The answer to that question determines the number of Olympic competitors. But, for any number of reasons, the answer isn't clear and never will be.

For years after the Paris Games, various committees and researchers tried to pin this down without much agreement. Throughout that summer there were few references to "Olympic Games." Events were given assorted names—*Concours Internationaux, Championnnats d'Exposition,* among others.

Some events such as the handicap competitions and professional only events were always considered simply as part of the Paris Exhibition, but the category of other events remains unclear.

The IOC had no control over the Exposition and the listings of official Olympic events. It wasn't until well after all events were finished that the IOC took up the issue of which events had been Olympic and which were not. They decided that the marathon was, but firefighting was not, that shooting was, but pigeon racing not. Some professional events were later considered by the IOC to be Olympic, some weren't.

To this day, confusion reigns over exactly how many events were truly Olympic. Of course, no question about the track and field scratch events. They have always been the foundation of the Olympics.

O O O O O

Some events drew only French competitors. Picard believed the value of the prizes may have been to blame.

When the modern Olympic Games began in 1896 winners received an olive wreath and a silver medal. But for most sports in Paris no medals were awarded although various prizes were. These were objects of art supposedly valued at 400 francs for first, 200 for second and 50 for third. The first and second prizes for the marathon, valued at Fr. 500 and 250 respectively, were the gifts of an American silver manufacturing company, the first being a large silver loving cup and the second one somewhat smaller. That company also gave prizes in the standing high and broad jumps.

CASPAR WHITNEY   The prizes were decidedly inartistic bronze birds, silver pins and studs, walking sticks, knives and that sort of thing.

ARTHUR ROWLEY   I won three prizes in Paris. One a little carriage clock, another a ladies' wove wire purse, and a silver stiletto paper-knife. There's only one word to describe these prizes: "paltry."

NORMAN PRITCHARD   I took second place in both the 200 meters and the 200-meter hurdles and for my accomplishments the French Olympic Committee awarded me a penknife, worth a few francs!

The program in Paris included three competitions for "Masters," this being a euphemism for professionals. The official document read: "all prizes will be paid out directly on the grounds."

ALBERT SPALDING   Another confusing incident: when the prizes were given out by the French officials, Mr. Tysoe, of England was called by the Frenchmen as "Monsieur Ti-so-a" and it was not until an interpreter called for Mr. Tysoe that the latter appeared. John Flanagan was also a victim of the French pronunciation. He was called "Monsieur Flan-i-gaw," and since the meeting the American champion hammer thrower is known among his Paris Associates as "Flan-i-gaw."

Competitors in some events weren't even aware that they were competing in the Olympics.

The words "Olympic Games" were nowhere to be found on the commemorative plaques eventually awarded to some winners.

Figure 136 Winner's plaque

Designed by Frédérique Vernon and produced by the Paris Mint, the rectangular plaque shows on the front, the winged goddess Nike holding laurel branches with Paris in the background. On the reverse side a victorious athlete holds a laurel branch with the Acropolis in the background.

Gold medals were never awarded. A silver medal was given for a first place and a bronze medal for second. It wasn't until years later that the IOC retroactively assigned gold, silver, and bronze medals to align with later awards.

Figure 137 Silver medal

Scads of awards were handed out for exhibitors at the Exposition. International juries awarded thousands of certificates of merit and plaques, ribbons, decorations and medals. Publishing houses in Paris worked overtime to print the multi-volumed lists of winners— Spalding Sporting Goods Company among them.

Figure 138 Exhibition certificate

O O O O O

Two big issues had a negative impact on the games: The ill will created by the Sabbath dispute and the question of amateurism.

True, the Paris Games precipitated an international outcry over the morality of Sabbath competition. However, to some of us at least, assured that we were the boldest and strongest proved more important than defending the sanctity of the Sabbath. The issue simmered for a while then mostly melted away.

Where Coubertin had wished to maintain strict adherence to the rules of amateurism, 1 million French francs were distributed to some as prize money.

The original Olympians, the Greeks, were all amateurs. Or so goes the popular thinking anyway. Except they weren't. Some were fully supported as they trained and although they may have officially received only an olive wreath for winning an event, when they returned to their homes they were amply rewarded. Some became rich and famous. The public loves winners.

The idea of amateurism probably dates to 17th century England when the aristocracy wanted to prevent any of their kind having to compete with the working classes. Since they didn't have to work for a living, the aristocracy were avid defenders of amateurism. They didn't need the money anyway. After all, there are standards.

The lower classes had either to work for a living or, if athletes, get paid as athletes.

The Baron, although a staunch member of the French aristocracy, saw the inequities in the divisive system. His answer was to enlist wealthy patrons to support working-class athletes.

Then, too, there was in 1900 just as there would remain for decades, the question of exactly what constituted an amateur.

Coubertin might have looked at American baseball which wrestled with that problem earlier in the 19th century. Baseball began as a sport pitting gentlemen's clubs against each other for the fun of the sport. Then as competition between the clubs ratcheted up, some clubs found "jobs" for talented players in shops and offices they never saw. Were they being paid? Were they professionals? Eventually, baseball gave up trying to enforce the distinction.

Coubertin was dead set against including professionals in his games. However, when some were admitted over his objections, he rationalized that at least if the amateurs could see the professionals they would work harder to achieve better results.

CASPAR WHITNEY   The games were conceived in the spirit of furthering healthful athletic competition, and of drawing the sportsmen of all countries closer together in protecting the amateur. Alas, that noble aim was not always evident. I was then, as I have remained, disgusted by the so-called amateur athlete who secretly performs for money. How vulgar that is.

O O O O O

It has to be said that the facilities were less than ideal—a great deal less. Actually they were lousy. But given our successes little was made of it. Uneven surfaces? Trees in the way? No matter, they were the same for everyone and we came out on top just as we would have on better facilities.

From the Official French Report: "Foot races and athletic competitions were the most beautiful such meeting ever given in any country of the world. They leave an unforgettable memory in the minds of all the competitors and spectators."

Most beautiful? Perhaps not.

Leaving unforgettable memories? Indubitably but perhaps some would be better forgotten.

O O O O O

Not even the French newspapers took much notice of the games. When a paper deigned to mention the games at all, there was no consistency which sporting activities were referred to as Olympic events.

Polo?

Some stories say yes, some no.

Cricket?

Ditto.

Archery.

Ditto again.

When the games were mentioned in the press, comments covered the whole range of opinions.

From a British paper: "The whole series of sports produced nothing but muddles, bad arrangements, bad management, bad prizes and any amount of ill-feeling amongst the nationalities engaged."

From a French paper: "The names of Kraenzlein—this extraordinary jumper—of Bauer, the superb discus thrower; of Tewksbury and Jarvis, the marvelous sprinters; of Sheldon the modern Apollo; Long, the winner of the 400 meters; of Bennet and Orton, the remarkable steeplechasers; of Baxter, the pole vaulter, the memories of these admirable athletes show what can be accomplished when moral courage and physical force come together in the same individual."

The American press, when it carried reports of the track and field results and some of the other events almost always waved a patriotic flag.

The *New York Times* wrote, "The feature of the meeting was not only the number of events the Americans won, but the ease with which they outstripped their competitors, often finishing first and second, laughing side-by-side and in a canter."

CASPAR WHITNEY   The athletic invasion of England and France, beginning at the English championships and ending at the Paris Exposition Games, was a triumphant tour for the Americans from first to last.

Leaving aside the handicap events, which meant nothing, there were 23 scratch track and field contests in the Paris Games, and the American athletes won 16 of the 22 in which we competed. Thankfully we did not enter the farce that became the 500-meter team race. The only three in which we didn't win any medal were the marathon and the two steeplechases. Kraenz led with four golds, while Bax and Tewks led in total medals with five each.

So those three headed home with 14 medals. Not a bad haul for the roommates.

Not only did Kraenz perform the astonishing feat of winning four individual championships but he set records in all four events. Several other athletes won four track and field gold medals in one Olympic Games—Paavo Nurmi and Jesse Owens among them— but all of them included victories and events other than individual contests. Kraenzlein's feat stands alone and will never be equaled because Olympic contestants are now limited to three individual events.

Bax is the only athlete in Olympic history to have won both the high jump and pole vault competitions.

Yale's Sheldon brothers won four medals between them.

The Ivy League was represented by 22 track and field athletes including the 13 from Penn. Had the Ivy League competed as its own country it would have placed third in total medals behind the United States and France. If none of the events had been held on Sunday that number would certainly have been higher yet. Only four track and field events did not have an Ivy League athlete finish with medals.

From the non-Ivy League contingent, Ray Ewry was the standout taking gold in all three standing jumps.

England captured three top spots, Hungary one, and Luxembourg one, assuming Théato won the marathon (maybe) representing that country. Australia, Bohemia, Canada, (unless you count Orton), Denmark, Austria, Germany, Norway, India, Italy, Sweden and

Greece had representative athletes entered in the different contests, but all failed to furnish the world a champion.

And the arrogant French? The record speaks for itself.

CASPAR WHITNEY   In point of popular interest and genuine international competition the Paris exhibition athletic games were utterly insignificant as compared with the Olympic Games, given at Athens, in '96 with its stadium and 70,000 spectators. In point of fact, the Paris Games were no more, no less, than an American intercollegiate meet, with Harvard out. Except for the English half miler, A.E. Tysoe who beat Cregan in the English championships, Prichard, the English hurdler and Stanley Rowley, the New South Wales champion sprinter, there were positively no really good men entered except from America. England, Ireland, Scotland and Germany sent no champions and but for the Americans the games would have been a complete fiasco.

There were only about 1000 spectators, mostly Americans, but the Americans provided a high class athletic entertainment for Paris.

SPALDING DE GARMENDIA   We demonstrated our superiority over other nations in almost every event.

JAMES SULLIVAN   I was pleased by the showing of our athletes and remain convinced this meeting did more to open the eyes of our legislators to athletics than anything that had been done for several years. The trip of our boys was one of triumphs. The performances of men like Kraenzlein, Long, Sheldon and Flanagan astounded the Frenchman.

While many exhibits from America, works of art, inventions, etc. were awarded prizes for their excellence, nevertheless there was some doubt in the minds as to the correctness of such awards. The decision was questioned and always will be, but on the athletic field there were no such questions. America just swept the board.

As I see it, here is exactly what we did: We loudly and proudly claimed we had won the Olympic Games again, even though when the medals in all the sports were counted, France had gathered more first-place wins than we did. The American press elevated our athletes to the Olympic championship by virtue of the U.S. domination in track and field. We defined the Olympic Games in our terms and then pronounced ourselves the world's best.

These games provided the U.S. with the perfect opportunity to measure itself against other countries. And didn't the results speak for themselves?

Yes, we demonstrated the strength of the American civilization and we did it with the highest embodiment of self-confidence.

Our press extolled our accomplishments with unbridled enthusiasm, often accompanied by chauvinistic bombast.

Look, we simply won more events not because of superior athleticism but because we came from a superior society enriched by taking in immigrants and turning them into productive citizens.

Isn't America the best, strongest country in the world? Don't our athletes prove that?

As would be proven in the years to come, our dominance in the games reflected a larger role for athletics in defending our place in the international scene.

There can be no doubt that our performances in Paris were good for our nation's self-esteem. Whether they were good for the Olympic movement is not as clear. Competitive balance engenders greater interest but we dominated these games as no other nation has ever since.

All hail the conquering missionaries!

O O O O O

Despite the shadow cast over them by the Exhibition, despite the many problems, despite the controversies, these games were notable for several reasons.

The Paris Games achieved wider international acceptance than was the case in Athens.

These were debut games for Spain, Canada, Cuba, the Netherlands, Norway and Haiti; and the first Asian countries—Iran and India

Women made their Olympic debut. They competed in tennis, golf, croquet, yachting and equestrian events.

Many competitions produced outstanding results including numerous world records.

Several athletes achieved worldwide recognition, most notably Kraenz and Ray Ewry.

The French took pride in the marathon and their dominance in fencing.

Considerable goodwill between nations was on display ... at times.

Whatever else might be said of these games they were the first great international sports meeting, bringing together nearly all the sports practiced in the world with athletes from most countries where sport was practiced.

These were strange games indeed, even farcical at times, nevertheless, they produced some sparkling contests, introduced women as competitors, established records, set precedents for future games ... and survived. The possibilities for *Citius, Altius, Fortius* were at least smoldering, ready to be whipped into a full flame.

O O O O O

For all they accomplished, the Paris Games remained a disappointment to Coubertin. His plans had been jettisoned, his dreams unfulfilled. Hadn't he brought a wonderful gift to the country he loved, only to have the gift thrown away? He was distraught but said little about it—at least publicly. He played the diplomat. He saw the scheduling as a big mistake so focus on the Games was badly diluted. Since the word "Olympic" was nowhere to be found on the official program, some athletes thought they were competing in demonstration events, only much later to realize they were in the Olympics.

He was also less than pleased that team sports were part of the Games. The Olympics as he envisioned them were to demonstrate how an individual could excel, how the individual could meet challenges. Yet these Games included soccer, rowing, cricket, croquet and even tug-of-war.

And women competitors! In Coubertin's mind, women should attend the Games by all means to provide applause and encouragement to the men, but step on the playing field? Never.

Figure 139 Baron de Coubertin

BARON de COUBERTIN   There is a place in the world where people are indifferent to the Olympic Games, and this place is Paris. We made a hash of our work. It's a miracle that the Olympic movement survived.

I have to say the athletes did their best. Interesting results were achieved, but with nothing Olympic about them. According to the words of one of our colleagues, "our idea had been used, but it had been torn to shreds in the process." What he said was very true. It typifies what happened in 1900.

Still, being the optimist he was, he sensed the Olympic flame was still burning, albeit dimly, and could and would be fanned into a full blaze at future games.

O O O O O

Coubertin may have been shunted aside during the Paris Games, but he never wavered in his commitment to the ideals of Olympism.

President Roosevelt, was so impressed with the Coubertin dream he wrote a letter to the French Baron asking his advice about the athletic prowess of the four Roosevelt children. Roosevelt felt he understood Coubertin's athletic philosophy declaring: "I think you preached just the right form of the gospel of physical development... When are you coming over here? I would like you to pay me a visit here in Washington and we will take some walks and rides together. If you come when I am in the country we will row or chop trees or shoot at a target, as well as ride and swim."

BARON de COUBERTIN   Of course the Olympian movement had enemies, like every other free and living work, but it also had staunch friends of great assistance. It was these to whom I appealed to celebrate the next games in America in 1904. I was convinced they would be a great success and draw across the ocean qualified representatives of all the sporting societies of the world for games which would be both worthy of the noble and ancient Olympian past and of the glorious future of the great American Republic.

Spalding, after corresponding with Coubertin, agreed to extend an invitation to the sportsmen of the world to come to America in 1904 for the third modern Olympics.

Not everyone thought that was a good idea.

Foreigners aren't going to come all the way over here unless England sends a big squad.

It looks as if we are to host the next games, they will be an almost entirely American competition.

The way we just beat up the Europeans, they most likely won't want to come here for more drubbings.

They did however. Twelve nations sent 631 athletes including six women to St. Louis. The participation was so limited that they might almost have been designated as the American championships. The Americans won 239 medals. The rest of the countries combined took 41 although there was confusion on the actual nationalities of some competitors.

Most officials had hoped that in the future any Olympic Games would be divorced from any big fair where the Olympic values vanish and their educational merit becomes nil. They vowed that never again would the Olympics be reduced to a humiliated vassal as it had in Paris. Alas, such was not to be. In both 1904 and 1908, for budgetary reasons they were unable to sever their relations with exhibitions. It was not until 1912 in Sweden that the break was firmly completed.

O O O O O

In his final years, Coubertin found himself marginalized and alone. His domestic life was a shambles. At age 72, his once considerable fortune, long since exhausted, he lived on the charity of friends and civic authorities—a white-whiskered old man in a frock coat of another era. After his funeral he was buried in Lausanne, Switzerland. At his request, his heart had been cut out of his corpse, placed in a white-satin-lined wooden box and sent to Olympia, Greece.

Maybe by the end, he thought that having Athens as the permanent home would have been a better idea after all.

If he did, it was a mistake. It is precisely because he refused to give in to the demands to make Athens a permanent site that has kept his dream alive. The Olympics have been embraced as a worldwide movement in a way it never would have had it been restricted to a one-country host. Today the Olympics remain the most popular entertainment/sports spectacle in the world.

APPENDIX 1
UNITED STATES TRACK AND FIELD MEDALISTS

Gold

Margaret Abbott	Women's Nine Hole Golf
Irving Baxter	High Jump Pole Vault
William Carr	Rowing Coxed Eights
Ray Ewry	Standing Long Jump Standing Triple Jump Standing High Jump
John Flanagan	Hammer Throw
Frank Jarvis	100 Meters
Foxhall Keene	Mixed Doubles Polo
Alvin Kraenzlein	60 Meters 110 Meter Hurdles 200 Meter Hurdles Long Jump
Maxie Long	400 Meters
Frank MacKey	Mixed Doubles Polo
Meyer Prinstein	Triple Jump
Charles Sands	Men's 36 Hole Golf
Richard Sheldon	Shot Put
Walter Tewksbury	200 Meters 400 Meter Hurdles

Silver

Irving Baxter   Standing Long Jump
                                   Standing Triple Jump
                                   Standing High Jump

Meredith Colket   Pole Vault

James Connolly   Triple Jump

John Cregan   800 Meters

Truxtun Hare   Hammer Throw

William Holland   400 Meters

Josiah McCracken   Shot Put

Walter McCreery   Polo

John McLean   110 Meter Hurdles

Meyer Prinstein   Long Jump

Basil Spalding de Garmendia   Doubles Tennis

Walter Tewksbury   60 Meters
                                   100 Meters

Pauline Whittier   Golf

Bronze

John Bray	1500 Meters
Robert Garrett	Shot Put Standing Triple Jump
David Hall	800 Meters
Marion Jones	Tennis
H. MacHenry	Sailing
Josiah McCracken	Hammer Throw
John Lake	Cycling
Fred Moloney	110 Meter Hurdles
Daria Pratt	Golf
Lewis Sheldon	Standing High Jump
Richard Sheldon	Discus Throw
Walter Tewksbury	200 Meter Hurdles

APPENDIX 2

After the Games …

Irving Knott Baxter (1876-1957) was admitted to the state bar of New York, worked on Wall Street and was appointed U.S. Commissioner of the Northern District of New York. His specialty was defending violators of the Volstead Act. He served as a private in World War I.

Meredith Bright Colket worked as an attorney for the General Accident Fire & Life Assurance Corporation.

James Connolly spent years on many different vessels, fishing boats, military ships all over the world and became an authority on maritime writing. He published more than 200 short stories, and 25 novels.

Walter Edwin Drumheller worked as a dentist for a few years before entering the hotel business with his father. He served in the army during World War I.

Arthur Duffey confessed in 1805 that he had been accepting sponsor money since 1898, and the AAU ordered all of his records expunged. Later, he became a columnist for the *Boston Post*.

Ray Ewry became a track official and served on the New York Board of Water Supply as a supervising engineer. In 1990, the United States Post Office issued a stamp commemorating his Olympic victories.

John Flanagan served with the New York City Police Department from 1902 to 1910, then returned to Ireland.

Robert Garrett became a banker and financier. His interest in archeology led to collecting more than 11,000 historic manuscripts, many containing rare examples of illuminated Byzantine art. He donated them all to Princeton University.

Alexander Grant, along with George Orton and Josiah McCracken, founded Camp Tecumseh, an all-boys summer camp in New Hampshire. Grant served as the director.

David Hall served as a Colonel in charge of the American Ambulance Corps on the Italian front during World War I and then taught at several universities.

Thomas Truxtun Hare was an outstanding archer and was president of the United Bowmen of America. He became an attorney specializing in corporate law, and published eight books of children's poems.

William Holland practiced medicine after his graduation from Georgetown Medical School.

After graduating from Princeton, Frank Jarvis took a law degree at the University of Pittsburgh and practiced law in that city for many years.

Alvin Kraenzlein practiced dentistry and coached track and field and football at the University of Michigan. In 1913 he signed a five-year $50,000 contract with the German government to train the 1916 German Olympic track team (this was canceled due to the outbreak of World War I). During the war he served in the U.S. Army as a physical training specialist. When the war ended, he returned to the University of Pennsylvania track where he was appointed assistant track and field coach.

Josiah C. McCracken worked for the Young Men's Christian Association. He went to China where he established the Christian Medical School in Canton and served as its president. Deported back to the United States when World War II broke out, he became Chief Resident Physician at the Pennsylvania Hospital in Philadelphia.

Edmund Minahan played one year—1907—for the Cincinnati Reds as a pitcher, appearing in two games, losing both. The only other American track and field Olympian to play Major League ball was Jim Thorpe.

George Washington Orton taught languages at several academies and preparatory schools. Along with Frank Ellis he managed the Penn Relays and wrote *History of Athletics at Pennsylvania.*

At the 1904 Olympic Games Meyer Prinstein won gold medals in both the long and triple jumps. He later practiced law in New York.

Norman Pritchard emigrated first to England and then the United States and became a performer in scores of silent films using the name Norman Trevor. He made his Broadway debut in 1914 and went on to appear in 20 productions.

John Rimmer joined the Liverpool City Police in 1901 and retired as sergeant 30 years later.

Richard Sheldon worked for the Cadillac Motor Company.

John Walter Beardsley Tewksbury practiced dentistry in Tunkhannock, Pennsylvania, for 34 years.

Alfred Tysoe's disappointing time in the 800 meters was to be the last race of his career. Early in 1901 he contracted pleurisy and died later that year at his father's home. He was 27.